Twisted Network Programming
Essentials

Other resources from O'Reilly

Related titles

Internet Core Protocols: The Definitive Guide

IPv6 Essentials

Managing IMAP

Network Security with OpenSSL

Programming Python

Python Cookbook™

Python in a Nutshell

Python Pocket Reference

SSH, The Secure Shell: The Definitive Guide

oreilly.com

oreilly.com is more than a complete catalog of O'Reilly books. You'll also find links to news, events, articles, weblogs, sample chapters, and code examples.

oreillynet.com is the essential portal for developers interested in open and emerging technologies, including new platforms, programming languages, and operating systems.

Conferences

O'Reilly brings diverse innovators together to nurture the ideas that spark revolutionary industries. We specialize in documenting the latest tools and systems, translating the innovator's knowledge into useful skills for those in the trenches. Visit *conferences.oreilly.com* for our upcoming events.

Safari Bookshelf (*safari.oreilly.com*) is the premier online reference library for programmers and IT professionals. Conduct searches across more than 1,000 books. Subscribers can zero in on answers to time-critical questions in a matter of seconds. Read the books on your Bookshelf from cover to cover or simply flip to the page you need. Try it today with a free trial.

Twisted Network Programming Essentials

Abe Fettig

O'REILLY®

Beijing · Cambridge · Farnham · Köln · Paris · Sebastopol · Taipei · Tokyo

Twisted Network Programming Essentials
by Abe Fettig

Published by O'Reilly Media, Inc., 1005 Gravenstein Highway North, Sebastopol, CA 95472.

O'Reilly books may be purchased for educational, business, or sales promotional use. Online editions are also available for most titles (*safari.oreilly.com*). For more information, contact our corporate/institutional sales department: (800) 998-9938 or *corporate@oreilly.com*.

Editor:	Jonathan Gennick
Production Editor:	Marlowe Shaeffer
Cover Designer:	Karen Montgomery
Interior Designer:	David Futato

Printing History:

October 2005:	First Edition.

 This book uses RepKover™, a durable and flexible lay-flat binding.

ISBN: 0-596-10032-9

[M]

Contents

Foreword

"My name is Ozymandius, king of kings:
Look on my words, ye Mighty, and despair!"
Nothing beside remains. Round the decay
Of that colossal wreck, boundless and bare
The lone and level sands stretch far away.

—Percy Bysshe Shelly
"Ozymandius"

As the Twisted project's originator and nominal leader—and as someone who is not being paid for writing this—I can very honestly say that this is a fine book, and it has made me proud of what I've started. You now hold in your hands a wondrous key that contains the knowledge to unlock a very powerful software system—a software system borne of a consistent, methodical vision; a vision half a decade in realization and hundreds of man-years in implementation; a vision for a video game that has yet to be written, called "Divunal."

I have been lauded many times for my role in Twisted's creation, and in this foreword I will attempt to disabuse you of the notion that any of it was on purpose. Not only was it an accident, but neither I, nor anyone else, has made one iota of progress towards my original goal of writing a game.

When I was eight years old, I decided I wanted to be a writer. I was going to write video games just like my favorite ones, the text-based games from Infocom. They were like books, but better. I knew how to write already—at a fourth-grade level, or so I'm told—and all I needed to figure out was the part where the computer wrote back. Lucky for you nobody thought to tell me how hard that step between the input and the output was, or Twisted would be a series of detective novels instead of a Python program.

Tolkien said it best: "The tale grew in the telling," and I'll say it worse: the code grew in the hacking. Twisted began over a decade after my aforementioned first plunge into the netherworld of software, as a solitary attempt to create a networking subsystem for a small online fantasy world. Since then, it has become an ongoing community quest to unify all manner of asynchronous communications. This book will take you on an adventure through Twisted for the Web, Twisted for email, Twisted for chat, and of course, Twisted for whatever new kind of networked application you want to dream up—maybe even an online video game.

Much as the tale of Twisted has grown and changed, its origins still have a profound effect on its nature, and on its future. Having origins in an eclectic* problem domain has attracted an eclectic† audience. As Mr. Fettig will warn you later in these pages, the community in the online support forum engages in discussions which are "often funny." I thank him for his tact, but to put it more directly: we're weird.

"Weird" is a badge I have long worn with pride, dear reader, so please take it as a compliment that I bestow it upon you. You're not simply non-average, you're better than average. Almost by definition, Twisted hackers are the ones for whom "good enough" isn't good enough. You are the web programmers who can't use their operating system's stock HTTP daemon because you need more power and more control over how it's run; the chat developers who aren't content with chatting on a perfectly working network just because it doesn't support some cool new features you want; the (dare I say it?) gamers who aren't content with the market's offerings of online games. You want to create something newer, different, better. To build higher than those who have come before, because you are building not merely upon the shoulders of giants, but upon the apex of an acrobatic balancing act of giants, or more literally an interlocking network of frameworks and libraries for different tasks, rather than just one at a time.

Twisted will let you do that, by letting you leverage code written by far more and far better programmers than I. Twisted provides a common method for that code to cooperate, which means you can use all of that code without performing a complex integration pass. In this spirit, I'd like to invite you to release your Twisted-based projects, or the infrastructure components of them, as open source software, so that we might together build a Twisted commons upon which many more fantastic applications will be built.

Don't mistake this friendly vision for altruism, however. I didn't have anything to do with the start of the Free Software or Open Source movements, respectively, but they came along at a convenient time for me. This feeling of share-and-share-alike has been a feature of the Twisted community since day one, not because I care about sharing.‡ It is because—I may have mentioned this—I want to write a video game

---

* And difficult! Making an online game work properly is *hard*.

† And intelligent! People who solve unusual problems are always learning.

‡ Caution for the humorless: this is a joke. I am not actually an enemy of freedom. Still, there is some truth to this.

one day. A game that effortlessly connects to the Web and to your email, that politely requests that you play when you have time, and that reminds you to get back to work when you do not.

You see, the majority of Twisted's core developers, including myself, suffer from Attention Deficit Disorder. This malady is the grease that makes the magic wheels of integration turn. While most developers—sane developers—would be content to write a perfectly good web server that could work only as a web server and leave it at that, we are always afraid we'll suddenly lose interest and need a chat application instead—or maybe it should be a mail server? Hey, there's a squirrel! I don't like this song.

What was I saying? Oh yes. The essence of Twisted is apparently paradoxical. Created on a whim by crazed eccentrics, designed to be a toy, and yet powerful enough to drive massive email systems, high-traffic web sites, transaction-processing systems, and inventory management applications.

However, the paradox is an illusion. People produce the best work when they are working and having fun at the same time. It takes a sense of humor to call yourself a crazed eccentric (whether it's true or not). You have to have a sense of fun to try and build a toy. In enjoying ourselves, we have brought to life a system that many of us have tried, and been unable, to create in more serious surroundings.

So, when I look out upon the "lone and level sands" of Divunal, a game whose incarnation today is little more than its name, I am not concerned. I am having a good time with Twisted. With this book in hand, I have no doubt that you will, too.

—Matthew "the Glyph" Lefkowitz
CTO at Divmod, Inc.
(not a game company)
(yet)
August 2005

Preface

This is a book about Twisted. Twisted is an open source Python framework for building network applications.* It gives developers a complete set of tools for communicating across networks and the Internet. Twisted includes both high- and low-level tools. You can create a web or mail server with just a few lines of code, or you can write your own protocol from scratch. At every level, Twisted provides a tested, well-designed API that makes it possible to rapidly develop powerful network software.

This book is for developers who want to start building applications using Twisted. It contains lots of examples of working code, with thorough notes and explanations. It focuses on practical examples of how you can use Twisted to do useful things.

Why Use Twisted?

If you're not already using Twisted, you may have some reservations about adopting it for your own applications. Why should you use Twisted instead of some other networking library or framework? Here are a few compelling reasons:

Python-powered

Twisted is written in Python, a powerful, object-oriented, interpreted language. Python is a language that inspires great enthusiasm among its fans, and for good reason. It's a joy to program in Python, which is easy to write, easy to read, and easy to run. And because Python is cross-platform, you can run the same Twisted application on Linux, Windows, Unix, and Mac OS X.

Asynchronous and event-based

Synchronous network libraries leave developers with a painful choice: either allow the application to become unresponsive during network operations, or introduce the additional complexity of threading. Twisted's event-based, asynchronous framework makes it possible to write applications that stay responsive

---

* See *http://open-source.org* for more information on open source software (OSS).

while processing events from multiple network connections, without using threads.

Full-featured

Twisted includes an amazing amount of functionality. Mail, web, news, chat, DNS, SSH, Telnet, RPC, database access, and more—it's all there, ready for you to use.

Flexible

Twisted provides high-level classes to let you get started quickly. But you'll never find yourself limited by the way things work out of the box. If you need advanced functionality, or you need to customize the way a protocol works, you can. You can also write your own protocol implementation, for complete control of every byte sent over the wire.

Open source

Twisted is free, both as in beer and as in freedom. It includes full source code, and is released under a liberal license. Want to distribute all or part of Twisted along with your application? You're welcome to do so, with no obligations to release your own code or pay any licensing fees. Want to get a better understanding of how an object in Twisted works? Take a look at the source. And when you get to the point where you're developing your own improvements and extensions to Twisted, you can contribute them to the community for the benefit of others.

Community-backed

Twisted has an active community of developers and users. If you run into a problem, you'll find many fellow developers ready to help on one of the Twisted mailing lists. See "Finding Answers to Your Questions," in Chapter 1. Or you can drop into the #twisted IRC channel, where the chances are good you'll be able to start a live conversation with the very person who wrote the code you're having trouble with.

An integration-friendly platform

A Twisted application can share data between several different services within the same process. This makes integration tasks a snap. You can write an SMTP-to-XMLRPC proxy, an SSH server that lets you update a website, or a web discussion board that includes an NNTP interface. If you need to transfer data between systems that don't speak the same protocol, Twisted will make your job a whole lot easier.

What This Book Covers

This book does not attempt to exhaustively document every module and class available for the Twisted framework. Instead, it focuses on presenting practical examples of the most common tasks that face developers building network applications. This book will also help you to understand the key concepts and design patterns used in Twisted applications. Here's a summary of the main topics covered:

Installing Twisted

Chapter 1 covers downloading and installing Twisted, and some additional libraries, on the operating system of your choice.

Working with TCP connections

Chapter 2 shows how you can use use Twisted to make TCP connections to servers, and how to write a server that accepts TCP connections from clients.

Web clients and servers

Chapters 3 and 4 show how to use Twisted to work with the Web. Chapter 3 covers HTTP clients. Chapter 4 demonstrates how to write a web server of your own, from the basics of responding to HTTP requests to higher-level concepts like managing a hierarchy of resources and storing data in an SQL database.

Web services and RPC

Twisted includes support for several different kinds of web services and remote procedure calls. Chapter 5 shows how you can design a Twisted web application for programmatic accessing using the REST architectural style. It also demonstrates how to write XML-RPC and SOAP clients and servers, and how you can use the Twisted Perspective Broker framework to transfer native Python objects over a network connection.

Authentication

Managing users and authentication is one of the core tasks in any server application. Chapter 6 discusses the Twisted authentication framework, which provides an extremely flexible approach to authenticating users against different backends.

Email clients and servers

Chapters 7 and 8 demonstrate Twisted's powerful support for mail clients and servers. Chapter 7 shows how to write clients that send and receive mail using SMTP, POP3, and IMAP. Chapter 8 shows how to build SMTP, POP3, and IMAP servers.

Usenet

Chapter 9 discusses Usenet clients and servers using the NNTP protocol. It shows how to read and post Usenet articles, how to run an NNTP server, and how to use NNTP as an interface for other kinds of messages, such as RSS feeds.

SSH clients and servers

Chapter 10 covers Twisted's support for SSH. It demonstrates how to write your own SSH server to give users remote shell access to your application, and how you can provide a live Python prompt over SSH for administering or debugging a running server. This chapter also shows how to write an SSH client to execute commands on a remote server.

Running and managing Twisted applications
    Chapter 11 shows how to use the tools Twisted provides for running and managing applications, which give you the ability to run daemon processes, use *setuid* and *chroot* to limit permissions, and write log files.

Conventions Used in This Book

This book uses standard typographical conventions to highlight different types of text. You'll see the following font styles used:

Italic
    Used for emphasis, to highlight technical terms the first time they appear, and for filenames, directories, and URLs.

`Constant width`
    Used for code samples, and for the names of variables, classes, objects, and functions when they are used within the main text of the book.

`Constant width bold`
    Shows user input at the command line and interactive prompts.

`Constant width bold italic`
    Shows placeholder user input that you should replace with something that makes sense for you.

    This icon signifies a tip, suggestion, or general note.

    This icon indicates a warning or caution.

What You'll Need

This book assumes a familiarity with programming in Python. If you're looking for a good introduction to Python, check out *Learning Python,* by Mark Lutz and David Ascher (O'Reilly), or *Dive Into Python*, by Mark Pilgrim (Apress). You should have a Linux, Mac OS X, or Windows computer with Python version 2.3 or later installed. Python 2.3 is included in Mac OS X 10.3 ("Jaguar") and higher, and in many Linux distributions. If you don't already have Python installed, you can download it for free from *http://www.python.org*.

Using Code Examples

This book is here to help you get your job done. In general, you may use the code in this book in your programs and documentation. You do not need to contact us for permission unless you're reproducing a significant portion of the code. For example, writing a program that uses several chunks of code from this book does not require permission. Selling or distributing a CD-ROM of examples from O'Reilly books does require permission. Answering a question by citing this book and quoting example code does not require permission. Incorporating a significant amount of example code from this book into your product's documentation does require permission.

We appreciate, but do not require, attribution. An attribution usually includes the title, author, publisher, and ISBN. For example: "*Twisted Network Programming Essentials* by Abe Fettig. Copyright 2006 O'Reilly Media, Inc., 0-596-10032-9."

If you feel your use of code examples falls outside fair use or the permission given here, feel free to contact us at *permissions@oreilly.com*.

Safari® Enabled

 When you see a Safari® Enabled icon on the cover of your favorite technology book, it means the book is available online through the O'Reilly Network Safari Bookshelf.

Safari offers a solution that's better than e-books. It's a virtual library that lets you easily search thousands of top technology books, cut and paste code samples, download chapters, and find quick answers when you need the most accurate, current information. Try it for free at *http://safari.oreilly.com*.

How to Contact Us

We have tested and verified the information in this book to the best of our ability, but you may find that features have changed or that we have made mistakes. If so, please notify us by writing to:

O'Reilly Media, Inc.
1005 Gravenstein Highway North
Sebastopol, CA 95472
(800) 998-9938 (in the United States or Canada)
(707) 829-0515 (international or local)
(707) 829-0104 (fax)

You can also send messages electronically. To be put on the mailing list or request a catalog, send email to:

info@oreilly.com

To ask technical questions or comment on the book, send email to:

bookquestions@oreilly.com

We have a web site for this book, where you can find examples and errata (previously reported errors and corrections are available for public view there). You can access this page at:

http://www.oreilly.com/catalog/twistedadn

For more information about this book and others, see the O'Reilly web site:

http://www.oreilly.com

Acknowledgments

I truly appreciate the work done by all the Twisted developers to make it the amazing framework it is today. Without the efforts of Glyph Lefkowitz, Sean Riley, Allen Short, Christopher Armstrong, Paul Swartz, Jürgen Hermann, Moshe Zadka, Benjamin Bruheim, Travis B. Hartwell, Itamar Shtull-Trauring, Andrew Bennetts, Kevin Turner, Donovan Preston, JP Calderone, Gavin Cooper, Jonathan Lange, Bob Ippolito, Pavel Pergamenshchik, Jonathan D. Simms, Brian Warner, Mary Gardiner, Eric Mangold, Tommi Virtanen, James Y. Knight, and many others, there would have been nothing for me to write about. Thank you all for your contributions to Twisted and open source software. I hope this book helps many more developers to appreciate what you've done in creating Twisted.

While working on this book, I received a great deal of valuable help and guidance from my editor, Jonathan Gennick, and the tech reviewers: Itamar Shtull-Trauring, Valentino Volonghi, and Greg Gennick. Thank you. I'd also like to thank James Y. Knight and Donovan Preston for helping with Chapter 5.

While working on this book I appreciated the support and encouragement of my parents, Mo and Peter Fettig, as well as Garrett Wilkin, Nellie Fettig, Sheri Smith, and many other friends and relatives. My colleagues at JotSpot were understanding when this project was taking its toll on my time and energy. Arabica Coffee in Portland, Maine, provided a great place to work and the world's best espresso. Mike and Jeannine Kertzman let us hide out in their old farmhouse when I needed a change of environment.

For some time, I've noticed that a feature of many acknowledgments sections is the part where the author somewhat guiltily thanks his wife for being so patient while he was working on the book. Now I have a better understanding of why this is the case. Writing a book is a lot of work, much more than I imagined when I began this project. Getting it done required many early mornings, late nights, and Sunday afternoons. Through it all, my wife Hannah was loving and supportive. She kept our schedule and our household on track during a time when I was busier than I had ever been in my life. She made it possible for me to get this book completed without losing my mind or my joy. Hannah, thank you. You're the best.

CHAPTER 1

Getting Started

Before you can start developing applications using Twisted, you'll need to download and install Twisted and its related packages. This chapter walks you through the installation process on various operating systems. It also shows you how to add the Twisted utilities to your path, familiarize yourself with the Twisted documentation, and get answers to your questions from the Twisted community.

Installing Twisted

First things first: you need to get Twisted installed on your computer. Downloads and instructions for installing Twisted on various operating systems can be found at *http://twistedmatrix.com/projects/core/*. To enable additional functionality in Twisted, you'll have to install a couple of optional packages as well.

How Do I Do That?

Begin by downloading the latest Twisted release from *http://www.twistedmatrix.com*. Then install PyOpenSSL (a Python wrapper of the popular OpenSSL library), which Twisted uses to make encrypted Secure Socket.Layer (*SSL*) connections. Finally, install PyCrypto, a package containing Python implementations of encryption algorithms used by the Secure SHell (*SSH*). Locations for these downloads are provided in each of the following platform-specific sections.

> You don't need to install PyOpenSSL or PyCrypto in order to use Twisted. Without these packages installed, you won't be able to use Twisted's SSL and SSH features, but everything else will still work.

Windows

Go to *http://twistedmatrix.com/projects/core/*. Download the Twisted Windows "Sumo" installer for Python 2.4 (or your Python version). The Sumo binary includes the Twisted core, as well as a number of extra modules to support specific groups of protocols like mail and web. You'll need the full Sumo version of Twisted installed to run most of the examples in this book. Then go to *http://twistedmatrix.com/products/download* and find the section labeled "Twisted Dependencies for Windows." There you'll find links to installers for the latest versions of PyOpenSSL and PyCrypto.

 It's possible that some of these packages might move to different pages as the Twisted web site grows and is restructured in the future. If one if these links doesn't work for you, try starting from the Twisted home page at *http://twistedmatrix.com*.

Once you've downloaded all three installers, run the Twisted Setup program. It's a simple installer, and it will automatically detect your existing Python installation. Next, run the PyOpenSSL and and PyCrypto installers. These are even simpler than the Twisted installer and take only a few seconds to complete.

 When byte-compiling the Twisted modules, the Twisted Setup program will throw up a tiny, floating progress bar that sits in a very tiny window of its own. The unpacking may take several minutes.

Verify that the installation worked by importing the twisted package from an interactive Python prompt:

```
$ python
Python 2.3 (#1, Sep 13 2003, 00:49:11)
Type "help", "copyright", "credits" or "license" for more information.
>>> import twisted
>>>
```

If the `import twisted` statement runs with no errors, you have a working Twisted install.

Mac OS X, Linux, and BSD

Many Linux distributions and BSD variants, including Debian, Ubuntu, Gentoo Linux, Red Hat Linux, and FreeBSD, have prepackaged versions of Twisted, PyOpenSSL, and PyCrypto available. Check the Twisted download page to see if it mentions your operating system, or search your favorite package repository. If there are packages available, make sure they are for Twisted 2.0 or higher, not the older 1.3 release.

If you can't find a prepackaged version of Twisted for your operating system or platform, refer to the following instructions on installing from source.

Installing from Source Files

If you're on an operating system for which no Twisted binary packages are available, you'll need to install from source. Don't worry, though; as source installs go, Python packages are among the easiest you'll find.

How Do I Do That?

First, download the full "Sumo" source package for Twisted (choosing the version with documentation) from *http://twistedmatrix.com/projects/core/*. The Sumo package is the core of Twisted, plus a number of bundled modules from other projects developed under the Twisted umbrella; you'll need the modules in the Sumo package to run most of the examples in this book. Once you've downloaded the package, extract it to a working directory:

```
$ tar -xjvf ~/downloads/TwistedSumo-2005-03-22.tar.bz2
TwistedSumo-2005-03-22/
TwistedSumo-2005-03-22/bin/
...
TwistedSumo-2005-03-22/README
TwistedSumo-2005-03-22/LICENSE
TwistedSumo-2005-03-22/setup.py
TwistedSumo-2005-03-22/ZopeInterface-3.0.1.tgz
```

Next, enter the *TwistedSumo-version* directory. Twisted depends on the zope. interface package, which is bundled in the Twisted Sumo distribution. Unzip the ZopeInterface tarball:

```
$ tar -xzvf ZopeInterface-3.0.1.tgz
ZopeInterface-3.0.1/
ZopeInterface-3.0.1/Support/
ZopeInterface-3.0.1/Support/zpkgsetup/
ZopeInterface-3.0.1/Support/zpkgsetup/publication.py
...
ZopeInterface-3.0.1/setup.py
ZopeInterface-3.0.1/setup.cfg
ZopeInterface-3.0.1/MANIFEST
```

Enter the *ZopeInterface-<version>* directory, and run the command *python setup.py install*. This command will build and install the zope.interface package in your python installation's *lib/site-packages/twisted* directory. You'll need to have administrative/root permissions to do this, so use *su* or *sudo* to increase your permission level if necessary:

```
$ cd ZopeInterface-3.0.1
$ python setup.py install
running install
running build
running build_py
running build_ext
building 'zope.interface._zope_interface_coptimizations' extension
```

```
...
running install_lib
copying build/lib.linux-i686-2.4/zope/interface/_zope_interface_coptimizations.so ->
/usr/lib/python2.4/site-packages/zope/interface
writing byte-compilation script '/tmp/tmpdY9dA9.py'
/usr/bin/python -O /tmp/tmpdY9dA9.py
removing /tmp/tmpdY9dA9.py
```

Once `zope.interface` is installed, you're ready to install Twisted. In this *TwistedSumo-<version>* directory, run the command *python setup.py install*. The command will compile the Twisted C modules and install Twisted:

```
$ cd TwistedSumo-2005-03-22
$ python setup.py install
Password:
running install
running build
running build_py
...
running install_data
```

If you have more than one version of Python installed, keep in mind that Twisted will be installed for only the version of Python you're using when you run *setup.py*. The examples in this book require Python 2.3 or higher. To check your Python version, run *python –V*.

Congratulations—you've installed Twisted! You can make sure the installation worked by importing the Twisted package from an interactive Python prompt:

```
$ python
Python 2.3 (#1, Sep 13 2003, 00:49:11)
[GCC 3.3 20030304 (Apple Computer, Inc. build 1495)] on darwin
Type "help", "copyright", "credits" or "license" for more information.
>>> import twisted
>>>
```

If the `import twisted` statement runs with no errors, you have a working Twisted install.

Next, download the latest release of PyOpenSSL from *http://pyopenssl.sourceforge. net*. PyOpenSSL works on top of the OpenSSL library, so you'll need to make sure you have OpenSSL installed first. Mac OS X comes with OpenSSL installed, along with its header files, and all Linux and BSD distributions should have a package available (if not installed by default).

If you're using a really obscure operating system that doesn't include OpenSSL, you can download and compile the source package from *http://www.openssl.org*.

To install PyOpenSSL, follow the same steps you did when installing Twisted. First, extract the contents of the downloaded file:

```
$ tar -zxvf pyOpenSSL-0.6.tar.gz
pyOpenSSL-0.6/
pyOpenSSL-0.6/doc/
pyOpenSSL-0.6/doc/html/
...
pyOpenSSL-0.6/__init__.py
pyOpenSSL-0.6/ChangeLog
pyOpenSSL-0.6/COPYING
pyOpenSSL-0.6/version.py
```

Next, switch to the *PyOpenSSL* directory and run *python setup.py install* as root or an administrative user:

```
$ cd pyOpenSSL-0.6
$ python setup.py install
running install
running build
running build_py
creating build
...
byte-compiling
/System/Library/Frameworks/Python.framework/Versions/2.3/lib/python2.3/site-packages/
OpenSSL/__init__.py to __init__.pyc
byte-compiling
/System/Library/Frameworks/Python.framework/Versions/2.3/lib/python2.3/site-packages/
OpenSSL/version.py to version.pyc
```

When the installation is complete, test to confirm that the OpenSSL package is now available, and that Twisted is making use of it in its internet.ssl module:

```
$ python
Python 2.3 (#1, Sep 13 2003, 00:49:11)
[GCC 3.3 20030304 (Apple Computer, Inc. build 1495)] on darwin
Type "help", "copyright", "credits" or "license" for more information.
>>> import OpenSSL
>>> import twisted.internet.ssl
>>> twisted.internet.ssl.SSL
<module 'OpenSSL.SSL' from
'/System/Library/Frameworks/Python.framework/Versions/2.3/lib/python2.3/site-
packages/OpenSSL/SSL.so'>
```

If you don't see any errors, you've successfully added SSL support to your Twisted installation.

The final package to install is PyCrypto. PyCrypto, the Python Cryptography Toolkit, is a package developed by A. M. Kuchling that contains implementations of many cryptographic functions. Twisted uses PyCrypto to support SSH connections.

Start by downloading PyCrypto from *http://www.amk.ca/python/code/crypto.html*. Then extract the package:

```
$ tar -xzvf pycrypto-2.0.tar.gz
pycrypto-2.0/
pycrypto-2.0/__init__.py
pycrypto-2.0/ACKS
pycrypto-2.0/ChangeLog
...
pycrypto-2.0/Util/test/prime_speed.py
pycrypto-2.0/Util/test.py
```

Run the now-familiar *python setup.py install* (as root or an administrative user) in the *PyCrypto* directory:

```
$ cd pycrypto-2.0
$ python setup.py install
running install
running build
running build_py
creating build
...
byte-compiling
/System/Library/Frameworks/Python.framework/Versions/2.3/lib/python2.3/site-packages/
Crypto/Util/RFC1751.py to RFC1751.pyc
byte-compiling
/System/Library/Frameworks/Python.framework/Versions/2.3/lib/python2.3/site-packages/
Crypto/Util/test.py to test.pyc
```

To verify that the package installed correctly, import it from an interactive Python prompt. You can also make sure Twisted's twisted.conch.ssh.transport module is now using PyCrypto's RSA implementation:

```
$ python
Python 2.3 (#1, Sep 13 2003, 00:49:11)
[GCC 3.3 20030304 (Apple Computer, Inc. build 1495)] on darwin
Type "help", "copyright", "credits" or "license" for more information.
>>> import Crypto
>>> import twisted.conch.ssh.transport
>>> twisted.conch.ssh.transport.RSA
<module 'Crypto.PublicKey.RSA' from
'/System/Library/Frameworks/Python.framework/Versions/2.3/lib/python2.3/site-
packages/Crypto/PublicKey/RSA.pyc'>
```

And that's it! You've installed PyCrypto from source. At this point you have a complete, working Twisted installation, including support for SSL and SSH connections.

Adding Twisted Utilities to Your Path

Twisted includes a number of scripts and utilities that you'll need to use. For convenience, you should make sure these are available in your path.

How Do I Do That?

Typically, all you have to do is add Twisted's utility directory to your operating system's command search path. Follow the specific instructions given in the following section for your platform.

Windows

Twisted's utilities will be installed in the Python *scripts* directory (typically in a location such as *c:\Python23\scripts*). Twisted includes a helpful Programs menu entry that launches a Windows command prompt with the Python *scripts* directory added to *%PATH%*. It's located under Programs → Twisted (Python [version]) → Twisted Command Prompt. Use this menu entry to launch your command prompt when you need to run the Twisted utilities, or edit your *%PATH%* to include the *scripts* directory.

Linux

Twisted's utilities will be installed in the same directory as your *python* binary (probably */usr/bin* or */usr/local/bin*), so you shouldn't need to make any changes to your *$PATH*.

Mac OS X

If you're using the version of Python included with Mac OS X 2.3 "Jaguar" or later, Twisted's utilities will be installed under */System/Library/Frameworks/Python. framework/Versions/Current/bin*. Add this directory to your *$PATH*:

```
$ set PATH=$PATH:/System/Library/Frameworks/Python.framework/Versions/Current/bin
```

Using the Twisted Documentation

Twisted includes a few different types of documentation: extensive API documentation, HOWTOs, a tutorial, and sample code. It's a good idea to familiarize yourself with this documentation now, so that you'll be able to refer to it during the development process.

How Do I Do That?

Documentation for Twisted is available online on the Twisted web site. A complete API reference can be found at *http://twistedmatrix.com/documents/current/api*. You'll probably refer to this documentation many times to see which classes a module contains or to see the list of arguments for a specific function. The pages in the API documentation are automatically generated from the source code using lore, a custom documentation tool developed as part of Twisted.

Twisted is developed as a set of subprojects, and each project has additional documentation in its section of the Twisted site. For example, documentation on the core modules is at *http://twistedmatrix.com/projects/core/documentation*, and documentation on web modules is at *http://twistedmatrix.com/projects/web/documentation*. There are links to the full list of projects and documentation on the home page.

Within each project's documentation, you'll find the following types of information:

HOWTOs
> These documents describe specific features of Twisted and how to use them. The HOWTOs don't cover every part of Twisted, but they can provide a helpful starting point for certain tasks. Included in the HOWTOs is a tutorial called "Twisted From Scratch," which shows how an application can be developed in Twisted, extended to take advantage of some advanced features, and then fully integrated with the Twisted utilities.

Examples
> These are examples of short and specific Twisted programs. Like the HOWTOs, these aren't comprehensive but can be an excellent resource when you need a working example of a certain feature.

Manual pages
> These are HTML versions of the manpages describing how to use the Twisted utilities.

What About...

...viewing the API documentation without using a browser? If you'd prefer, you can view the API documentation using the standard *pydoc* utility. *pydoc* doesn't understand all of the conventions used in the Twisted internal documentation, but it's still quite usable. Figure 1-1 shows output from the command *pydoc twisted.web.http*.

Also, when you *really* want to understand how a part of Twisted works, you can always read the source code. With the exception of a few modules that are written in C for better performance, you don't even need the source distribution—just go to your Python *lib* directory, look under *site-packages/twisted*, and open the appropriate *.py* file in your favorite editor.

Finding Answers to Your Questions

Even with this book, and the Twisted documentation, you'll eventually run into a question whose answer you can't figure out on your own. When that happens, it's time to get help from the Twisted community.

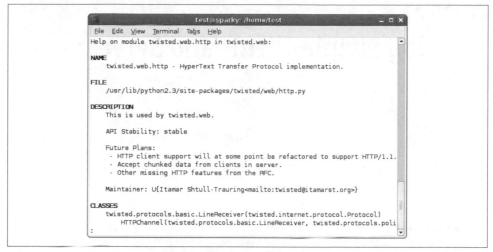

Figure 1-1. Using pydoc to view API documentation

How Do I Do That?

There are a few excellent community resources you can look to for help. First, there are the mailing lists. The *twisted-python* list is for general discussion of Twisted. The *twisted-web* list is dedicated to discussion of web applications. It's good etiquette to use the proper list; if you ask web-related questions on the *twisted-python* list, you'll probably be asked to move the discussion to *twisted-web*. You can sign up for the *twisted-python* and *twisted-web* mailing lists at *http://twistedmatrix.com/cgi-bin/ mailman/listinfo/twisted-python* and *http://twistedmatrix.com/cgi-bin/mailman/listinfo/ twisted-web*.

Second, you can talk with Twisted users and developers in the #twisted and #twisted.web IRC channels on the freenode network (see *http://freenode.net* for a list of servers). These channels feature lively, and often funny, discussion, and give you the unique opportunity to ask questions directly to members of the Twisted development team. Keep in mind, though, that such real-time support is a privilege, not a right. Be polite, and understand that developers might not always have time to answer your questions right at that moment. If you don't get an immediate answer on IRC, try sending a message to the appropriate mailing list. This approach will give the question to a wider audience, and let people answer when they have more time.

A final resource available to the Twisted community is Planet Twisted. Located at *http://planet.twistedmatrix.com*, this web site aggregates weblog posts made by members of the Twisted development team. It's an excellent way to keep track of what's going on with Twisted development, as well as to get to know the personalities of the Twisted team. Planet Twisted also provides an RSS feed at *http://planet. twistedmatrix.com/rss.xml*.

CHAPTER 2

Building Simple Clients and Servers

To develop with Twisted, you'll need to learn how to use several new classes and objects. These classes are at the core of Twisted, and you'll use them over and over in your applications. They also represent the steepest part of the Twisted learning curve. Understand how to use them, and the rest of Twisted will be easy; otherwise, you'll struggle (or write lots of unnecessary code).

This chapter shows how to write simple clients and servers with Twisted. Along the way, it introduces Twisted's basic classes, explains how they work, and demonstrates how to use them.

Starting the Twisted Event Loop

Twisted is an *event-driven* framework. This means that instead of having the program's functions called in a sequence specified by the program's logic, they are called in response to external actions, or *events*. For example, a GUI program might have code for responding to the "button pressed" event. The designer of the program can't be sure exactly when such an event will occur; but she writes a function to respond to this event whenever it does happen. Such a function is known as an *event handler*.

Every event-driven framework includes a special function called an *event loop*. Once started, an event loop runs indefinitely. While it's running, it waits for events. When an event occurs, the event loop triggers the appropriate event handler function.

Using an event loop requires a different mindset on the part of the programmer than traditional sequential programming. Once you start the event loop, you no longer have the ability to directly instruct your program what to do; it can perform actions only in response to events. Therefore, you need to think in terms of events and event handlers when you design your program. What are the events you want your program to respond to? How do you want it to react when a given event occurs?

In Twisted, there's a special object that implements the event loop. This object is called the reactor. You can think of the reactor as the central nervous system of a Twisted application. In addition to being responsible for the event loop, the reactor handles many other important tasks: scheduling, threading, establishing network connections, and listening for connections from other machines. To allow the reactor to do all these things, you must start its event loop, handing off control of your program.

How Do I Do That?

Starting the reactor is easy. Import the `reactor` object from the `twisted.internet` module. Then call `reactor.run( )` to start the reactor's event loop. Example 2-1 shows all the code you need.

Example 2-1. runreactor.py

```
from twisted.internet import reactor
print "Running the reactor..."
reactor.run( )
print "Reactor stopped."
```

The reactor will continue to run until it's told to stop. Press Ctrl-C to exit the event loop and end the application:

```
$ python runreactor.py
Running the reactor...
<ctrl-c>
^CReactor stopped.
```

That's a pretty boring example. Although the reactor was running, it hadn't been given anything to do. Example 2-2 provides a more interesting bit of code, which introduces the reactor's `callLater` method. `reactor.callLater` is used to set up scheduled events. This method is useful when you want to schedule a function to run in the future. (Such a function is still an event handler, with the event in this case being the passage of time.) In Example 2-2, functions are called after a predetermined number of seconds have passed.

Example 2-2. calllater.py

```
from twisted.internet import reactor
import time

def printTime( ):
    print "Current time is", time.strftime("%H:%M:%S")

def stopReactor( ):
    print "Stopping reactor"
    reactor.stop( )
```

Example 2-2. calllater.py (continued)

```
reactor.callLater(1, printTime)
reactor.callLater(2, printTime)
reactor.callLater(3, printTime)
reactor.callLater(4, printTime)
reactor.callLater(5, stopReactor)

print "Running the reactor..."
reactor.run( )
print "Reactor stopped."
```

Run this program, and you'll see output like the following:

```
$ python calllater.py
Running the reactor...
Current time is 10:33:44
Current time is 10:33:45
Current time is 10:33:46
Current time is 10:33:47
Stopping reactor
Reactor stopped.
```

How Does That Work?

Example 2-1 simply imports the reactor and calls reactor.run( ) to start it. The reactor will keep running (although it hadn't been giving anything to do) until you press Ctrl-C. At that point, the reactor stops, and the program proceeds to the final line of code, which prints out a message informing you that the reactor has been stopped.

The second example uses the reactor.callLater function to schedule some function calls. reactor.callLater has two required arguments: the number of seconds to wait, and the function to run. After setting up the scheduled function calls, control is handed off to the reactor's event loop using reactor.run( ).

> You can pass additional arguments and keyword arguments to reactor.callLater, and they will be used to invoke your function. For example, reactor.callLater(1, func, True, x="hello") would result in the function call func(True, x="hello"), after a one-second delay.

The first four scheduled function calls were to printTime( ), which simply printed out the current time. However, the fifth scheduled function, stopReactor( ), did something interesting. It called reactor.stop( ), which caused the reactor to exit the event loop. That's why you didn't have to press Ctrl-C to stop the reactor this time. It stopped itself.

> You can still manually stop the reactor. Try pressing Ctrl-C halfway through this example and see what happens.

Notice the order in which things happened. First, the reactor was given instructions to run certain functions at specific times. Then the reactor was started, which handed control of the program to the reactor's event loop and allowed it to manage the scheduled function calls. The reactor continued to run until it was told to stop—this time through a call to reactor.stop( ). Once the reactor had stopped, the program could proceed with the final line of code, which printed a "Reactor stopped" message.

> In real applications, reactor.callLater is typically used for timeouts and scheduled events. You might want to set up a function that runs at set intervals to do something like shut down inactive connections or save snapshots of in-memory data to disk.

Establishing a TCP Connection

All networked programs have to start with one basic step: making a connection. Eventually, of course, you'll want to send email, transfer files, and stream live video, but before any of that can happen, a connection between two computers must be established. This section shows how to use the Twisted reactor to open a TCP connection.

How Do I Do That?

Call the reactor.connectTCP( ) method to start a TCP connection, passing a ClientFactory object as the third parameter. The ClientFactory object waits for the connection to be established, and then creates a Protocol object that manages the flow of data back and forth along that connection. Example 2-3 shows how to establish a connection between your computer and a server on the Internet (in this case, *www.google.com*).

Example 2-3. tcpconnection.py

```
from twisted.internet import reactor, protocol

class QuickDisconnectProtocol(protocol.Protocol):
    def connectionMade(self):
        print "Connected to %s." % self.transport.getPeer( ).host
        self.transport.loseConnection( )

class BasicClientFactory(protocol.ClientFactory):
    protocol = QuickDisconnectProtocol

    def clientConnectionLost(self, connector, reason):
        print "Lost connection: %s" % reason.getErrorMessage( )
        reactor.stop( )
```

Example 2-3. tcpconnection.py (continued)

```
    def clientConnectionFailed(self, connector, reason):
        print "Connection failed: %s" % reason.getErrorMessage()
        reactor.stop()

reactor.connectTCP('www.google.com', 80, BasicClientFactory())
reactor.run()
```

When you run this example, you should get the following output:

```
$ python connection.py
Connected to www.google.com.
Lost connection: Connection was closed cleanly.
```

unless, of course, your computer is offline. In that case, you'll see an error message, such as this:

```
$ python connection.py
Connection failed: DNS lookup failed: address 'www.google.com' not found.
```

How Does That Work?

There are two main classes used for working with client connections, ClientFactory and Protocol. These classes are designed to handle all the potential events that arise when you start working with connections: when a connection is established, when a connection attempt fails, when an existing connection is broken, or when data is received from the other side.

ClientFactory and Protocol have specific and distinct roles. The ClientFactory's job is to manage connection-related events, and to create a new Protocol object for each successful connection. Once the connection is established, the Protocol object takes over, and is put in charge of sending and receiving data across the connection and deciding when (if ever) to close the connection.

The name "Factory" in ClientFactory comes from the fact that it creates Protocol instances on demand, in response to each successful connection.

Example 2-3 defines a custom Protocol called QuickDisconnectProtocol, which inherits from protocol.Protocol. It overrides a single method, connectionMade. This method is run as soon as the connection is up and running, just after the reactor has successfully established the connection and the ClientFactory has created this instance of QuickDisconnectProtocol. True to its name, the QuickDisconnectProtocol object quickly closes its connection (after printing the name of the host it's connected to).

Protocol objects have an attribute called transport, which is used for interacting with the current connection.

BasicClientFactory is a class inheriting from protocol.ClientFactory. It first sets the class-level attribute protocol to QuickDisconnectProtocol. An instance of this class will be created to manage each successful connection. BasicClientFactory overrides two methods of ClientFactory, clientConnectionLost and clientConnectionFailed. These methods are event handlers. clientConnectionFailed will be called if the reactor is unable to establish the connection. clientConnectionLost will be called when an established connection is closed or broken.

To tell the reactor to establish a TCP connection, Example 2-3 calls reactor.connectTCP:

```
reactor.connectTCP('www.google.com', 80, BasicClientFactory())
```

This line tells the reactor to attempt a TCP connection to the server *www.google.com*, port 80, managed by an instance of BasicClientFactory.

Working with Asynchronous Results

After the reactor, Deferreds are probably the most important objects used in Twisted. You'll work with Deferreds frequently in Twisted applications, so it's essential to understand how they work. Deferreds can be a little confusing at first, but their purpose is simple: to keep track of an asynchronous action, and to get the result when the action is completed.

Deferreds can be illustrated this way: perhaps you've had the experience of going to one of those restaurants where, if there's going to be a wait for a table, you're given a little pager that will buzz when your table is ready. Having the pager is nice, because it gives you freedom to do other things while you're waiting for your table, instead of standing around the front of the restaurant feeling bored. You can take a walk outside, or even go next door and do some shopping. When a table (finally!) becomes available, the pager buzzes, and you head back inside the restaurant to be seated.

A Deferred is like that pager. It gives your program a way of finding out when some asynchronous task is finished, which frees it up to do other things in the meantime. When a function returns a Deferred object, it's saying that there's going to be some delay before the final result of the function is available. To control what happens when the result does become available, you can assign event handlers to the Deferred.

How Do I Do That?

When writing a function that starts an asynchronous action, return a Deferred object. When the action is competed, call the Deferred's callback method with the return value. If the action fails, call Deferred.errback with an exception. Example 2-4 shows a program that uses an asynchronous action to test connectivity to a given server and port.

When calling a function that returns a Deferred object, use the Deferred.addCallback method to assign a function to handle the results of the deferred action if it completes successfully. Use the Deferred.addErrback method to assign a function to handle the exception if the deferred action fails.

Example 2-4. connectiontest.py

```python
from twisted.internet import reactor, defer, protocol

class CallbackAndDisconnectProtocol(protocol.Protocol):
    def connectionMade(self):
        self.factory.deferred.callback("Connected!")
        self.transport.loseConnection()

class ConnectionTestFactory(protocol.ClientFactory):
    protocol = CallbackAndDisconnectProtocol

    def __init__(self):
        self.deferred = defer.Deferred()

    def clientConnectionFailed(self, connector, reason):
        self.deferred.errback(reason)

def testConnect(host, port):
    testFactory = ConnectionTestFactory()
    reactor.connectTCP(host, port, testFactory)
    return testFactory.deferred

def handleSuccess(result, port):
    print "Connected to port %i" % port
    reactor.stop()

def handleFailure(failure, port):
    print "Error connecting to port %i: %s" % (
        port, failure.getErrorMessage())
    reactor.stop()

if __name__ == "__main__":
    import sys
    if not len(sys.argv) == 3:
        print "Usage: connectiontest.py host port"
        sys.exit(1)
```

Example 2-4. connectiontest.py (continued)

```
host = sys.argv[1]
port = int(sys.argv[2])
connecting = testConnect(host, port)
connecting.addCallback(handleSuccess, port)
connecting.addErrback(handleFailure, port)
reactor.run( )
```

Run this script from the command line with two arguments: the name of the server to connect to and the port to connect on. The output will look something like this:

```
$ python connectiontest.py oreilly.com 80
Connection to port 80.
```

Or, if you try to connect to a closed port:

```
$ python connectiontest.py oreilly.com 81
Error connecting to port 81: Connection was refused by other side: 22: Invalid
argument.
```

Or if you try to connect to a server that doesn't really exist:

```
$ python connectiontest.py fakesite 80
Error connecting to port 80: DNS lookup failed: address 'fakesite' not found.
```

How Does That Work?

The ConnectionTestFactory is a ClientFactory that has a Deferred object as an attribute (called, predictably enough, deferred). When the connection is completed, the connectionMade method of the CallbackAndDisconnectProtocol will be called. connectionMade then calls self.factory.deferred.callback with an arbitrary value to indicate a successful result. If the connection fails, the ConnectionTestFactory's clientConnectionFailed method will be called. The second argument to clientConnectionFailed, reason, is a twisted.python.failure.Failure object encapsulating an exception describing why the connection failed. clientConnectionFailed passes the Failure to self.deferred.errback to indicate that the action failed.

The testConnect function takes two arguments: host and port. It creates a ConnectionTestFactory called testFactory, and passes it to reactor.connectTCP along with the host and port. It then returns a testFactory.deferred attribute, which is the Deferred object used to track whether the connection attempt succeeds.

Example 2-4 also defines two event handler functions: handleSuccess and handleFailure. When run from the command line, it takes the arguments for host and port and uses them to call testConnect, assigning the resulting Deferred to the variable connecting. It then uses connecting.addCallback and connecting.addErrback to set up the event handler functions. In each case, it passes port as an additional argument. Because any extra arguments or keyword arguments given to addCallback or addErrback will be passed on to the event handler, this has the effect of calling handleSuccess or handleFailure with the port as the second argument.

When your function returns a Deferred, you must make sure to eventually call either that Deferred's callback or errback method. Otherwise, the code that calls your function will be stuck waiting forever for a result.

After calling testConnect and setting up the event handlers, control is handed off to the reactor with a call to reactor.run( ). Depending on the success of testConnect, either handleSuccess or handleFailure will eventually be called, printing a description of what happened and stopping the reactor.

What About...

...keeping track of a bunch of related Deferreds? Sometimes you might want to write a program that does many asynchronous tasks at the same time, and then exits when they've all completed. For example, you might want to build a simple port scanner that runs the testConnect function from Example 2-4 against a range of ports. To do this, use the DeferredList object, as shown in Example 2-5, to manage a group of Deferreds.

Example 2-5. portscan.py

```
from twisted.internet import reactor, defer
from connectiontester import testConnect

def handleAllResults(results, ports):
    for port, resultInfo in zip(ports, results):
        success, result = resultInfo
        if success:
            print "Connected to port %i" % port
    reactor.stop( )

import sys
host = sys.argv[1]
ports = range(1, 201)
testers = [testConnect(host, port) for port in ports]
defer.DeferredList(testers, consumeErrors=True).addCallback(
    handleAllResults, ports)
reactor.run( )
```

Run *portscan.py* with a single argument: the host to scan. It will try to connect to that host on ports 1–200 and report on the results:

```
$ python portscan.py localhost
Connected to port 22
Connected to port 23
Connected to port 25
Connected to port 80
Connected to port 110
Connected to port 139
Connected to port 143
```

Example 2-5 uses a Python list comprehension to create a list of Deferred objects returned from testConnect(). Each call to testConnect uses the host provided from the command line, and a port from 1 to 200:

```
testers = [testConnect(host, port) for port in ports]
```

Then Example 2-5 wraps the list of Deferred objects in a DeferredList object. The DeferredList will track the results of all the Deferreds in the list passed in as its first argument. When they've all finished, it will call back with a list of tuples in the format (success, result) for each Deferred in the list. If the Deferred completed successfully, the first value in each tuple will be True and the second will contain the results returned by the Deferred; if it fails, the first value will be False and the second will contain a Failure object wrapping an exception. The consumeErrors keyword is set to True to tell the DeferredList to completely absorb any errors in its Deferreds. Otherwise, you'd see a bunch of messages about unhandled errors.

When the DeferredList is complete, the results are passed to the handleAllResults function, along with a list of which ports were scanned. handleAllResults uses the zip function to match each port with its results. For each port that had a successful connection, it prints a message. Finally, it stops the reactor to end the program.

Sending and Receiving Data

Once a TCP connection is established, it can be used for communication. A program can send data to the computer on the other end, or respond to data received from the connection.

How Do I Do That?

Use a subclass of Protocol to send and receive data. Override the dataReceived method to control what happens when data is received from the connection. Use self.transport.write to send data.

Example 2-6 includes a class called DataForwardingProtocol, which takes any data received and writes it to self.output. This usage makes it possible to create a simple application, similar to the classic utility *netcat*, that passes any data received on standard input to a server, while printing any data received from the server to standard output.

Example 2-6. dataforward.py

```
from twisted.internet import stdio, reactor, protocol
from twisted.protocols import basic
import re

class DataForwardingProtocol(protocol.Protocol):
    def __init__(self):
        self.output = None
        self.normalizeNewlines = False
```

Example 2-6. dataforward.py (continued)

```
    def dataReceived(self, data):
        if self.normalizeNewlines:
            data = re.sub(r"(\r\n|\n)", "\r\n", data)
        if self.output:
            self.output.write(data)

class StdioProxyProtocol(DataForwardingProtocol):
    def connectionMade(self):
        inputForwarder = DataForwardingProtocol( )
        inputForwarder.output = self.transport
        inputForwarder.normalizeNewlines = True
        stdioWrapper = stdio.StandardIO(inputForwarder)
        self.output = stdioWrapper
        print "Connected to server.  Press ctrl-C to close connection."

class StdioProxyFactory(protocol.ClientFactory):
    protocol = StdioProxyProtocol

    def clientConnectionLost(self, transport, reason):
        reactor.stop( )

    def clientConnectionFailed(self, transport, reason):
        print reason.getErrorMessage( )
        reactor.stop( )

if __name__ == '__main__':
    import sys
    if not len(sys.argv) == 3:
        print "Usage: %s host port" % __file__
        sys.exit(1)

    reactor.connectTCP(sys.argv[1], int(sys.argv[2]), StdioProxyFactory( ))
    reactor.run( )
```

Run *dataforward.py* with two arguments: the host and port to connect to. Once connected, you can interact with the server from the command line. Anything you type will be sent to the server, and any data received from the server will be printed to your screen. For example, you can do a manual HTTP request to oreilly.com:

```
$ python dataforward.py oreilly.com 80
Connected to server.  Press ctrl-C to close connection.
HEAD / HTTP/1.0
Host: oreilly.com
                      <-- blank line
HTTP/1.1 200 OK
Date: Fri, 17 Dec 2004 06:25:53 GMT
Server: Apache/1.3.33 (Unix) PHP/4.3.9 mod_perl/1.29
P3P: policyref="http://www.oreillynet.com/w3c/p3p.xml",CP="CAO DSP COR CURa ADMa DEVa
TAIa PSAa PSDa IVAa IVDa CONo OUR DELa PUBi OTRa IND PHY ONL UNI PUR COM NAV INT DEM
CNT STA PRE"
```

```
Last-Modified: Fri, 17 Dec 2004 00:58:06 GMT
ETag: "8352-de9f-41c22f1e"
Accept-Ranges: bytes
Content-Length: 56991
Content-Type: text/html
X-Cache: MISS from www.oreilly.com
Connection: close
```

How Does That Work?

Example 2-6 starts by defining a class called DataForwardingProtocol. Whenever this Protocol receives data, it will pass that data along to self.output (which can be any object with a write method) by calling self.output.write. DataForwardingProtocol has an attribute called normalizeNewLines. If this is set to true, it will normalize Unix-style \n newlines to the \r\n newlines used by most standard network protocols.

A subclass of DataForwardingProtocol, StdioProxyProtocol, does all the setup work. Once its connection is established, it creates a DataForwardingProtocol instance called inputForwarder and sets its output to self.transport. Then it wraps inputForwarder in an instance of the twisted.internet.stdio.StandardIO utility class, which hooks inputForwarder up to standard I/O instead of a network connection. This step has the effect of forwarding any data received on standard input to the StdioProxyProtocol's network connection. Finally, it sets the StdioProxyProtocol's output attribute to stdioWrapper, so that data received from the connection will be forwarded to standard output.

Once these protocols have been defined, it's simply a matter of defining StdioProxyFactory, which sets StdioProxyProtocol as its protocol, and handles stopping the reactor when the connection is closed (or fails). A call to reactor.connectTCP kicks off the connection attempt, and then control is given to the reactor with reactor.run( ).

Accepting Connections from Clients

The previous labs in this chapter dealt with client connections, where an application initiated a connection to a remote server. However, Twisted can also be used for writing network servers, where the application waits for connections from clients. This lab will show you how to write a Twisted server that accepts connections from clients and interacts with them.

How Do I Do That?

Create a `Protocol` object defining your server's behavior. Create a `ServerFactory` object using the `Protocol`, and pass it to `reactor.listenTCP`. Example 2-7 shows a simple echo server that accepts a client connection and then repeats back all client messages.

Example 2-7. echoserver.py

```python
from twisted.internet import reactor, protocol
from twisted.protocols import basic

class EchoProtocol(basic.LineReceiver):
    def lineReceived(self, line):
        if line == 'quit':
            self.sendLine("Goodbye.")
            self.transport.loseConnection()
        else:
            self.sendLine("You said: " + line)

class EchoServerFactory(protocol.ServerFactory):
    protocol  = EchoProtocol

if __name__ == "__main__":
    port = 5001
    reactor.listenTCP(port, EchoServerFactory())
    reactor.run()
```

When you run this example, it will listen on port 5001, and report client connections as they are made:

```
$ python echoserver.py
Server running, press ctrl-C to stop.
Connection from  127.0.0.1
Connection from  127.0.0.1
```

In another terminal, use *netcat*, *telnet*, or the *dataforward.py* application from Example 2-6 to connect to the server. It will echo anything you type back to you. Type **quit** to close your connection:

```
$ python dataforward.py localhost 5001
Connected to server.  Press ctrl-C to close connection.
hello
You said: hello
twisted is fun
You said: twisted is fun
quit
Goodbye.
$ How does that work?
```

Twisted servers use the same Protocol classes as clients. To save some work, the EchoProtocol in Example 2-6 inherits from twisted.protocols.basic.LineReciever, which is a slightly higher-level implementation of Protocol. LineReceiver is a Protocol that automatically breaks its input into separate lines, making it easier to process a single line at a time. When EchoProtocol receives a line, it will echo it back to the client—unless the line is "quit", in which case it sends a goodbye message and closes the connection.

Next, a class called EchoServerFactory is defined. EchoServerFactory inherits from ServerFactory, the server-side sibling of ClientFactory, and sets EchoProtocol as its protocol. An instance of EchoServerFactory is then passed as the second argument to reactor.listenTCP, with the first argument being the port to listen on.

CHAPTER 3
Web Clients

The most common way to interact with the Web is through a web browser. But as more data and services are made available on the Web, it's important to be able to write web clients that can communicate with web servers through HTTP. This chapter shows how to use the twisted.web.client module to interact with web resources, including downloading pages, using HTTP authentication, uploading files, and working with HTTP headers.

Downloading a Web Page

The simplest and most common task for a web client application is fetching the contents of a web page. The client connects to the server, sends an HTTP GET request, and receives an HTTP response containing the requested page.

How Do I Do That?

Here's where you can begin to experience the usefulness of Twisted's built-in protocol support. The twisted.web package includes a complete HTTP implementation, saving you the work of developing the necessary Protocol and ClientFactory classes. Furthermore, it includes utility functions that allow you to make an HTTP request with a single function call. To fetch the contents of a web page, use the function twisted.web.client.getPage. Example 3-1 is a Python script called *webcat.py*, which fetches a URL that you specify.

Example 3-1. webcat.py

```
from twisted.web import client
from twisted.internet import reactor
import sys

def printPage(data):
    print data
    reactor.stop( )
```

Example 3-1. webcat.py (continued)

```
def printError(failure):
    print >> sys.stderr, "Error:", failure.getErrorMessage( )
    reactor.stop( )

if len(sys.argv) == 2:
    url = sys.argv[1]
    client.getPage(url).addCallback(
        printPage).addErrback(
        printError)
    reactor.run( )
else:
    print "Usage: webcat.py <URL>"
```

Give *webcat.py* a URL as its first argument, and it will fetch and print the contents of
the page:

```
$ python webcat.py http://www.oreilly.com/
<!DOCTYPE HTML PUBLIC "-//W3C//DTD HTML 4.01 Transitional//EN">
<html xmlns="http://www.w3.org/1999/xhtml" lang="en-US" xml:lang="en-US">
<head>
<title>oreilly.com -- Welcome to O'Reilly Media, Inc. -- computer books, software
conferences, online publishing</title>
...
```

How Does That Work?

The printPage and printError functions are simple event handlers that print the
downloaded page contents or an error message, respectively. The most important
line in Example 3-1 is the call to client.getPage(url). This function returns a
Deferred object that will be called back with the contents of the page once it has
been completely downloaded.

Notice how the callbacks are added to the Deferred in a single line. This is possible
because addCallback and addErrback both return a reference to their Deferred object.
Therefore, the statements:

```
d = deferredFunction( )
d.addCallback(resultHandler)
d.addErrback(errorHandler)
```

can be expressed as:

```
deferredFunction( ).addCallback(resultsHandler).addErrback(errorHandler)
```

Which of these two forms is more readable is probably a matter of personal opinion,
but the latter is an idiom that appears frequently in Twisted code.

What About...

...writing the page to disk as it's being downloaded? One disadvantage to the *webcat.py* script in Example 3-1 is that it loads the entire contents of the downloading page into memory, which could present a problem if you're downloading a large file. A better approach might be to write the data to a temporary file on disk as it's being downloaded, and then read the contents back from the temp file once the download is complete.

twisted.web.client includes downloadPage, a function that is similar to getPage but that writes data to a file. Call downloadPage with a URL as the first argument, and a filename or file object as the second. The script *webcat2.py* in Example 3-2 does this.

Example 3-2. webcat2.py

```python
from twisted.web import client
import tempfile

def downloadToTempFile(url):
    """
    Given a URL, returns a Deferred that will be called back with
    the name of a temporary file containing the downloaded data.
    """
    tmpfd, tempfilename = tempfile.mkstemp()
    os.close(tmpfd)
    return client.downloadPage(url, tempfilename).addCallback(
        returnFilename, tempfilename)

def returnFilename(result, filename):
    return filename

if __name__ == "__main__":
    import sys, os
    from twisted.internet import reactor

    def printFile(filename):
        for line in file(filename, 'r+b'):
            sys.stdout.write(line)
        os.unlink(filename) # delete file once we're done with it
        reactor.stop()

    def printError(failure):
        print >> sys.stderr, "Error:", failure.getErrorMessage()
        reactor.stop()

    if len(sys.argv) == 2:
        url = sys.argv[1]
        downloadToTempFile(url).addCallback(
        printFile).addErrback(
        printError)
        reactor.run()
    else:
        print "Usage: %s <URL>" % sys.argv[0]
```

The `downloadToTempFile` function in Example 3-2 returns the `Deferred` that results from calling `twisted.web.client.downloadPage`. `downloadToTempFile` adds `returnFilename` as a callback to this `Deferred`, with the temp filename as an additional argument. This means that when the result of `downloadToTempFile` comes in, the reactor will call `returnFileName` with the result of `downloadToTempFile` as the first argument and the filename as the second argument.

Example 3-2 registers another callback for the result of `downloadToTempFile`. Remember that the `Deferred` returned from `downloadToTempFile` already has `returnFilename` as a callback handler. Therefore, when the result comes in, `returnFilename` will be called first. The result of this function (the filename) will be used to call `printFile`.

Accessing a Password-Protected Page

Web pages can require authentication. If you're developing an HTTP client application, it's a good idea to be prepared to handle this case, and give the user some way of entering his login name and password.

How Do I Do That?

If an HTTP request fails with a 401 status code, authentication is required. Try the request again, this time passing a user-supplied login and password in an `Authorization` header, as shown in the script *webcat3.py* in Example 3-3.

Example 3-3. webcat3.py

```python
from twisted.web import client, error as weberror
from twisted.internet import reactor
import sys, getpass, base64

def printPage(data):
    print data
    reactor.stop()

def checkHTTPError(failure, url):
    failure.trap(weberror.Error)
    if failure.value.status == '401':
        print >> sys.stderr, failure.getErrorMessage()
        # prompt for user name and password
        username = raw_input("User name: ")
        password = getpass.getpass("Password: ")
        basicAuth = base64.encodestring("%s:%s" % (username, password))
        authHeader = "Basic " + basicAuth.strip()
        # try to fetch the page again with authentication
        return client.getPage(
            url, headers={"Authorization": authHeader})
    else:
        return failure
```

Example 3-3. webcat3.py (continued)

```
def printError(failure):
    print >> sys.stderr, "Error:", failure.getErrorMessage()
    reactor.stop()

if len(sys.argv) == 2:
    url = sys.argv[1]
    client.getPage(url).addErrback(
        checkHTTPError, url).addCallback(
        printPage).addErrback(
        printError)
    reactor.run()
else:
    print "Usage: %s <URL>" % sys.argv[0]
```

Run *webcat3.py* with a URL as the first argument, and it will attempt to download and print the page. If it receives a 401 error, it will ask for a username and password and try the request again:

```
$ python webcat3.py http://example.com/protected/page
401 Authorization Required
User name: User
Password: <enter password>
<html>
<title>A Password Protected Page</title>
...
```

How Does That Work?

This example uses an extra error handler, checkHTTPError. It is added to the Deferred returned from client.getPage first, before adding the printPage and printError handler functions. This gives checkHTTPError the opportunity to handle any errors returned by client.getPage before either of the other handler functions is called.

As an errback handler, checkHTTPError will be called with a twisted.python.failure. Failure object. The Failure object encapsulates the exception that was raised, records a traceback at the time of the exception, and adds several useful methods. checkHTTPError starts by using the Failure.trap method to verify that the exception was of type twisted.web.error.Error. If it wasn't, trap will reraise the exception, exiting the current function and letting the error pass on to the next errback handler in line, printError.

Next, checkHTTPError checks the HTTP response status code. failure.value is an Exception object, and since it's already been verified as type twisted.web.error. Error, it's known to have a status attribute containing the status code. If the status is not 401, the original failure is simply returned, which again has the effect of letting the error pass through to printError.

But if the status is 401, checkHTTPError takes action. It prompts the user for his login name and password, and encodes the results into an HTTP Authorization header. Then it calls client.getPage again, and returns the resulting Deferred. This causes something very cool to happen: the reactor waits for the results of this second call to getPage, and then calls printPage or printError with those results. In effect, checkHTTPError is saying, "Handling the error resulted in another Deferred—wait for the result of that Deferred and pass it to the next event handler in line." This technique is very powerful and is used many times in Twisted applications.

The end result is the same as in previous examples: either printPage is called with the downloaded page data, or printError is called with an error. Of course, if the initial request was successful, and didn't require authentication, checkHTTPError is never called at all, and the result passes directly to printPage.

Uploading a File

From a user's perspective, there's no easier way to upload a file than going to a web page, using an HTML form to select the file, and pressing the submit button. Because of this, many web sites have adopted HTTP as a means of allowing file uploads. There are times, however, when you might need to perform a file upload without using a browser. Perhaps you want to develop an application that can upload image files to a photo-sharing service, or HTML documents to a web-based content management system. This lab shows how to use Twisted's HTTP client support to perform a file upload.

How Do I Do That?

First, encode the field/value pairs and file data that you wish to upload as a multipart/form-data MIME document. Neither the Python standard library nor Twisted provides an easy way to do this, but you can do it yourself without too much effort. Then pass the encoded form data as the formdata keyword argument to client.getPage or client.downloadPage, along with POST as the HTTP method. You can then work with the results of getPage or downloadPage as you would any other HTTP response. Example 3-4 shows a script named *validate.py* that uploads a file to the W3C validation service, saves the response to a local file, and then displays it in the user's browser.

Example 3-4. validate.py

```
from twisted.web import client
import os, tempfile, webbrowser, random

def encodeForm(inputs):
    """
    Takes a dict of inputs and returns a multipart/form-data string
    containing the utf-8 encoded data. Keys must be strings, values
```

Example 3-4. validate.py (continued)

```
    can be either strings or file-like objects.
    """
    getRandomChar = lambda: chr(random.choice(range(97, 123)))
    randomChars = [getRandomChar() for x in range(20)]
    boundary = "---%s---" % ''.join(randomChars)
    lines = [boundary]
    for key, val in inputs.items():
        header = 'Content-Disposition: form-data; name="%s"' % key
        if hasattr(val, 'name'):
            header += '; filename="%s"' % os.path.split(val.name)[1]
        lines.append(header)
        if hasattr(val, 'read'):
            lines.append(val.read())
        else:
            lines.append(val.encode('utf-8'))
        lines.append('')
        lines.append(boundary)
    return "\r\n".join(lines)

def showPage(pageData):
    # write data to temp .html file, show file in browser
    tmpfd, tmp = tempfile.mkstemp('.html')
    os.close(tmpfd)
    file(tmp, 'w+b').write(pageData)
    webbrowser.open('file://' + tmp)
    reactor.stop()

def handleError(failure):
    print "Error:", failure.getErrorMessage()
    reactor.stop()

if __name__ == "__main__":
    import sys
    from twisted.internet import reactor

    filename = sys.argv[1]
    fileToCheck = file(filename)
    form = encodeForm({'uploaded_file': fileToCheck})
    postRequest = client.getPage(
        'http://validator.w3.org/check',
        method='POST',
        headers={'Content-Type': 'multipart/form-data; charset=utf-8',
                 'Content-Length': str(len(form))},
        postdata=form)
    postRequest.addCallback(showPage).addErrback(handleError)
    reactor.run()
```

Run *validate.py* with the name of an HTML file as the first argument:

```
    $ python validate.py test.html
```

As long as there are no errors, you should get a validation report in your default browser, similar to the report shown in Figure 3-1.

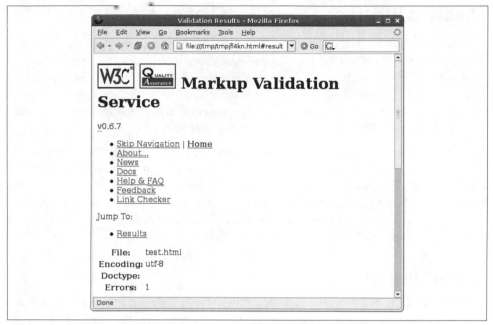

Figure 3-1. Result of running validate.py

How Does That Work?

The W3C validate page, *http://validator.w3.org*, contains a form that looks like this:

```
<form method="post" enctype="multipart/form-data" action="check">
  <label title="Choose a Local File to Upload and Validate"
         for="uploaded_file">Local File:
  <input type="file" id="uploaded_file" name="uploaded_file" size="30" /></label>
  <label title="Submit file for validation">
  <input type="submit" value="Check" /></label>
</form>
```

You can build an HTTP client that sends the same data a browser would use when submitting that form. The encodeForm function takes a dictionary that maps keys to string values or file-like objects, and returns a string containing the data as a multipart/form-encoded MIME document. When *validate.py* runs, it opens the file specified as its first argument and passes it to encodeForm as the 'uploaded_file' value of a dictionary. This returns the data that should be posted to the validator service.

validate.py then uses client.getPage to post the form data, passing headers to advise the server of the Content-Length and Content-Type of the data being posted. The showPage callback handler takes the data returned from the validator service and writes it to a temporary file. Then it uses Python's webbrowser module to open the file in the user's default browser.

Checking Whether a Page Has Changed

One popular HTTP application is RSS (Really Simple Syndication) aggregators, which download news items or blog posts in RSS (or Atom) format. RSS aggregators download a new copy of each RSS feed at regular intervals, typically once an hour. This process can end up wasting a lot of bandwidth for the publisher of the RSS feed, though: the contents of the feed may change infrequently, which means that the client will be downloading the same data over and over again.

To prevent this waste of network resources, RSS aggregators (and other applications that request the same page multiple times) are encouraged to use a *conditional HTTP GET* request. By including conditional HTTP headers with a request, a client instructs the server to return the page data only if certain conditions are met. And, of course, one of those conditions might be whether the page has been modified since it was last checked.

How Do I Do That?

Keep track of the headers returned the first time you download the page. Look for either an ETag header, which identifies the unique revision of the page, or the Last-Modified header, which gives the page's modification time. The next time you request the page, send the headers If-None-Match, with the ETag value, and If-Modified-Since, with the Last-Modified value. If the server supports conditional GET requests, it will return a 304 Unchanged response if the page has not been modified since the last request.

The getPage and downloadPage functions provided by twisted.web.client are handy, but they don't allow for the level of control necessary to use conditional requests. Therefore, you'll need to use the slightly lower-level HTTPClientFactory interface. Example 3-5 demonstrates using HTTPClientFactory to test whether a page has been updated.

Example 3-5. updatecheck.py

```
from twisted.web import client

class HTTPStatusChecker(client.HTTPClientFactory):

    def __init__(self, url, headers=None):
        client.HTTPClientFactory.__init__(self, url, headers=headers)
        self.status = None
        self.deferred.addCallback(
            lambda data: (data, self.status, self.response_headers))

    def noPage(self, reason): # called for non-200 responses
        if self.status == '304': # Page hadn't changed
            client.HTTPClientFactory.page(self, '')
```

Example 3-5. updatecheck.py (continued)

```
        else:
            client.HTTPClientFactory.noPage(self, reason)

def checkStatus(url, contextFactory=None, *args, **kwargs):
    scheme, host, port, path = client._parse(url)
    factory = HTTPStatusChecker(url, *args, **kwargs)
    if scheme == 'https':
        from twisted.internet import ssl
        if contextFactory is None:
            contextFactory = ssl.ClientContextFactory()
        reactor.connectSSL(host, port, factory, contextFactory)
    else:
        reactor.connectTCP(host, port, factory)
    return factory.deferred

def handleFirstResult(result, url):
    data, status, headers = result
    nextRequestHeaders = {}
    eTag = headers.get('etag')
    if eTag:
        nextRequestHeaders['If-None-Match'] = eTag[0]
    modified = headers.get('last-modified')
    if modified:
        nextRequestHeaders['If-Modified-Since'] = modified[0]
    return checkStatus(url, headers=nextRequestHeaders).addCallback(
        handleSecondResult)

def handleSecondResult(result):
    data, status, headers = result
    print 'Second request returned status %s:' % status,
    if status == '200':
        print 'Page changed (or server does not support conditional requests).'
    elif status == '304':
        print 'Page is unchanged.'
    else:
        print 'Unexpected Response.'
    reactor.stop()

def handleError(failure):
    print "Error", failure.getErrorMessage()
    reactor.stop()

if __name__ == "__main__":
    import sys
    from twisted.internet import reactor

    url = sys.argv[1]
    checkStatus(url).addCallback(
        handleFirstResult, url).addErrback(
        handleError)
    reactor.run()
```

Run updatecheck.py from the command line with a web URL as the first argument. It will download the page once, and then download it again using a conditional GET. It then indicates whether the second response was a 304, indicating that the server understood the conditional headers and indicated that the page had not changed. It's fairly typical for servers to support conditional GET requests for static files, such as RSS feeds, but not dynamically generated content, such as the home page:

```
$ python updatecheck.py http://slashdot.org/slashdot.rss
Second request returned status 304: Page is unchanged
$ python updatecheck.py http://slashdot.org/
Second request returned status 200: Page changed
(or server does not support conditional requests).
```

How Does That Work?

The HTTPStatusChecker class is a subclass of client.HTTPClientFactory. It does a couple of notable things. During initialization, it adds an additional callback to self.deferred, using a lambda function. This anonymous function will catch the result of self.deferred before it gets passed to any external callback handlers. It will then replace this result (the downloaded data) with a tuple containing more information: the data, the HTTP status code, and self.response_headers, which is a dictionary of the headers returned with the response.

HTTPStatusChecker also overrides the noPage method, which HTTPClientFactory calls to indicate an unsuccessful response code. If the response status is 304 (the Unchanged status code), the noPage method calls HTTPClientFactory.page instead of the original noPage method, which indicates a successful response. In the case of a success, of course, the noPage in HTTPStatusChecker passes the call on to the overridden noPage in HTTPClientFactory. In this way, it prevents a 304 response from being considered an error.

The checkStatus function takes a URL and parses it using the twisted.web.client._parse utility function. It looks at the parts of the URL, gets the hostname it needs to connect to, and whether it's using HTTP (which runs over straight TCP) or HTTPS (which runs over SSL, and establishes the connection using reactor.connectSSL). Next, checkStatus creates an HTTPStatusChecker factory object, and opens the connection. All this code is basically lifted from twisted.web.client.getPage and modified to use the HTTPStatusChecker factory instead of the vanilla HTTPClientFactory.

When updatecheck.py runs, it calls checkStatus, setting handleFirstResult as the callback handler. handleFirstResult, in turn, makes a second request using the If-None-Match and If-Modified-Since conditional headers, setting handleSecondResult as the callback handler. The handleSecondResult function reports whether the server returned a 304 response, and then stops the reactor.

`handleFirstResult` actually returns the deferred result of `handleSecondResult`. This allows `printError`, the error handler function assigned to the first call to `checkStatus`, to handle any errors that come up in the second call to `checkStatus` as well.

Monitoring Download Progress

One potential weakness in the examples presented so far in this chapter is that there hasn't been a way to monitor a download in progress. Sure, it's nice that a `Deferred` will pass you the results of a page once it's completely downloaded, but sometimes what you really need is to keep an eye on the download as it's happening.

How Do I Do That?

Again, the utility functions provided by `twisted.web.client` don't give you quite enough control. Define a subclass of `client.HTTPDownloader`, the factory class used for downloading a web page to a file. By overriding a couple of methods, you can keep track of a download in progress. The *webdownload.py* script in Example 3-6 shows how.

Example 3-6. webdownload.py

```python
from twisted.web import client

class HTTPProgressDownloader(client.HTTPDownloader):

    def gotHeaders(self, headers):
        if self.status == '200': # page data is on the way
            if headers.has_key('content-length'):
                self.totalLength = int(headers['content-length'][0])
            else:
                self.totalLength = 0
            self.currentLength = 0.0
            print ''
        return client.HTTPDownloader.gotHeaders(self, headers)

    def pagePart(self, data):
        if self.status == '200':
            self.currentLength += len(data)
            if self.totalLength:
                percent = "%i%%" % (
                    (self.currentLength/self.totalLength)*100)
            else:
                percent = '%dK' % (self.currentLength/1000)
            print "\033[1FProgress: " + percent
        return client.HTTPDownloader.pagePart(self, data)

def downloadWithProgress(url, file, contextFactory=None, *args, **kwargs):
    scheme, host, port, path = client._parse(url)
    factory = HTTPProgressDownloader(url, file, *args, **kwargs)
```

Example 3-6. webdownload.py (continued)

```
    if scheme == 'https':
        from twisted.internet import ssl
        if contextFactory is None:
            contextFactory = ssl.ClientContextFactory()
        reactor.connectSSL(host, port, factory, contextFactory)
    else:
        reactor.connectTCP(host, port, factory)
    return factory.deferred

if __name__ == "__main__":
    import sys
    from twisted.internet import reactor

    def downloadComplete(result):
        print "Download Complete."
        reactor.stop()

    def downloadError(failure):
        print "Error:", failure.getErrorMessage()
        reactor.stop()

    url, outputFile = sys.argv[1:]
    downloadWithProgress(url, outputFile).addCallback(
        downloadComplete).addErrback(
        downloadError)
    reactor.run()
```

Run *webdownload.py* with two arguments: the URL of a page to download and a filename in which to save it. As the command works, it will print updates on the download progress:

```
$ python webdownload.py http://www.oreilly.com/ oreilly.html
Progress: 100%  <- updated during the download
Download Complete.
```

If the web server doesn't return a Content-Length header indicating the total length of the download, it isn't possible to calculate the percentage complete. In this case, *webdownload.py* prints the number of kilobytes downloaded:

```
$ python webdownload.py http://www.slashdot.org/ slashdot.html
Progress: 60K <- updated during the download
Download Complete.
```

How Does That Work?

HTTPProgressDownloader is a subclass of client.HTTPDownloader. It overrides the gotHeaders method to check for a Content-Length header that would indicate the total size of the page being downloaded. It also overrides the pagePart method, which is called each time a chunk of page data is received, to keep track of the number of bytes downloaded so far.

Each time a chunk of data comes in, HTTPProgressDownloader prints out a progress report. The string \033[1F is a terminal escape sequence that causes each line of the progress report to be written over the preceding line. This effect makes it look like the progress information is being updated in place.

The downloadWithProgress function contains code similar to that in Example 3-5 for parsing the requested URL, creating the HTTPProgressDownloader factory object, and initializing the connection. downloadComplete and downloadError are simple callback and errback handlers that print a message and stop the reactor.

CHAPTER 4

Web Servers

It's probably safe to say that these days, most new software is being developed in the form of web applications. People spend an increasingly large part of their day in their web browser, not just reading HTML pages but sending email, managing calendars, entering records into databases, updating Wiki pages, and writing weblog posts.

Even if you're not writing an application strictly for the Web, a web interface is often the easiest way to provide a cross-platform UI for things like administration and reporting. The ability to include a lightweight web server inside your app without introducing any additional dependencies is one of the great things about developing with Twisted. This chapter shows you how to run a web server using Twisted, and introduces you to some building blocks for creating web applications. It also offers an example of a custom HTTP proxy server.

 This chapter provides some introductory information about the HTTP protocol used by web servers and web clients. There are many additional details of HTTP that you should know if you're serious about building web applications. In fact, there's enough information to write an entire book on the subject, such as *HTTP: The Definitive Guide* by David Gourley and Brian Totty (O'Reilly). There's also no substitute for reading the HTTP spec, RFC 2616 (*http://www.faqs.org/rfcs/rfc2616.html*).

Responding to HTTP Requests

HTTP is, on its surface, a simple protocol. A client sends a request, the server sends a response, the connection closes. You can experiment with HTTP by writing your own Protocol that accepts a connection, reads the request, and sends back an HTTP-formatted response.

How Do I Do That?

Every HTTP request starts with a single line containing the HTTP method, a partial *Uniform Resource Identifier* (URI), and the HTTP version. Following this line are an arbitrary number of header lines. A blank line indicates the end of the headers. The header section is optionally followed by additional data called the *body* of the request, such as data being posted from an HTML form.

Here's an example of a minimal HTTP request. This request asks the server to perform the method GET on the resource www.example.com/index.html, preferably using HTTP version 1.1:

```
GET /index.html HTTP/1.1
Host: www.example.com
```

The first line of the server's response tells the client the HTTP version being used for the response and the HTTP status code. Like the request, the response also contains header lines followed by a blank line and the message body. Here's a minimal HTTP response:

```
HTTP/1.1 200 OK
Content-Type: text/plain
Content-Length: 17
Connection: Close

Hello HTTP world!
```

To set up a very basic HTTP server, write a Protocol that accepts input from the client. Look for the blank line that identifies the end of the headers. Then send an HTTP response. Example 4-1 shows a simple HTTP implementation that echoes each request back to the client.

Example 4-1. webecho.py

```
from twisted.protocols import basic
from twisted.internet import protocol, reactor

class HttpEchoProtocol(basic.LineReceiver):

    def __init__(self):
        self.lines = []
        self.gotRequest = False

    def lineReceived(self, line):
        self.lines.append(line)
        if not line and not self.gotRequest:
            self.sendResponse()
            self.gotRequest = True
```

Example 4-1. webecho.py (continued)

```python
    def sendResponse(self):
        responseBody = "You said:\r\n\r\n" + "\r\n".join(self.lines)
        self.sendLine("HTTP/1.0 200 OK")
        self.sendLine("Content-Type: text/plain")
        self.sendLine("Content-Length: %i" % len(responseBody))
        self.sendLine("")
        self.transport.write(responseBody)
        self.transport.loseConnection( )

f = protocol.ServerFactory( )
f.protocol = HttpEchoProtocol
reactor.listenTCP(8000, f)
reactor.run( )
```

Run *webecho.py* to start the server. You can see the server in action by pointing your web browser to *http://localhost:8000*. You'll get a response echoing the request your browser sends to the server, as shown in Figure 4-1.

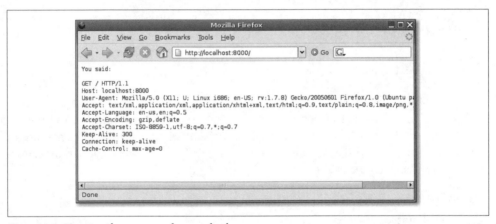

Figure 4-1. Viewing the response from webecho.py

How Does That Work?

HTTPEchoProtocol understands just enough about HTTP to return a response to each request. As data is received from the client, it appends each incoming line to self.lines. When it sees a blank line, it knows that it has come to the end of the headers. It then sends back an HTTP response. The first line contains the HTTP version and status code; in this case, 200 for OK (the string "OK" is a human-readable version of the status code; it could just as easily be another phrase with the same meaning, like "No problem!"). The next couple of lines are the Content-Type and Content-Length headers, which tell the client the format and length of the body. HTTPEchoProtocol sends a blank line to indicate the end of the headers, and then the body itself, which in this case is just an echo of the request sent by the client.

Parsing HTTP Requests

The `HTTPEchoProtocol` class in Example 4-1 provides an interesting glimpse into HTTP in action, but it's a long way from being ready for use in a real web server. It doesn't even parse the request to figure out what resource the client is trying to access, or what HTTP method she's using. Before you try to build a real web application, you need a better way to parse and respond to requests. This lab shows you how.

How Do I Do That?

Write a subclass of `twisted.web.http.Request` with a process method that processes the current request. The Request object will already contain all the important information about an HTTP request when process is called, so all you have to do is decide how to respond. Example 4-2 demonstrates how to run an HTTP server based on a subclass of `http.Request`.

Example 4-2. requesthandler.py

```python
from twisted.web import http

class MyRequestHandler(http.Request):
    pages = {
        '/': '<h1>Home</h1>Home page',
        '/test': '<h1>Test</h1>Test page',
        }

    def process(self):
        if self.pages.has_key(self.path):
            self.write(self.pages[self.path])
        else:
            self.setResponseCode(http.NOT_FOUND)
            self.write("<h1>Not Found</h1>Sorry, no such page.")
        self.finish()

class MyHttp(http.HTTPChannel):
    requestFactory = MyRequestHandler

class MyHttpFactory(http.HTTPFactory):
    protocol = MyHttp

if __name__ == "__main__":
    from twisted.internet import reactor
    reactor.listenTCP(8000, MyHttpFactory())
    reactor.run()
```

Run *requesthandler.py* and it will start up a web server on port 8000. You should be able to view both the home page (*http://localhost:8000/*) and the page /test (*http://localhost:8000/test*) in your browser. Figure 4-2 shows you how the page /test will look in your browser.

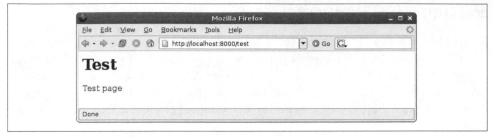

Figure 4-2. A page generated by the requesthandler.py web server

If you attempt to load any other page, you should get an error message, as shown in Figure 4-3.

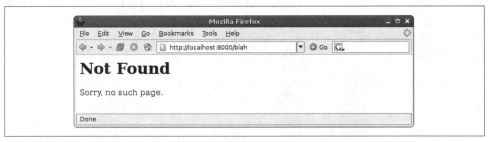

Figure 4-3. The requesthandler.py 404 page

How Does That Work?

The `http.Request` class parses an incoming HTTP request and provides an interface for working with the request and generating a response. In Example 4-2, `MyRequestHandler` is a subclass of `http.Request` that provides a custom `process` method. The `process` method will be called after the request has been completely received. It is responsible for generating a response and then calling `self.finish()` to indicate that the response is complete. `MyRequestHandler` uses the `path` property to find out which path is being requested, and attempts to find a matching path in the `pages` dictionary. If a matching page is found, `MyRequestHandler` uses the `write` method to send back the text of the page as the response.

Note that `write` is used only to write the body portion of the response, not to generate the raw HTTP response itself. The `setResponseCode` method can be used to change the HTTP status code. The `twisted.web.http` module provides constants for all the status codes defined by HTTP, so you can write `http.NOT_FOUND` instead of 404.

> `Request.setResponseCode` takes an optional second argument, a human-readable status message. You can feel free to leave this out—the `twisted.web.http` module includes a built-in list of descriptions for common status codes, which it will use by default.

The Request class also provides a setHeader method for adding headers to the response. MyRequestHandler uses setHeader to set the Content-Type header to text/html; this setting tells the browser that the response body is in HTML format.

The twisted.web.http module provides two additional classes that you'll need to turn your subclass of Request into a functioning web server. The HTTPChannel class is a Protocol that creates Request objects for each connection. To make the HTTPChannel use your subclass of Request, override the requestFactory class attribute. HTTPFactory is a ServerFactory that adds some extra features, including a log method that takes a Request object and generates a log message in the standard Combined log format used by Apache and other web servers.

Working with POST Data from HTML Forms

The previous lab showed how to take a request from a client and return a response containing static HTML. This lab shows how you could write code to control how each response is generated, and act on data submitted from an HTML form.

How Do I Do That?

Write functions that take a Request object and work with it to generate a response. Set up a dictionary to map each available path in your web site to a function that will handle requests for that path. Use the Request.args dictionary to access data submitted from an HTML form. Example 4-3 shows a web server that generates one page containing an HTML form, and another page that processes the form and displays the results.

Example 4-3. formhandler.py

```
from twisted.web import http

def renderHomePage(request):
    colors = 'red', 'blue', 'green'
    flavors - 'vanilla', 'chocolate', 'strawberry', 'coffee'
    request.write("""
    <html>
    <head>
      <title>Form Test</html>
    </head>
    <body>
      <form action='posthandler' method='post'>
        Your name:
        <p>
          <input type='text' name='name'>
        </p>
        What's your favorite color?
        <p>
```

Example 4-3. formhandler.py (continued)

```python
    """)
    for color in colors:
        request.write(
            "<input type='radio' name='color' value='%s'>%s<br />" % (
            color, color.capitalize()))
    request.write("""
        </p>
        What kinds of ice cream do you like?
        <p>
        """)
    for flavor in flavors:
        request.write(
            "<input type='checkbox' name='flavor' value='%s'>%s<br />" % (
            flavor, flavor.capitalize()))
    request.write("""
        </p>
        <input type='submit' />
      </form>
    </body>
    </html>
    """)
    request.finish()

def handlePost(request):
    request.write("""
    <html>
      <head>
        <title>Posted Form Datagg</title>
      </head>
      <body>
      <h1>Form Data</h1>
    """)

    for key, values in request.args.items():
        request.write("<h2>%s</h2>" % key)
        request.write("<ul>")
        for value in values:
            request.write("<li>%s</li>" % value)
        request.write("</ul>")

    request.write("""
      </body>
    </html>
    """)
    request.finish()

class FunctionHandledRequest(http.Request):
    pageHandlers = {
        '/': renderHomePage,
        '/posthandler': handlePost,
        }
```

Example 4-3. formhandler.py (continued)

```python
    def process(self):
        self.setHeader('Content-Type', 'text/html')
        if self.pageHandlers.has_key(self.path):
            handler = self.pageHandlers[self.path]
            handler(self)
        else:
            self.setResponseCode(http.NOT_FOUND)
            self.write("<h1>Not Found</h1>Sorry, no such page.")
            self.finish( )

class MyHttp(http.HTTPChannel):
    requestFactory = FunctionHandledRequest

class MyHttpFactory(http.HTTPFactory):
    protocol = MyHttp

if __name__ == "__main__":
    from twisted.internet import reactor
    reactor.listenTCP(8000, MyHttpFactory( ))
    reactor.run( )
```

Run *formhandler.py*. It will start a web server on port 8000. Go to *http://localhost:8000/* and fill out the form on the home page. Figure 4-4 shows the home page with some fields already filled in.

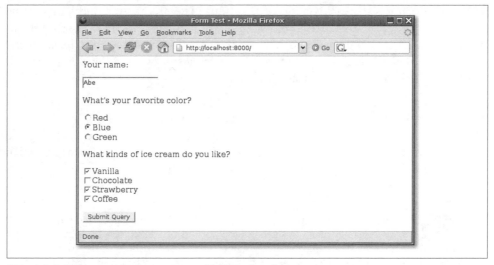

Figure 4-4. Filling out the form generated by formhandler.py

When you click the Submit button, your browser will send the form data to the page *formhandler* using an HTTP POST request. When it receives the form data, *formhandler* will show you the fields and values that were submitted, as shown in Figure 4-5.

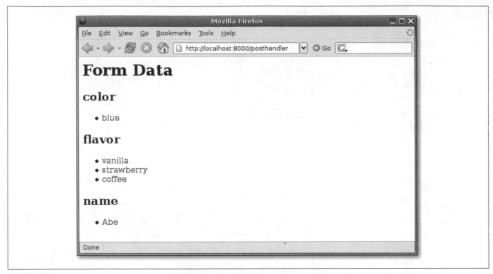

Figure 4-5. Displaying data submitted from a form

How Does That Work?

Example 4-3 defines two different functions for handling requests, renderHomePage and handlePost. FunctionHandledRequest is a subclass of Request with an attribute called pageHandlers that maps paths to functions. The process method looks at the path this particular request is using and tries to find a matching path in pageHandlers. If a match is found, the FunctionHandledRequest passes itself to the matching function, which is free to process the request however it likes; if no match is found, it generates a 404 "Not Found" response.

The renderHomePage function is set as the handler for /, the root page of the site. It generates an HTML form that will submit data to the page */formhandler*. The handler function for */formhandler* is handlePost, which responds with a page listing the posted data. handlePost iterates through the keys and values in Request args, which is a dictionary representing all the form data sent with the request.

> In this case, the form data is sent as the body of an HTTP POST request. When a request is sent using HTTP GET, Request.args will contain values taken from the query portion of the request URI. You can verify this behavior by changing the method attribute of the form generated by renderHomePage from post to get, restarting the server, and resubmitting the form.

An HTML form can have multiple fields with the same name. For example, the form in Example 4-3 lets you check off multiple checkboxes, all which have the name of a flavor. Unlike many other web frameworks, http.Request doesn't hide this from you: instead of a mapping each field name to a string, `Request.args` maps each field name to a *list*. If you know there's going to be one value for a particular field, just grab the first value from the list.

Managing a Hierarchy of Resources

The paths in a web application usually imply a hierarchy of resources. For example, look at these URIs:

```
http://example.com/people
http://example.com/people/charles
http://example.com/people/charles/contact
```

It's easy to see the hierarchy here. The page */people/charles* is a child of */people*, and the page */people/charles/contact* is a child of */people/charles*. Each page in the hierarchy is more specific: */people/charles* is one specific person, and */people/charles/contact* is one specific type of data (in this case, contact information) related to *charles*.

The default behavior for most web servers is to map request paths to a hierarchy of files and folders on disk. Each time a client requests the resource at a certain path, the web server tries to find a file at the corresponding path on disk, and responds with either the content of the file itself or (as in the case of a CGI script) the output created by executing the file. But in web applications, it can be artificially constraining to have to have a file on disk for every path that might be requested. For example, the data in your application might not be stored on disk, but in a relational database in another server. Or you might want to create resources on demand when they are requested. In cases like this, it's useful to be able to write your own logic for navigating a hierarchy of resources.

Writing your own logic for managing resources can also help you to manage security. Rather than opening up an entire directory to web access, you can selectively control which files are made available.

How Do I Do That?

The `twisted.web.resource`, `twisted.web.static`, and `twisted.web.server` modules provide classes for working with requests at a higher level than `twisted.web.http.Resource`, which you can use to set up a web server that combines several different kinds of resources into a logical hierarchy. Example 4-4 uses these classes to build an application for testing hexadecimal color codes. Request the resource */colors/hex*, where *hex* is a hexadecimal color code, and you'll get a page with the background color *#hex*. Rather than trying to generate a page for every possible color in advance, this server creates resources on demand.

Example 4-4. resourcetree.py

```python
from twisted.web import resource, static, server

class ColorPage(resource.Resource):
    def __init__(self, color):
        self.color = color

    def render(self, request):
        return """
        <html>
        <head>
          <title>Color: %s</title>
          <link type='text/css' href='/styles.css' rel='Stylesheet' />
        </head>
        <body style='background-color: #%s'>
          <h1>This is #%s.</h1>
          <p style='background-color: white'>
          <a href='/color/'>Back</a>
          </p>
        </body>
        </html>
        """ % (self.color, self.color, self.color)

class ColorRoot(resource.Resource):
    def __init__(self):
        resource.Resource.__init__(self)
        self.requestedColors = []
        self.putChild('', ColorIndexPage(self.requestedColors))

    def render(self, request):
        # redirect /color -> /color/
        request.redirect(request.path + '/')
        return "Please use /colors/ instead."

    def getChild(self, path, request):
        if path not in self.requestedColors:
            self.requestedColors.append(path)
        return ColorPage(path)

class ColorIndexPage(resource.Resource):
    def __init__(self, requestedColorsList):
        resource.Resource.__init__(self)
        self.requestedColors = requestedColorsList

    def render(self, request):
        request.write("""
        <html>
        <head>
          <title>Colors</title>
          <link type='text/css' href='/styles.css' rel='Stylesheet' />
        </head>
```

Example 4-4. resourcetree.py (continued)

```
        <body>
        <h1>Colors</h1>
        To see a color, enter a url like
        <a href='/color/ff0000'>/color/ff0000</a>. <br />
        Colors viewed so far:
        <ul>""")
        for color in self.requestedColors:
            request.write(
                "<li><a href='%s' style='color: #%s'>%s</a></li>" % (
                color, color, color))
        request.write("""
        </ul>
        </body>
        </html>
        """)
        return ""

class HomePage(resource.Resource):
    def render(self, request):
        return """
        <html>
        <head>
          <title>Colors</title>
          <link type='text/css' href='/styles.css' rel='Stylesheet' />
        </head>
        <body>
        <h1>Colors Demo</h1>
        What's here:
        <ul>
          <li><a href='/color'>Color viewer</a></li>
        </ul>
        </body>
        </html>
        """

if __name__ == "__main__":
    from twisted.internet import reactor
    root = resource.Resource()
    root.putChild('', HomePage())
    root.putChild('color', ColorRoot())
    root.putChild('styles.css', static.File('styles.css'))
    site = server.Site(root)
    reactor.listenTCP(8000, site)
    reactor.run()
```

Example 4-4 requires one static file, a CSS stylesheet. Create a file in the same directory as *resourcetree.py* called *styles.css*, with the content shown in Example 4-5.

Example 4-5. styles.css

```
body {
  font-family: Georgia, Times, serif;
  font-size: 11pt;
}

h1 {
  margin: 10px 0;
  padding: 5px;
  background-color: black;
  color: white;
}

a {
  font-family: monospace;
}

p {
  padding: 10px;
}
```

Run *resourcetree.py* to start a web server on port 8000. Here's a complete list of resources that the server provides:

/	Home page
/css	Virtual resource for holding CSS stylesheets
/css/styles.css	The static file *styles.css*
/colors/	Index of colors people have viewed so far
/colors/hexcolor	A page with the background color #hexcolor

Try going to the URI *http://localhost:8000/colors/00abef*, and you'll see the page in Figure 4-6 with the background color #00abef (which may not look like much printed in monochrome, but in real life is a bright shade of blue).

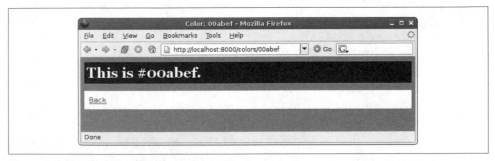

Figure 4-6. Viewing a hexadecimal color

Feel free to try other colors as well. You can also go to the page *http://localhost:8000/colors/*, shown in Figure 4-7, to see a list of the colors you've viewed so far.

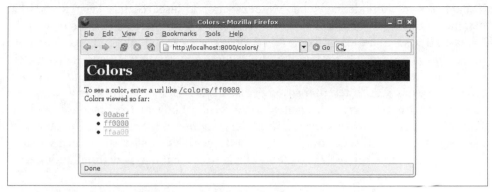

Figure 4-7. The /colors/ page showing a list of viewed colors

How Does That Work?

Example 4-4 introduces several new classes from the `twisted.web` package: `resource. Resource`, `static.File`, and `server.Site`. Each `resource.Resource` object does two things. First, it defines how requests for that resource should be handled. Second, it defines which `Resource` objects should be used for requests for *child resources*—resources whose path puts them below this resource in the hierarchy.

For example, take a look at the class `ColorRoot` in Example 4-4. An instance of this class will later be inserted into the resource hierarchy at the path */colors*. When initialized, `ColorRoot` uses the `putChild` method to insert a `ColorIndexPage` `Resource` as the child resource `''`. What does that mean? It means that requests for */colors/* (the path of `ColorRoot` plus a trailing slash) should be handled by the `ColorIndexPage` object.

You might think of them as being equivalent, but the URIs *http://example.com/stuff* and *http://example.com/stuff/* (note the trailing slash) are not the same. They are different URIs identifying different resources. Browsers will expand relative links differently depending on whether the trailing slash is part of the URI. In the first example, a link to "*otherpage*" will expand to *http://example.com/otherpage*; in the second example, it will expand to *http://example.com/stuff/otherpage*.

If you're not explicit in your server code, this problem can come back to bite you. It's a good idea to decide whether you want to have trailing slashes in your URIs, and redirect requests from one form to the other. The Resource class makes this easy to do. If you set the attribute `addSlash` to True, a `Resource` will automatically add a trailing slash to any requests that don't already have them and redirect those requests to the updated URI.

The render method defines what happens after a Resource has been found that matches the path of a request. Resource.render works basically the same way as the request handler methods in Example 4-3: it takes a Request object as its only argument, and is responsible for handing the request and sending a response to the client. Resource.render has a few caveats that you'll need to keep in mind, however. First, it expects you to return a string. This is a useful shortcut in many cases: you can just return the data you want to send as the body of the response, and the Resource will send it to the client and end the response. But even when you choose to use request.write to write the response body yourself, render still expects you to return a string. You can return an empty string to make it happy without adding anything to the response.

At times, you might want to start a deferred operation inside a render method. In this case, you won't be ready to write the response until your Deferred calls back. You might wonder, "Can I just return a Deferred that calls back with a string?" Well, sadly, you can't. (This is one of many deficiencies in the Resource object; see the note at the end of this lab for a discussion of why you shouldn't use the classes discussed here for major web development projects.) Instead, you return the magic value twisted.web.server.NOT_DONE_YET, which tells the Resource that you've started something asynchronous and aren't done with this request yet, so it shouldn't call request.finish(). Then you can call request.finish() yourself later after you're done writing the response. (See Example 4-5 for an example of this technique.)

The ColorRoot Resource will be used to render requests for the path /colors. In reality, though, ColorRoot is just a container for child resources. ColorRoot.render calls request.redirect, a helper function that sets the HTTP status code of the response to 302 ("Moved Temporarily") and writes a Location: header directing the client to request a page from another location, in this case /colors/ (with a trailing slash). Note that even though it's told the client to go somewhere else, render still has to return a string.

Resource offers an alternative to the render method. You can write separate methods to handle different HTTP methods: render_GET, render_POST, and so on. This approach is discussed in detail in Example 5-1 in Chapter 5.

ColorRoot has one more method, getChild. Here the possibilities for doing interesting things with resource hierarchies start to expand. The getChild method is designed for dynamically managing child resources. A Resource's getChild method is called when the client has sent a request for a path beneath the Resource in the hierarchy, and no matching path has been registered using putChild. By default, getChild will send a 404 ("Not Found") response. But you can override it, as ColorRoot does. ColorRoot's getChild method takes the child path and uses it to initialize a ColorPage object. The ColorPage can then respond to the request, using the last part of the path as a hexadecimal color code.

The static.File class is a subclass of Resource that serves the contents of a file or directory on disk. Initialize a static.File object with a filename as an argument. Using static.File is better than loading files from disk yourself because static.File is smart about handling large files: it won't take up too much memory, and it won't cause your entire server process to become unresponsive while it reads data from disk. If you initialize a static.File with the path of a directory, it will serve all the files and subdirectories under that directory.

 Even if you're not using server.Site and a tree of Resource objects to manage your web server, you can still use a static.File object to handle a request. You can use a temporary static.File to push the contents of a file as the response to a request like this:

```
static.File('file.txt').render(request)
```

You can change the MIME type static.File uses when serving files by making changes to the contentTypes attribute. That attribute functions as a dictionary for the purpose of mapping file extensions (such as .png) to MIME types.

The server.Site class is a Factory that you initialize with a Resource object. It will handle HTTP requests by splitting the requested path into segments and then walking the tree of Resource objects to find the Resource that it should use to handle the request.

Storing Web Data in an SQL Database

Lots of web applications use an SQL backend for data storage. With a Twisted application, though, you wouldn't want to use a regular Python SQL library. Standard SQL libraries have blocking function calls: every time you run a query, the query function will pause your application until the server returns a result. This can take a long time, especially if the query requires a lot of processing, or if the network connection to the server is slow. To use an SQL database with Twisted, you need a way to run queries using Deferreds, allowing your app to continue doing other things while it's waiting for the results.

Twisted provides such an SQL library in the twisted.enterprise package. twisted. enterprise doesn't actually include SQL drivers; it would be far too much work to support every database you might potentially want to use. Instead, twisted. enterprise provides an asynchronous API on top of the standard DB-API interface used by many Python database modules. When necessary, it uses threads to prevent database queries from blocking. You can use twisted.enterprise to work with any SQL database, as long as you have a DB-API compatible Python module for that database installed.

The Future of Twisted Web Development

The classes in `twisted.web.resource` and `twisted.web.server` are, as of this writing, widely considered to be past their prime. They have some serious shortcomings, especially their lack of support for `Deferred` results in `Resource.render` and `Resource.getChild`. Both are scheduled to be deprecated in the future in favor of improved classes provided by a next-generation web package known as `twisted.web2`. Unfortunately, `twisted.web2` is under such heavy development at this time that any examples included in this book would probably stop working soon after it went to press. While `twisted.web2` will have a different API, it will continue to use the concepts introduced here of a hierarchy of objects rendering requests.

Since `twisted.web.resource` and `twisted.web.server` will eventually be deprecated, you should avoid depending on them too heavily in your code. For a simple web server, you can take the approach in Example 4-3 and use a subclass of `twisted.http.Request`. `twisted.web2` will also provide a backward-compatible interface for `Resource` objects, so you should be able to port code such as that in Examples 4-5 and 4-6 with little to no effort.

If you're building a major web application with Twisted, you should use the Nevow (pronounced "nouveau") web server framework, which you can download from *http://www.nevow.com*. Nevow gives you more than just classes for working with HTTP requests: it provides many of the goodies you'd expect in a modern web application framework, including an XML templating system. It also includes some unique features like `livepage`, which gives you a way to send JavaScript code to the browser through a persistent connection. Nevow is designed from the ground up for Twisted, which means you can use `Deferred`s everywhere, and it's released under an extremely liberal open source license.

Like `twisted.web2`, Nevow hasn't yet reached the point where it has stable APIs that can be documented here. But it is mature enough that people are already using it for production web sites. You can find up-to-date documentation and examples at *http://www.nevow.com*.

How Do I Do That?

First, make sure you have a DB-API compatible Python module installed for your particular database. Then create a `twisted.enterprise.adbapi.ConnectionPool` object using your database driver and connection information. Example 4-6 uses the `MySQLdb` module (which you can download from *http://sourceforge.net/projects/mysql-python*) to connect to a MySQL database. It runs a minimal weblog application that stores posts in a database table.

Example 4-6. databaseblog.py

```python
from twisted.web import resource, static, server, http
from twisted.enterprise import adbapi, util as dbutil

DB_DRIVER = "MySQLdb"
DB_ARGS = {
    'db': 'test',
    'user': 'your_user_here',
    'passwd': 'your_pass_here',
    }


class HomePage(resource.Resource):
    def __init__(self, dbConnection):
        self.db = dbConnection
        resource.Resource.__init__(self)

    def render(self, request):
        query = "select title, body from posts order by post_id desc"
        self.db.runQuery(query).addCallback(
            self._gotPosts, request).addErrback(
            self._dbError, request)
        return server.NOT_DONE_YET

    def _gotPosts(self, results, request):
        request.write("""
        <html>
        <head><title>MicroBlog</title></head>
        <body>
          <h1>MicroBlog</h1>
          <i>Like a blog, but less useful</i>
          <p><a href='/new'>New Post</a></p>
        """)

        for title, body in results:
            request.write("<h2>%s</h2>" % title)
            request.write(body)

        request.write("""
        </body>
        </html>
        """)
        request.finish()

    def _dbError(self, failure, request):
        request.setResponseCode(http.INTERNAL_SERVER_ERROR)
        request.write("Error fetching posts: %s" % failure.getErrorMessage())
        request.finish()
```

Example 4-6. databaseblog.py (continued)

```python
class NewPage(resource.Resource):
    def render(self, request):
        return """
        <html>
        <head><title>New Post</title></head>
        <body>
          <h1>New Post</h1>
          <form action='save' method='post'>
          Title: <input type='text' name='title' /> <br />
          Body: <br />
          <textarea cols='70' name='body'></textarea> <br />
          <input type='submit' value='Save' />
          </form>
        </body>
        </html>
        """


class SavePage(resource.Resource):
    def __init__(self, dbConnection):
        self.db = dbConnection
        resource.Resource.__init__(self)

    def render(self, request):
        title = request.args['title'][0]
        body = request.args['body'][0]
        query = """
        Insert into posts (title, body) values (%s, %s)
        """ % (dbutil.quote(title, "char"),
               dbutil.quote(body, "text"))
        self.db.runQuery(query).addCallback(
            self._saved, request).addErrback(
            self._saveFailed, request)
        return server.NOT_DONE_YET

    def _saved(self, result, request):
        request.redirect("/")
        request.finish( )

    def _saveFailed(self, failure, request):
        request.setResponseCode(http.INTERNAL_SERVER_ERROR)
        request.write("Error saving record: %s" % (
            failure.getErrorMessage( )))
        request.finish( )

class RootResource(resource.Resource):
    def __init__(self, dbConnection):
        resource.Resource.__init__(self)
        self.putChild('', HomePage(dbConnection))
        self.putChild('new', NewPage( ))
        self.putChild('save', SavePage(dbConnection))
```

Example 4-6. databaseblog.py (continued)

```
if __name__ == "__main__":
    from twisted.internet import reactor
    dbConnection = adbapi.ConnectionPool(DB_DRIVER, **DB_ARGS)
    f = server.Site(RootResource(dbConnection))
    reactor.listenTCP(8000, f)
    reactor.run()
```

Example 4-6's code uses a simple SQL table called posts. You can create it by running the following SQL statement in a MySQL database:

```
CREATE TABLE posts (
    post_id int NOT NULL auto_increment,
    title varchar(255) NOT NULL,
    body text,
    PRIMARY KEY (post_id)
)
```

Then run *databaseblog.py* to start the server on port 8000. You should be able to view the home page in your browser. If you get this far without any errors, the database connection is working correctly. Try clicking the *New Post* link and composing a blog entry, as shown in Figure 4-8.

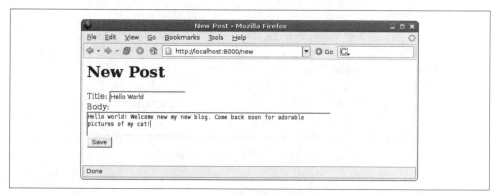

Figure 4-8. Composing a weblog post

Submit the form, and you'll be taken back to the main page. You should see your post, which is now saved in the database. See Figure 4-9.

How Does That Work?

Example 4-6 uses three Resource classes: HomePage, NewPage, and SavePage. HomePage connects to the database and displays the current posts in reverse order. NewPage provides a form for entering new posts. SavePage processes the form and inserts a new record in the database.

Figure 4-9. Displaying a post from the database

First, the *databaseblog.py* script creates a `twisted.enterprise.adbapi.ConnectionPool` object. A ConnectionPool represents a managed group of one or more database connections that you can use to send queries to an SQL database. Initialize a ConnectionPool with the name of the database driver module as the first argument. Any additional arguments or keyword arguments will be passed along to the driver when it is initialized.

After the ConnectionPool object in Example 4-6 is created, it gets passed to the HomePage and SavePage classes so that they can run database queries. In order to run these queries, HomePage and SavePage have to process requests asynchronously. They start by using the ConnectionPool.runQuery method to run a database query. This returns a Deferred. Example 4-6 shows how to set up callback and errback handlers for the Deferred so that a response is sent to the client once each query is complete. In each case, the render method returns the special value server.NOT_DONE_YET to indicate that the response is being processed asynchronously.

Running an HTTP Proxy Server

Besides HTTP servers and clients, `twisted.web` includes support for writing HTTP *proxies*. A proxy is a client and server in one: it accepts requests from clients (acting as a server) and forwards them to servers (acting as a client). Then it sends the response back to the client who originally sent the request. HTTP proxies are useful mostly for the additional services they can provide, such as caching, filtering, and usage reporting. This lab shows how to build an HTTP proxy using Twisted.

How Do I Do That?

The `twisted.web` package includes `twisted.web.proxy`, a module with classes for building HTTP proxies. Example 4-7 shows how easy it is to set up a basic proxy.

Example 4-7. simpleproxy.py

```
from twisted.web import proxy, http
from twisted.internet import reactor
from twisted.python import log
import sys
log.startLogging(sys.stdout)

class ProxyFactory(http.HTTPFactory):
    protocol = proxy.Proxy


reactor.listenTCP(8001, ProxyFactory())
reactor.run()
```

Run *simpleproxy.py* from the command line and you'll have an HTTP proxy running on *localhost* port 8001. Set up a web browser to use this proxy and try surfing some web pages. The call to log.startLogging prints all HTTP log messages to stdout so you can watch the proxy at work:

```
$ python simpleproxy.py
2005/06/13 00:22 EDT [-] Log opened.
2005/06/13 00:22 EDT [-] __main__.ProxyFactory starting on 8001
2005/06/13 00:22 EDT [-] Starting factory <__main__.ProxyFactory instance at
0xb7d9d10c>
2005/06/13 00:23 EDT [Proxy,0,127.0.0.1] Starting factory <twisted.web.proxy.
ProxyClientFactory instance at 0xb78a99ac>
2005/06/13 00:23 EDT [-] Enabling Multithreading.
2005/06/13 00:23 EDT [Proxy,1,127.0.0.1] Starting factory <twisted.web.proxy.
ProxyClientFactory instance at 0xb781ee8c>
2005/06/13 00:23 EDT [Proxy,2,127.0.0.1] Starting factory <twisted.web.proxy.
ProxyClientFactory instance at 0xb782534c>
...
```

That gives you a working proxy, but not one that does anything useful. Example 4-8 dives deeper into the twisted.web.proxy module to build a proxy that keeps track of the most frequently used words in the HTML documents being browsed.

Example 4-8. wordcountproxy.py

```
import sgmllib, re
from twisted.web import proxy, http
import sys
from twisted.python import log
log.startLogging(sys.stdout)

WEB_PORT = 8000
PROXY_PORT = 8001

class WordParser(sgmllib.SGMLParser):
    def __init__(self):
        sgmllib.SGMLParser.__init__(self)
        self.chardata = []
        self.inBody = False
```

Example 4-8. wordcountproxy.py (continued)

```python
    def start_body(self, attrs):
        self.inBody = True

    def end_body(self):
        self.inBody = False

    def handle_data(self, data):
        if self.inBody:
            self.chardata.append(data)

    def getWords(self):
        # extract words
        wordFinder = re.compile(r'\w*')
        words = wordFinder.findall("".join(self.chardata))
        words = filter(lambda word: word.strip(), words)
        print "WORDS ARE", words
        return words

class WordCounter(object):
    ignoredWords = "the a of in from to this that and or but is was be can could i you
they we at".split()

    def __init__(self):
        self.words = {}

    def addWords(self, words):
        for word in words:
            word = word.lower()
            if not word in self.ignoredWords:
                currentCount = self.words.get(word, 0)
                self.words[word] = currentCount + 1

class WordCountProxyClient(proxy.ProxyClient):
    def handleHeader(self, key, value):
        proxy.ProxyClient.handleHeader(self, key, value)
        if key.lower() == "content-type":
            if value.split(';')[0] == 'text/html':
                self.parser = WordParser()


    def handleResponsePart(self, data):
        proxy.ProxyClient.handleResponsePart(self, data)
        if hasattr(self, 'parser'): self.parser.feed(data)


    def handleResponseEnd(self):
        proxy.ProxyClient.handleResponseEnd(self)
        if hasattr(self, 'parser'):
            self.parser.close()
            self.father.wordCounter.addWords(self.parser.getWords())
            del(self.parser)
```

Example 4-8. wordcountproxy.py (continued)

```python
class WordCountProxyClientFactory(proxy.ProxyClientFactory):
    def buildProtocol(self, addr):
        client = proxy.ProxyClientFactory.buildProtocol(self, addr)
        # upgrade proxy.proxyClient object to WordCountProxyClient
        client.__class__ = WordCountProxyClient
        return client

class WordCountProxyRequest(proxy.ProxyRequest):
    protocols = {'http': WordCountProxyClientFactory}

    def __init__(self, wordCounter, *args):
        self.wordCounter = wordCounter
        proxy.ProxyRequest.__init__(self, *args)

class WordCountProxy(proxy.Proxy):
    def __init__(self, wordCounter):
        self.wordCounter = wordCounter
        proxy.Proxy.__init__(self)

    def requestFactory(self, *args):
        return WordCountProxyRequest(self.wordCounter, *args)

class WordCountProxyFactory(http.HTTPFactory):
    def __init__(self, wordCounter):
        self.wordCounter = wordCounter
        http.HTTPFactory.__init__(self)

    def buildProtocol(self, addr):
        protocol = WordCountProxy(self.wordCounter)
        return protocol

# classes for web reporting interface
class WebReportRequest(http.Request):
    def __init__(self, wordCounter, *args):
        self.wordCounter = wordCounter
        http.Request.__init__(self, *args)

    def process(self):
        self.setHeader("Content-Type", "text/html")
        words = self.wordCounter.words.items()
        words.sort(lambda (w1, c1), (w2, c2): cmp(c2, c1))
        for word, count in words:
            self.write("<li>%s %s</li>" % (word, count))
        self.finish()

class WebReportChannel(http.HTTPChannel):
    def __init__(self, wordCounter):
        self.wordCounter = wordCounter
        http.HTTPChannel.__init__(self)

    def requestFactory(self, *args):
        return WebReportRequest(self.wordCounter, *args)
```

Example 4-8. wordcountproxy.py (continued)

```python
class WebReportFactory(http.HTTPFactory):
    def __init__(self, wordCounter):
        self.wordCounter = wordCounter
        http.HTTPFactory.__init__(self)

    def buildProtocol(self, addr):
        return WebReportChannel(self.wordCounter)

if __name__ == "__main__":
    from twisted.internet import reactor
    counter = WordCounter()
    prox = WordCountProxyFactory(counter)
    reactor.listenTCP(PROXY_PORT, prox)
    reactor.listenTCP(WEB_PORT, WebReportFactory(counter))
    reactor.run()
```

Run wordcountproxy.py and set your browser to use the proxy server localhost port 8001. Browse to a couple of sites to test the proxy. Then go to *http://localhost:8000/* to see a report of word frequency in the sites you've visited. Figure 4-10 shows what your browser might look like after visiting *http://www.twistedmatrix.com*.

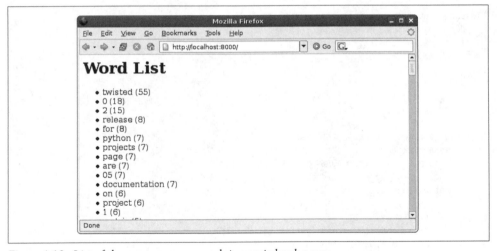

Figure 4-10. List of the most common words in proxied web pages

How Does That Work?

There are a lot of classes in Example 4-8, but the majority of them are just glue. Only a few are doing real work. The first two classes, WordParser and WordCounter, do the work of extracting words from the text of HTML documents and counting their frequency. The third class, WordCountProxy client, contains the code that looks for HTML documents and runs them through a WordParser as it comes back from the server. That's it for code specific to the problem of counting words.

Because a proxy acts as both a client and server, it uses a lot of classes. There's a ProxyClientFactory and ProxyClient, which provide the Factory/Protocol pair for client connections to other servers. To accept connections from clients, the proxy module provides the class ProxyRequest, a subclass of http.Request, and Proxy, a subclass of http.HTTPChannel. These are used the same way as they would be in a regular HTTP server: an HTTPFactory uses Proxy for its Protocol, and the Proxy HTTPChannel uses ProxyRequest as its RequestFactory. Here's the sequence of events when a client sends a request for a web page:

1. The client establishes a connection to the proxy server. This connection is handled by the HTTPFactory.

2. The HTTPFactory.buildProtocol creates a Proxy object to send and receive data over the client connection.

3. When the client sends a request over the connection, the Proxy creates a ProxyRequest to handle it.

4. The ProxyRequest looks at the request to see what server the client is trying to connect to. It creates a ProxyClientFactory and calls reactor.connectTCP to connect the factory to the server.

5. Once the ProxyClientFactory is connected to the server, it creates a ProxyClient Protocol object to send and receive data over the connection.

6. ProxyClient sends the original request to the server. As it receives the reply, it sends it back to the client that sent the request. This is done by calling self.father.transport.write: self.father is the Proxy object that is managing the client's connection.

With such a long chain of classes, it becomes a lot of work to pass an object from one end of the chain to the other. But it is possible, as Example 4-8 demonstrates. By creating a subclass of each class provided by the proxy module, you can have complete control over every step of the process.

At only one step in Example 4-8 is it necessary to resort to a bit of a hack. The ProxyClientFactory class has a buildProtocol method that's hardcoded to use ProxyClient as the protocol. It doesn't give you any easy way to substitute your own subclass of ProxyClient instead. The solution is to use the special Python __class__ attribute to do an in-place upgrade of the ProxyClient object returned by ProxyClientFactory.buildProtocol, which changes the object from a ProxyClient to a WordCountProxyClient.

In addition to the proxy server, Example 4-8 runs a regular web server on port 8000, which displays the current word count data from the proxy server. The ability to include a lightweight embedded HTTP server in your application is extremely handy, and can be used in any Twisted application where you want to provide a way to view status information remotely.

CHAPTER 5

Web Services and RPC

When you write a networked application, you make information or services accessible over a computer network. Sometimes this is done with the goal of letting people use your program remotely. But more often it's done to enable other applications to communicate with yours. Providing a way for other programs to communicate with your application makes it more flexible and more valuable. It allows other developers to use your application's data and services in new ways—possibly even to write new features that you might not have the time or expertise to write yourself.

The concept of one program calling a function in another program over a network is called *RPC*, or Remote Procedure Calls. RPC can be done in any number of ways, but these days the most common way is to make functions available through the Web. Programmatic interfaces that are available on the Web, meant for use by other applications instead of by a user with a web browser, are known as *web services*.

This chapter shows how to use web services and RPC in your applications. It demonstrates how to make services available across the network, and how to write client applications that use these services. It discusses four different ways to do this using Twisted: REST, XML-RPC, SOAP, and Twisted's own Perspective Broker.

Using the REST Architecture for Web Services

In 2000, Roy Thomas Fielding published the paper "Architectural Styles and the Design of Network-based Software Architectures" (*http://www.ics.uci.edu/~fielding/pubs/dissertation/top.htm*). This paper described a software architecture style called *REST* (short for "Representational State Transfer") and explained how this architecture could be seen in the design of the Web. REST isn't tied to any particular technology or data formats. Instead, it offers a set of principles for designing web applications that take advantage of the fundamental design of the Web.

Applications that use the REST architectural style use the Web the way it was designed to be used. Instead of struggling to overcome the limitations of the Web, REST embraces those constraints to give developers an elegant, powerful approach to designing and thinking about web applications.

How Do I Do That?

Design your web application in terms of *resources*. Every URI on the Web identifies a resource. A resource may be any information or service, including a document, an image, or a web service that takes input data and performs some action. What information and services is your application going to provide? Each should be available through the Web at a logical URI. HTTP defines four actions that can be taken on resources: GET, POST, PUT, and DELETE. Web browsers generally support only two of these: GET, for retrieving the representation of a resource, and POST, for submitting data to a service for processing. But when designing services meant for use by non-browser clients you can take advantage of PUT and DELETE as well.

Example 5-1 shows how you can use the REST architecture to design a web application that's usable through both a web browser and web services. In this case, the application is a Wiki, a simple set of user-editable linked web pages.

Example 5-1. wiki.py

```
import re, pickle, os
from twisted.web import server, resource, http

reWikiWord = re.compile(r"\b(([A-Z][a-z]+){2,})\b")

class WikiData(object):
    "class for managing Wiki data"

    def __init__(self, filename):
        self.filename = filename
        if os.path.exists(filename):
            self.pages = pickle.load(file(filename, 'r+b'))
        else:
            self.pages = {'WikiHome': 'This is your Wiki home page.'}

    def save(self):
        pickle.dump(self.pages, file(self.filename, 'w+b'))

    def hasPage(self, path):
        return self.pages.has_key(path)

    def listPages(self):
        return self.pages.keys( )
```

Example 5-1. wiki.py (continued)

```
    def getPage(self, path):
        return self.pages.get(path, '')

    def getRenderedPage(self, path):
        pageData = self.getPage(path)
        "get content with linked WikiWords"
        wikiWords = [match[0] for match in reWikiWord.findall(pageData)]
        for word in wikiWords:
            pageData = pageData.replace(
                word, "<a href='%s'>%s</a>" % (word, word))
        return pageData

    def setPage(self, path, content):
        self.pages[path] = content
        self.save( )

    def deletePage(self, path):
        del(self.pages[path])

class RootResource(resource.Resource):
    def __init__(self, wikiData):
        self.wikiData = wikiData
        resource.Resource.__init__(self)
        self.putChild('edit', EditFactory(self.wikiData))
        self.putChild('save', SavePage(self.wikiData))
        self.putChild('index', IndexPage(self.wikiData))

    def getChild(self, path, request):
        return WikiPage(self.wikiData, path or 'WikiHome')

class EditFactory(resource.Resource):
    def __init__(self, wikiData):
        self.wikiData = wikiData
        resource.Resource.__init__(self)

    def getChild(self, path, request):
        return EditPage(self.wikiData, path)

class EditPage(resource.Resource):
    def __init__(self, wikiData, path):
        self.wikiData = wikiData
        self.path = path
        resource.Resource.__init__(self)

    def render(self, request):
        return """
        <html>
        <head><title>Editing: %(path)s</title></head>
        <body>
        Editing: %(path)s
        <form method='post' action='/save'>
        <input type='hidden' name='path' value='%(path)s'>
```

Example 5-1. wiki.py (continued)

```
            <textarea name='data' rows='30' cols='80'>%(data)s</textarea>
            <br />
            <input type='submit' value='Save'>
            </form>
            </body>
            </html>
            """ % {'path':self.path,
                   'data':self.wikiData.getPage(self.path)}

class SavePage(resource.Resource):
    def __init__(self, wikiData):
        self.wikiData = wikiData
        resource.Resource.__init__(self)

    def render_POST(self, request):
        data = request.args['data'][0]
        path = request.args['path'][0]
        self.wikiData.setPage(path, data)
        request.redirect('/' + path)
        return ""

    def render_GET(self, request):
        return """
        To add a page to the Wiki, send data to this page using
        HTTP POST. Arguments:
        <ul>
        <li><code>path</code>: the name of a Wiki page</li>
        <li><code>data</code>: the content to use for that page</li>
        </ul>
        """

class WikiPage(resource.Resource):
    def __init__(self, wikiData, path):
        self.wikiData = wikiData
        self.path = path
        resource.Resource.__init__(self)

    def render_GET(self, request):
        if self.wikiData.hasPage(self.path):
            return """
            <html>
            <head><title>%s</title></head>
            <body>
            <p>
            <a href='/edit/%s'>Edit Page</a>
            <a href='/index'>Index</a>
            <a href='/'>Home</a>
            </p>
            %s
            </body>
            </html>
```

Example 5-1. wiki.py (continued)

```
        """ % (self.path, self.path,
               self.wikiData.getRenderedPage(self.path))
        else:
            request.redirect('/edit/%s' % self.path)
            return ""

    def render_PUT(self, request):
        "accept a PUT request to set the contents of this page"
        if not self.wikiData.hasPage(self.path):
            request.setResponseCode(http.CREATED, "Created new page")
        else:
            request.setResponseCode(http.OK, "Modified existing page")
        request.content.seek(0)
        self.wikiData.setPage(self.path, request.content.read())
        return ""

    def render_DELETE(self, request):
        "accept a DELETE request to remove this page"
        if self.wikiData.hasPage(self.path):
            self.wikiData.deletePage(self.path)
            return "Deleted."
        else:
            request.setResponseCode(http.NOT_FOUND)
            return "No such page."

class IndexPage(resource.Resource):
    def __init__(self, wikiData):
        self.wikiData = wikiData
        resource.Resource.__init__(self)

    def render(self, request):
        pages = self.wikiData.listPages()
        pages.sort()
        links = ["<li><a href='%s'>%s</a></li>" % (p, p)
                 for p in pages]
        return """
        <html>
        <head><title>Wiki Index</title></head>
        <a href='/'>Home</a>
        <h1>Index</h1>
        <body>
        <ul>
        %s
        </ul>
        </body>
        """ % "".join(links)

if __name__ == "__main__":
    import sys
    from twisted.internet import reactor
    wikiData = WikiData(sys.argv[1])
    reactor.listenTCP(8082, server.Site(RootResource(wikiData)))
    reactor.run()
```

Run *wiki.py* with a single argument, the name of a file to use for data storage:

```
$ python wiki.py wiki.dat
```

The script starts up a web server on port 8082. Go to *http://localhost:8082/*, and you'll be able to view and edit pages in the Wiki. WikiWords will automatically be converted into links. Figure 5-1 shows the default Wiki home page. Figure 5-2 shows the Edit Page form.

Figure 5-1. Browsing the Wiki

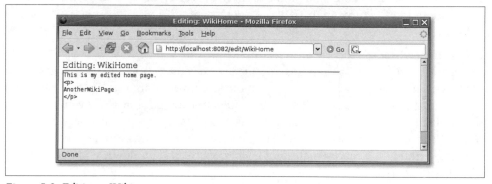

Figure 5-2. Editing a Wiki page

You're not limited to using a web browser to update the Wiki, however. For example, you can use command-line tools like *wget* or *curl* to create pages by posting data to the resource */save* at *http://localhost:8082/save*:

```
$ wget -q --post-data="path=WgetTest&data=Hello%20from%20wget"  \
  --output-document=- http://localhost:8082/save
```

```
$ curl -d "path=CurlTest&data=Hello%20from%20curl" \
  http://localhost:8082/save
```

> Example 5-2 shows how to use a Twisted HTTP client to create, modify, and delete pages in this Wiki.

How Does That Work?

The *wiki.py* application in Example 5-1 uses a class called WikiData to manage a dictionary of Wiki pages. Then it defines a series of resources, makes them available through a twisted.web.server.Server, and starts the server on port 8082. All the resource classes inherit from twisted.web.resource.Resource (for the basics on the resource.Resource class, see Chapter 4).

The WikiPage class represents a single page in the Wiki. In keeping with the REST architectural style, the class provides a two-way mechanism for transferring a representation of the page. When a client sends a GET request, WikiPage will return a rendered HTML version of the page, suitable for viewing in the browser. To update the page, a client can send an HTTP PUT request containing the new version of the page. PUT is an oft-neglected part of HTTP that allows a client to send the server data that should be used to create or replace the resource at a given URI. WikiPage also supports the HTTP DELETE method, which will completely remove the page. The separate functions render_GET, render_PUT, and render_DELETE take advantage of a built-in feature of the resource.Resource class: if these methods are defined separately, then resource.Resource will use a method matching the HTTP method used in the incoming request (and return an HTTP 405 "Method not Allowed" response if none is defined).

Unfortunately, most modern browsers don't provide a nice way to use PUT, so the server needs to offer an alternative means to create and update pages. The PageSaverResource class accepts a POST request with two arguments: the path of a page, and the page data. It will set the contents of the page at the given path, and then redirect the client so he can view it. PageSaverResource is purely a service, meant to accept input in the form of a POST request. Still, it responds to a GET request with the closest thing to a representation of itself: documentation describing how the service should be used.

The EditPage class generates an HTML form for posting to the PageSaverResource. EditPage objects are dynamically created in the getChild method of EditPageFactory, so you can get an edit form for any page by requesting the resource /edit/PageName. In traditional script-based web programming, this same thing might have been done using a URI with an appended query, something like edit.php?path=PageName. Twisted's web server gives you more control, so you can design a URI that looks nicer and isn't so closely tied to the underlying technology.

For convenience, WikiPage will respond to a request for a page that doesn't exist by returning a 302 response that redirects the client to the URI of the corresponding EditPage. This response makes it possible to link to pages in the Wiki whether or not they currently exist; if they don't, the server will do the right thing and prompt the client to create the page.

A final class, IndexPage, renders an HTML list of all the pages in the Wiki. Working together, these classes make up a web application that follows the principles of REST. It invites the client to view the application as a set of resources whose state can be retrieved or set through HTTP requests. These resources provide an HTML interface that can be used by a web browser, but they simultaneously define an API for web services. The next example shows how you can write a Twisted client to work with these resources.

Using a Web Client to Update Resources Through REST

The Web itself is an example of REST architecture. You can look at any web site as a set of resources whose state can be retrieved and updated using HTTP methods like GET and POST. Thus a web application doesn't have to support special web service protocols like XML-RPC or SOAP for you to be able to work with it from a client program: straight HTTP is all you need.

How Do I Do That?

Use the twisted.web.client.getPage function to send HTTP requests to web resources. Despite its name, getPage supports HTTP methods beyond GET, as demonstrated in Example 5-2.

Example 5-2. rest_client.py

```
from twisted.web import client
import urllib

class RestResource(object):
    def __init__(self, uri):
        self.uri = uri

    def get(self):
        return self._sendRequest('GET')

    def post(self, **kwargs):
        postData = urllib.urlencode(kwargs)
        mimeType = 'application/x-www-form-urlencoded'
        return self._sendRequest('POST', postData, mimeType)

    def put(self, data, mimeType):
        return self._sendRequest('PUT', data, mimeType)

    def delete(self):
        return self._sendRequest('DELETE')

    def _sendRequest(self, method, data="", mimeType=None):
        headers = {}
        if mimeType:
            headers['Content-Type'] = mimeType
```

Example 5-2. rest_client.py (continued)

```
        if data:
            headers['Content-Length'] = str(len(data))
        return client.getPage(
            self.uri, method=method, postdata=data, headers=headers)

class RestWikiTester(object):
    def __init__(self, baseUri):
        self.baseUri = baseUri

    def test(self):
        return self.createPage("RestTestTmp").addCallback(
            lambda _: self.deletePage("RestTestTmp")).addCallback(
            lambda _: self.createPage("RestTest")).addCallback(
            lambda _: self.getPage("RestTest")).addErrback(
            self.handleFailure)

    def createPage(self, page):
        print "Creating page %s..." % page
        return RestResource(self.baseUri + page).put(
            "Created using HttpPut!", "text/html")

    def deletePage(self, page):
        print "Deleting page %s..." % page
        return RestResource(self.baseUri + page).delete()

    def getPage(self, page):
        uri = self.baseUri + page
        return RestResource(uri).get().addCallback(
            self._gotPage, uri)

    def _gotPage(self, pageData, uri):
        print "Got representation of %s:" % uri
        print pageData

    def handleFailure(self, failure):
        print "Error:", failure.getErrorMessage()

if __name__ == "__main__":
    from twisted.internet import reactor
    tester = RestWikiTester('http://localhost:8082/')
    tester.test().addCallback(lambda _: reactor.stop())
    reactor.run()
```

When you run *rest_client.py*, it creates and deletes a page called *RestTestTmp*, creates a page called *RestTest*, and then displays the contents of *RestTest* as rendered by the server:

```
$ python rest_client.py
Creating page RestTestTmp...
Deleting page RestTestTmp...
Creating page RestTest...
Got representation of http://localhost:8082/RestTest:
```

```
<html>
<head><title>RestTest</title></head>
<body>
<p>
<a href='/edit/RestTest'>Edit Page</a>
<a href='/index'>Index</a>
<a href='/'>Home</a>
</p>
Created using <a href='HttpPut'>HttpPut</a>!
</body>
</html>
```

How Does That Work?

The RestResource class takes a URI and provides methods for sending HTTP GET, PUT, POST, and DELETE requests to that resource. All of these use twisted.web.client. getPage to send the request. The post method will take an arbitrary number of keyword arguments, URL-encode them, and use the resulting string as the body of the request sent to the server. The put method will take arbitrary data representing the new state of the resource, along with a MIME type identifying the data format. The other methods, get and delete, don't need to pass any additional information.

The RestWikiTester class has a test method that chains together a series of tests to be run on the server. While not a comprehensive test, it demonstrates the use of the GET, PUT, and DELETE methods on the Wiki application from Example 5-1.

Enabling Web Services Using XML-RPC

XML-RPC is a system for making function calls through HTTP using XML message formats. XML-RPC is very different from the REST style of architecture; while both can be elegant solutions in the right hands, they have almost opposite design principles. Where REST invites you to think about the nature of the web and design your application accordingly, XML-RPC tries to make web services fit into the way most developers already think about programming: you call functions and get back results.

In XML-RPC, a function call is encoded as XML and sent to the server using an HTTP POST request. The server then replies with an XML document containing the result of the function call. Here's an example XML-RPC request, calling the function echo with the string argument 'cheese':

```
POST /RPC2 HTTP/1.0
Host: localhost
Content-Type: text/xml
Content-length: 190
```

```
<?xml version="1.0"?>
<methodCall>
  <methodName>echo</methodName>
  <params>
    <param>
      <value>
        <string>cheese</string>
      </value>
    </param>
  </params>
</methodCall>
```

And here's the response sent back from the server:

```
HTTP/1.1 200 OK
Connection: close
Content-Length: 158
Content-Type: text/xml
Date: Mon, 6 Jun 2005 12:55:00 GMT

<?xml version="1.0"?>
<methodResponse>
  <params>
    <param>
      <value>
        <string>You said: cheese</string>
      </value>
    </param>
  </params>
</methodResponse>
```

The XML format is simple and uses a limited set of common data types. For more information on XML-RPC, see the book *Programming Web Services with XML-RPC*, by Simon St.Laurent, Joe Johnston, and Edd Dumbill (O'Reilly).

XML-RPC has the advantage of being extremely easy to learn and use. Its limited set of supported data types makes it easy to implement, so you can find XML-RPC modules for almost any programming language. The twisted.web package supports XML-RPC out of the box, making it very easy to support XML-RPC web services in your application.

How Do I Do That?

The twisted.web.xmlrpc.XMLRPC class is a subclass of twisted.web.resource.Resource that does just about all the work of handling XML-RPC. All you have to do is define methods beginning with xmlrpc_, and it will make them available as XML-RPC functions. The script in Example 5-3 imports the *wiki.py* Wiki server from Example 5-1 and adds an XML-RPC interface.

Example 5-3. xmlrpc_server.py

```
import wiki
from twisted.web import server, xmlrpc

class WikiXmlRpc(xmlrpc.XMLRPC):
    def __init__(self, wikiData):
        self.wikiData = wikiData

    def xmlrpc_hasPage(self, path):
        return self.wikiData.hasPage(path)

    def xmlrpc_listPages(self):
        return self.wikiData.listPages()

    def xmlrpc_getPage(self, path):
        return self.wikiData.getPage(path)

    def xmlrpc_getRenderedPage(self, path):
        return self.wikiData.getRenderedPage(path)

    def xmlrpc_setPage(self, path, data):
        self.wikiData.setPage(path, data)
        # wikiData.setPage returns None, which has no xmlrpc
        # representation, so you have to return something else
        return path

if __name__ == "__main__":
    import sys
    from twisted.internet import reactor
    datafile = sys.argv[1]
    wikiData = wiki.WikiData(datafile)
    siteRoot = rest_wiki.RootResource(wikiData)
    siteRoot.putChild('RPC2', WikiXmlRpc(wikiData))
    reactor.listenTCP(8082, server.Site(siteRoot))
    reactor.run()
```

Run *xmlrpc_server.py* with a single argument, the name of your Wiki data file:

```
python xmlrpc_server.py
```

This command runs a web server on port 8082 that works just like *wiki.py* from Example 5-1, but with the addition of a resource providing XML-RPC access at */RPC2* (which is somewhat of a standard location for XML-RPC services).

You can test the XML-RPC interface using the xmlrpclib module in the Python standard library:

```
$ python
Python 2.4.1 (#2, Apr 14 2005, 09:13:52)
[GCC 4.0.0 20050413 (prerelease) (Debian 4.0-0pre11)] on linux2
Type "help", "copyright", "credits" or "license" for more information.
>>> import xmlrpclib
```

```
>>> wiki = xmlrpclib.ServerProxy('http://localhost:8082/RPC2')
>>> wiki.listPages()
['WikiHome', 'CurlTest', 'WgetTest', 'RestTest']
>>> wiki.setPage('PythonXmlRpcTest', 'Creating this through XmlRpc!')
'PythonXmlRpcTest'
>>> wiki.getRenderedPage('PythonXmlRpcTest')
"Creating this through <a href='XmlRpc'>XmlRpc</a>!"
>>> wiki.listPages()
['WikiHome', 'CurlTest', 'WgetTest', 'PythonXmlRpcTest', 'RestTest']
```

How Does That Work?

The `xmlrpc.XMLRPC` class is a `Resource` designed to handle XML-RPC requests. When it receives a `POST` request, it parses the incoming XML to extract the name of the function being called and the arguments. Then it looks for a matching method with an `xmlrpc_` prefix and calls it with the arguments provided by the client. This function can return a `Deferred` result or a direct value. The XMLRPC class encodes the result as XML and returns it to the client.

XML-RPC has a limited set of data types. You can return strings, integers, floating-point numbers, Booleans, dictionaries, tuples, or lists, and they will be converted automatically to their XML-RPC representations. To send a date value, wrap a date tuple such as the result of `time.localtime()` in an `xmlrpc.DateTime` object. To send binary data, wrap a binary string in an `xmlrpc.Binary` object. Other data types, including `None`, have no equivalent in XML-RPC. Attempting to return an unsupported data type will result in an error, so make sure that you limit your return values to the supported types.

Calling XML-RPC Functions

The `twisted.web.xmlrpc` module includes client support for sending XML-RPC method calls to a server. Unlike the `xmlrpclib` module in the Python standard library, Twisted's XML-RPC client doesn't try to hide the fact that you're making a function call over the network (for one thing, method calls return a `Deferred`, so that your program can do other things while it's waiting for a response from the server). But it's still very easy to use.

How Do I Do That?

Create a `twisted.web.xmlrpc.Proxy` object pointing to the URI of your XML-RPC service. Use the `callRemote` method to call XML-RPC functions. Example 5-4 demonstrates a client that uses the XML-RPC services from Example 5-3.

Example 5-4. xmlrpc_client.py

```python
from twisted.web import xmlrpc
from twisted.internet import reactor

class WikiTester(object):
    def __init__(self):
        self.wiki = xmlrpc.Proxy('http://localhost:8082/RPC2')

    def runTests(self):
        self.listPages().addCallback(
            lambda _:self.createTestPage()).addCallback(
            lambda _: self.getTestPage()).addErrback(
            self._catchFailure).addCallback(
            lambda _: reactor.stop())

    def listPages(self):
        print "Getting page list..."
        return self.wiki.callRemote('listPages').addCallback(
            self._gotList)

    def _gotList(self, pages):
        print "Got page list:", pages

    def createTestPage(self):
        print "Creating test page XmlRpcTest..."
        pageData = "This is a test of XmlRpc"
        return self.wiki.callRemote('setPage', 'XmlRpcTest', pageData)

    def getTestPage(self):
        print "Getting test page content..."
        return self.wiki.callRemote(
            'getRenderedPage', 'XmlRpcTest').addCallback(
            self._gotTestPage)

    def _gotTestPage(self, content):
        print "Got page content:"
        print content
        return self.listPages()

    def _catchFailure(self, failure):
        print "Error:", failure.getErrorMessage()

w = WikiTester()
w.runTests()
reactor.run()
```

Run *xmlrpc_client.py*, and it will run a few commands over XML-RPC:

```
$ python xmlrpc_client.py
Getting page list...
Got page list: ['WikiHome', 'CurlTest', 'WgetTest', 'RestTest', 'PythonXmlRpcTest']
Creating test page XmlRpcTest...
Getting test page content...
```

```
Got page content:
This is a test of <a href='XmlRpc'>XmlRpc</a>
Getting page list...
Got page list: ['WikiHome', 'CurlTest', 'XmlRpcTest', 'WgetTest', 'RestTest',
'PythonXmlRpcTest']
```

How Does That Work?

The `callRemote` method of `xmlrpc.Proxy` takes the name of the function to be called as the first argument, followed by an arbitrary number of additional arguments that will be passed to the function. When you use `callRemote`, the `Proxy` encodes your function call as XML, sends it to the server using an HTTP `POST`, and returns a `Deferred`. When the server responds, the `Proxy` decodes the XML and calls back the `Deferred` with the returned value.

Installing SOAP Libraries

SOAP (for Simple Object Access Protocol) is another way to make remote function calls using XML over HTTP. SOAP and XML-RPC were both developed as part of the same project; XML-RPC is basically an early working version of what eventually became SOAP. While XML-RPC was intentionally kept simple, SOAP grew to become more powerful and more complicated.

Here's an example of the SOAP XML format, calling the function echo with the string argument `'cheese'`:

```
<?xml version="1.0" encoding="UTF-8"?>
<SOAP-ENV:Envelope
  SOAP-ENV:encodingStyle="http://schemas.xmlsoap.org/soap/encoding/"
  xmlns:SOAP-ENC="http://schemas.xmlsoap.org/soap/encoding/"
  xmlns:xsi="http://www.w3.org/1999/XMLSchema-instance"
  xmlns:SOAP-ENV="http://schemas.xmlsoap.org/soap/envelope/"
  xmlns:xsd="http://www.w3.org/1999/XMLSchema">
  <SOAP-ENV:Body>
    <echo SOAP-ENC:root="1">
      <v1 xsi:type="xsd:string">cheese</v1>
    </echo>
  </SOAP-ENV:Body>
</SOAP-ENV:Envelope>
```

And here's the XML returned from the server:

```
<?xml version="1.0" encoding="UTF-8"?>
<SOAP-ENV:Envelope
  SOAP-ENV:encodingStyle="http://schemas.xmlsoap.org/soap/encoding/"
  xmlns:SOAP-ENC="http://schemas.xmlsoap.org/soap/encoding/"
  xmlns:xsi="http://www.w3.org/1999/XMLSchema-instance"
  xmlns:SOAP-ENV="http://schemas.xmlsoap.org/soap/envelope/"
  xmlns:xsd="http://www.w3.org/1999/XMLSchema">
```

```
<SOAP-ENV:Body>
  <echoResponse SOAP-ENC:root="1">
    <Result xsi:type="xsd:string">You said: cheese</Result>
  </echoResponse>
</SOAP-ENV:Body>
</SOAP-ENV:Envelope>
```

Twisted uses an external library called SOAPpy to create and parse SOAP messages. You'll have to install SOAPpy to run the next two examples. SOAPpy also requires two additional libraries to be installed: *PyXML* and *fpconst*.

To install PyXML, download the package for your platform from *http://pyxml. sourceforge.net*. If there is an installer available, use it to install PyXML. Otherwise, you can install from the source by extracting the package, entering the package directory, and running the command python setup.py install. You can test to make sure PyXML is installed correctly by importing it in a Python shell:

```
$ python
Python 2.4.1 (#2, Apr 14 2005, 09:13:52)
[GCC 4.0.0 20050413 (prerelease) (Debian 4.0-0pre11)] on linux2
Type "help", "copyright", "credits" or "license" for more information.
>>> import xml
>>> xml.__version__
'0.8.4'
```

The xml.__version__ property should be the same as the PyXML package you installed.

The next prerequisite for SOAPpy is fpconst—a Python library for working with floating-point special values. fpconst doesn't have installer packages available, so you'll have to install from the source. Download and extract the latest version. In the directory containing the extracted files, run the command python setup.py install. Once the install is completed, you can verify that fpconst is correctly installed by importing it in a Python shell:

```
$ python
Python 2.4.1 (#2, Apr 14 2005, 09:13:52)
[GCC 4.0.0 20050413 (prerelease) (Debian 4.0-0pre11)] on linux2
Type "help", "copyright", "credits" or "license" for more information.
>>> import fpconst
>>> fpconst.__version__
'0.6.0'
```

Now that the dependencies are installed, you can install SOAPpy. Like fpconst, it's available only as a source package. Download the latest release from *http:// pywebsvcs.sourceforge.net/* and extract it. In the directory containing the extracted files, run the command python setup.py install to install SOAPpy. Again, it's a good idea to make sure the install was successful by importing the module:

```
$ python
Python 2.4.1 (#2, Apr 14 2005, 09:13:52)
[GCC 4.0.0 20050413 (prerelease) (Debian 4.0-0pre11)] on linux2
```

```
Type "help", "copyright", "credits" or "license" for more information.
>>> import SOAPpy
>>> SOAPpy.__version__
'0.11.3'
```

 For more information on installing SOAPpy, see the file README in the SOAPpy package.

Sharing Web Services with SOAP

Once you have SOAPpy installed, you can write a Twisted server that provides web services through SOAP.

How Do I Do That?

Because SOAP is based on HTTP, you enable SOAP web services by adding a special type of Resource to a twisted web server. Write a class that inherits from soap. SOAPPublisher and has methods starting with soap_. Make your class available as a web resource, as shown in Example 5-5, and you're ready to handle SOAP requests.

Example 5-5. soap_server.py

```
import wiki, rest_wiki
from twisted.web import server, soap

class WikiSoap(soap.SOAPPublisher):
    def __init__(self, wikiData):
        self.wikiData = wikiData

    def soap_hasPage(self, path):
        return self.wikiData.hasPage(path)

    def soap_listPages(self):
        return self.wikiData.listPages()

    def soap_getPage(self, path):
        return self.wikiData.getPage(path)

    def soap_getRenderedPage(self, path):
        return self.wikiData.getRenderedPage(path)

    def soap_setPage(self, path, data):
        self.wikiData.setPage(path, data)

if __name__ == "__main__":
    import sys
    from twisted.internet import reactor
    datafile = sys.argv[1]
```

Example 5-5. soap_server.py (continued)

```
wikiData = wiki.WikiData(datafile)
siteRoot = rest_wiki.RootResource(wikiData)
siteRoot.putChild('SOAP', WikiSoap(wikiData))
reactor.listenTCP(8082, server.Site(siteRoot))
reactor.run()
```

Run *soap_server.py* from the command line with the name of your Wiki datafile as an argument:

```
$ python soap_server.py wiki.dat
```

Once again, it will start up a web server on port 8082, but this time it will listen for SOAP requests at *http://localhost:8082/SOAP*. You should be able to test this using a SOAP library in any language; the next lab shows how to do so using a Twisted SOAP client.

How Does That Work?

The `soap.SOAPPublisher` class is the SOAP equivalent of the `xmlrpc.XMLRPC` class in Example 5-3. It's a subclass of `Resource` that parses the SOAP message in an incoming HTTP `POST`, runs the requested function, and then returns the SOAP-formatted result. Note that unlike XML-RPC, SOAP supports null values, so you don't have to avoid returning `None` from your methods.

Calling SOAP Web Services

The `twisted.web.soap` module contains a soap client. You can use it to communicate with the SOAP Wiki service defined in Example 5-5.

How Do I Do That?

The `twisted.web.soap.Proxy` class provides the same `callRemote` method as `twisted.web.xmlrpc.Proxy`. Use `callRemote` to call a SOAP method and get a `Deferred` result. Example 5-6 demonstrates a SOAP client that communicates with the SOAP Wiki service from Example 5-5.

Example 5-6. soap_client.py

```
from twisted.web import soap
from twisted.internet import reactor

class WikiTester(object):
    def __init__(self):
        self.wiki = soap.Proxy('http://localhost:8082/SOAP')

    def runTests(self):
        self.listPages().addCallback(
```

Example 5-6. soap_client.py (continued)

```
                lambda _:self.createTestPage( )).addCallback(
                lambda _: self.getTestPage( )).addErrback(
                self._catchFailure).addCallback(
                lambda _: reactor.stop( ))

    def listPages(self):
        print "Getting page list..."
        return self.wiki.callRemote('listPages').addCallback(
            self._gotList)

    def _gotList(self, pages):
        print "Got page list:", pages

    def createTestPage(self):
        print "Creating test page SoapTest..."
        pageData = "This is a test of SoapRpc"
        return self.wiki.callRemote('setPage', 'SoapTest', pageData)

    def getTestPage(self):
        print "Getting test page content..."
        return self.wiki.callRemote(
            'getRenderedPage', 'SoapTest').addCallback(
            self._gotTestPage)

    def _gotTestPage(self, content):
        print "Got page content:"
        print content
        return self.listPages( )

    def _catchFailure(self, failure):
        print "Error:", failure.getErrorMessage( )

w = WikiTester( )
w.runTests( )
reactor.run( )
```

Run *soap_client.py*, and it will test calling some methods through SOAP:

```
$ python soap_client.py
Getting page list...
Got page list: <SOAPpy.Types.typedArrayType Result at -1226273460>:
['WikiHome', 'CurlTest', 'XmlRpcTest', 'WgetTest', 'RestTest', 'PythonXmlRpcTest']
Creating test page SoapTest...
Getting test page content...
Got page content:
This is a test of <a href='SoapRpc'>SoapRpc</a>
Getting page list...
Got page list: <SOAPpy.Types.typedArrayType Result at -1226245012>:
['WikiHome', 'CurlTest', 'SoapTest', 'XmlRpcTest', 'WgetTest', 'RestTest',
'PythonXmlRpcTest']
```

How Does That Work?

The `callRemote` method of `soap.Proxy` takes the name of a function as the first argument, followed by any number of additional arguments that will be passed to the function. You can use keyword arguments instead, if the SOAP service you're using supports named arguments. When you use `callRemote`, the `Proxy` encodes your function call as a SOAP XML document, sends it to the server using an HTTP `POST` request, and returns a `Deferred`. When the server responds, the `Proxy` parses the result using SOAPpy and calls back the `Deferred` with the returned value.

Sharing Python Objects with Perspective Broker

XML-RPC and SOAP both transfer data using XML, which makes them language- and platform-neutral. This is an advantage most of the time. But what if you want to communicate between two Twisted applications without having to interoperate with anything else? In that case, the cross-platform advantages of XML could introduce a lot of work, as you have to convert your objects into formats that can be serialized as XML elements. A better approach might be to use Twisted Spread, a system for RPC that uses serialized Python objects.

How Do I Do That?

The core of Twisted Spread is Perspective Broker, which manages connections and handles calls to and from remote objects. The Perspective Broker module is named pb, which has resulted in a large number of peanut-butter-sandwich-related puns and module names (two of the other modules in Spread are `banana` and `jelly`).

Perspective Broker is conservative about what it exposes to the network. To avoid security holes, you have to specify exactly which objects should be able to be accessed remotely, and which methods you want to make available over the network. The pb module contains several different classes that you can inherit from to provide remotely accessible objects and methods. It also provides a `PBServerFactory` class for managing a Perspective Broker server. Example 5-7 shows how to run a server that shares Wiki data using Perspective Broker.

Example 5-7. pb_wiki.py

```
from twisted.spread import pb
import wiki

class WikiPerspective(pb.Root):
    def __init__(self, wikiData):
        self.wikiData = wikiData

    def remote_hasPage(self, path):
        return self.wikiData.hasPage(path)
```

Example 5-7. pb_wiki.py (continued)

```
    def remote_listPages(self):
        return self.wikiData.listPages( )

    def remote_getPage(self, path):
        return self.wikiData.getPage(path)

    def remote_getRenderedPage(self, path):
        return self.wikiData.getRenderedPage(path)

    def remote_setPage(self, path, data):
        self.wikiData.setPage(path, data)

    def remote_getReporter(self):
        return RemoteWikiReporter(self.wikiData)

class WikiReporter(pb.Referenceable):
    "I do simple reporting tasks in the wiki"
    def __init__(self, wikiData):
        self.wikiData = wikiData

    def listNeededPages(self):
        "return a list of pages that are linked to but don't exist yet"
        allPages = [self.wikiData.getPage(p)
                    for p in self.wikiData.listPages( )]
        neededPages = []
        for page in allPages:
            wikiWords = [match[0]
                        for match in wiki.reWikiWord.findall(page)]
            for pageName in wikiWords:
                if not self.wikiData.hasPage(pageName):
                    neededPages.append(pageName)
        return neededPages

if __name__ == "__main__":
    import sys
    from twisted.internet import reactor
    datafile = sys.argv[1]
    wikiData = wiki.WikiData(datafile)
    wikiPerspective = WikiPerspective(wikiData)
    reactor.listenTCP(8789, pb.PBServerFactory(wikiPerspective))
    reactor.run( )
```

Run *pb_server.py* with one argument, the name of the Wiki datafile:

```
$ python pb_server.py wiki.dat
```

Now you need a client to connect to the server. Example 5-8 shows a basic Perspective Broker client.

Example 5-8. pb_client.py

```python
from twisted.spread import pb
from twisted.internet import reactor

class PbTester(object):
    def __init__(self):
        self.wiki = None

    def runTests(self):
        self.connect().addCallback(
            lambda _: self.listPages()).addCallback(
            lambda _: self.createTestPage()).addCallback(
            lambda _: self.getTestPage()).addCallback(
            lambda _: self.runReports()).addErrback(
            self._catchFailure).addCallback(
            lambda _: reactor.stop())

    def connect(self):
        factory = pb.PBClientFactory()
        reactor.connectTCP("localhost", 8789, factory)
        return factory.getRootObject().addCallback(self._connected)

    def _connected(self, rootObj):
        self.wiki = rootObj

    def listPages(self):
        print "Getting page list..."
        return self.wiki.callRemote('listPages').addCallback(
            self._gotList)

    def _gotList(self, pages):
        print "Got page list:", pages

    def createTestPage(self):
        print "Creating test page PbTest..."
        pageData = "This is a test of PerspectiveBroker"
        return self.wiki.callRemote('setPage', 'PbTest', pageData)

    def getTestPage(self):
        print "Getting test page content..."
        return self.wiki.callRemote(
            'getRenderedPage', 'PbTest').addCallback(
            self._gotTestPage)

    def _gotTestPage(self, content):
        print "Got page content:"
        print content
        return self.listPages()
```

Example 5-8. pb_client.py (continued)

```
    def runReports(self):
        print "Running report..."
        return self.wiki.callRemote('getReporter').addCallback(
            self._gotReporter)

    def _gotReporter(self, reporter):
        print "Got remote reporter object"
        return reporter.callRemote('listNeededPages').addCallback(
            self._gotNeededPages)

    def _gotNeededPages(self, pages):
        print "These pages are needed:", pages

    def _catchFailure(self, failure):
        print "Error:", failure.getErrorMessage()

t = PbTester()
t.runTests()
reactor.run()
```

Run *pb_client.py*, and it will call functions on the server using the Perspective Broker protocol:

```
$ python pb_client.py
Getting page list...
Got page list: ['WikiHome', 'CurlTest', 'SoapTest',  'XmlRpcTest', 'WgetTest',
'RestTest', 'PythonXmlRpcTest']
Creating test page PbTest...
Getting test page content...
Got page content:
This is a test of <a href='PerspectiveBroker'>PerspectiveBroker</a>
Getting page list...
Got page list: ['WikiHome', 'CurlTest', 'SoapTest', 'XmlRpcTest', 'WgetTest',
'RestTest', 'PbTest', 'PythonXmlRpcTest']
Running report...
Got remote reporter object
These pages are needed: ['AnotherWikiPage', 'SoapRpc', 'XmlRpc', 'HttpPut',
'PerspectiveBroker', 'XmlRpc']
```

How Does That Work?

The *pb_server.py* server creates subclasses of classes in the twisted.spread.pb module. WikiPerspective is a subclass of pb.Root, and WikiReporter is a subclass of pb.Referenceable. Inheriting from these special classes tells Perspective Broker that these objects should be made available for remote access. Methods that should be available remotely must be named with a remote_ prefix.

WikiPerspective inherits from pb.Root, and is passed to the PBServerFactory when it gets created. This makes a WikiPerspective instance available to any client that establishes a connection.

The WikiReporter class in Example 5-7 is an example of how you could expose a second object through Perspective Broker. To make this object available over the network, it inherits from pb.Referenceable. WikiReporter has one method, remote_listNeededPages, which crawls through the Wiki data and returns a list of pages that are mentioned in other pages but have yet to be created.

On the client side, *pb_client.py* opens a connection to the server. The first thing it has to do is call getRootObject on a PBClientFactory. This returns a Deferred that will call back with a reference to the root object on the remote server once the connection has been established. Once you have the root object, you can call remote methods with the same callRemote syntax used in the XML-RPC and SOAP clients earlier in this chapter.

The server method remote_getReporter is interesting because instead of returning a simple Python type it returns a WikiReporter object. Since WikiReporter inherits from pb.Referenceable, the server knows to give the client a reference to the server-side object. Once it receives this reference, the client can use its callRemote method to call methods on the WikiReporter object that was created on the server.

Example 5-7 doesn't require authentication, and makes no distinction between different users who might be connecting to the server. To learn how to manage authentication and user permissions in Perspective Broker, see Example 6-5.

CHAPTER 6
Authentication

A requirement in almost any server application is a system for managing authentication. You need to be able to verify the identity of every user who attempts to access your server, based on their password or some other credentials. Once you allow a user to log in, you need to manage his permissions, controlling what he can and cannot do. The `twisted.cred` package is designed to facilitate these kinds of tasks.

Many parts of Twisted rely on `twisted.cred`, including the POP3, IMAP, SSH, and FTP servers. You can also use `twisted.cred` to add authentication to a web application, an SMTP server, a Perspective Broker server, or your own custom protocol. This chapter explains how `twisted.cred` works, and how to use it in your applications.

Using Authentication in a Twisted Server

There are quite a few different classes and interfaces used in `twisted.cred`. These classes and interfaces work together to form a flexible authentication system. This lab introduces the individual pieces of `twisted.cred` and shows how to tie them together to add authentication to a server.

How Do I Do That?

Set up a `portal.Portal` object that takes the username and password provided by a user, verifies her identity, and returns an object representing the actions and data available to that user. To do this you'll need to implement a few different `twisted.cred` interfaces. Example 6-1 demonstrates how to do this, adding authentication to a simple line-based server protocol.

Example 6-1. simplecred.py

```
from twisted.cred import portal, checkers, credentials, error as credError
from twisted.protocols import basic
from twisted.internet import protocol, reactor, defer
from zope.interface import Interface, implements
```

Example 6-1. simplecred.py (continued)

```
class PasswordDictChecker(object):
    implements(checkers.ICredentialsChecker)
    credentialInterfaces = (credentials.IUsernamePassword,)

    def __init__(self, passwords):
        "passwords: a dict-like object mapping usernames to passwords"
        self.passwords = passwords

    def requestAvatarId(self, credentials):
        username = credentials.username
        if self.passwords.has_key(username):
            if credentials.password == self.passwords[username]:
                return defer.succeed(username)
            else:
                return defer.fail(
                    credError.UnauthorizedLogin("Bad password"))
        else:
            return defer.fail(
                credError.UnauthorizedLogin("No such user"))

class INamedUserAvatar(Interface):
    "should have attributes username and fullname"

class NamedUserAvatar:
    implements(INamedUserAvatar)
    def __init__(self, username, fullname):
        self.username = username
        self.fullname = fullname

class TestRealm:
    implements(portal.IRealm)

    def __init__(self, users):
        self.users = users

    def requestAvatar(self, avatarId, mind, *interfaces):
        if INamedUserAvatar in interfaces:
            fullname = self.users[avatarId]
            logout = lambda: None
            return (INamedUserAvatar,
                    NamedUserAvatar(avatarId, fullname),

                    logout)
        else:
            raise KeyError("None of the requested interfaces is supported")

class LoginTestProtocol(basic.LineReceiver):
    def lineReceived(self, line):
        cmd = getattr(self, 'handle_' + self.currentCommand)
        cmd(line.strip())
```

Example 6-1. simplecred.py (continued)

```python
    def connectionMade(self):
        self.transport.write("User Name: ")
        self.currentCommand = 'user'

    def handle_user(self, username):
        self.username = username
        self.transport.write("Password: ")
        self.currentCommand = 'pass'

    def handle_pass(self, password):
        creds = credentials.UsernamePassword(self.username, password)
        self.factory.portal.login(creds, None, INamedUserAvatar).addCallback(
            self._loginSucceeded).addErrback(
            self._loginFailed)

    def _loginSucceeded(self, avatarInfo):
        avatarInterface, avatar, logout = avatarInfo
        self.transport.write("Welcome %s!\r\n" % avatar.fullname)
        defer.maybeDeferred(logout).addBoth(self._logoutFinished)

    def _logoutFinished(self, result):
        self.transport.loseConnection( )

    def _loginFailed(self, failure):
        self.transport.write("Denied: %s.\r\n" % failure.getErrorMessage( ))
        self.transport.loseConnection( )

class LoginTestFactory(protocol.ServerFactory):
    protocol = LoginTestProtocol

    def __init__(self, portal):
        self.portal = portal

users = {
    'admin': 'Admin User',
    'user1': 'Joe Smith',
    'user2': 'Bob King',
    }

passwords = {
    'admin': 'aaa',
    'user1': 'bbb',
    'user2': 'ccc'
    }

if __name__ == "__main__":
    p = portal.Portal(TestRealm(users))
    p.registerChecker(PasswordDictChecker(passwords))
    factory = LoginTestFactory(p)
    reactor.listenTCP(2323, factory)
    reactor.run( )
```

When you run *simplecred.py*, it will start up a server on port 2323. You can then communicate with the server using *Telnet*. Each time you make a connection, it will ask for your username and password, attempt to log you in, and then disconnect:

```
$ telnet localhost 2323
Trying 127.0.0.1...
Connected to sparky.
Escape character is '^]'.
User Name: admin
Password: aaa
Welcome Admin User!
Connection closed by foreign host.

$ telnet localhost 2323
Trying 127.0.0.1...
Connected to sparky.
Escape character is '^]'.
User Name: admin
Password: 123
Denied: Bad password.
Connection closed by foreign host.

$ telnet localhost 2323
Trying 127.0.0.1...
Connected to sparky.
Escape character is '^]'.
User Name: someotherguy
Password: pass
Denied: No such user.
Connection closed by foreign host.
```

How Does That Work?

Before you try to understand how all the classes in Example 6-1 work, you should familiarize yourself with the vocabulary `twisted.cred` uses to talk about users and authentication. Here are some of the terms you'll see in Example 6-1, and other applications using `twisted.cred`:

Credentials

Information used to identify and authenticate a user. This is typically a username and password, but it can be any data or object used to prove a user's identity. Objects that provide credentials will implement `twisted.cred.credentials.ICredentials`.

Avatar

An object on the server that does things on behalf of a user. The concept of an avatar can seem a little fuzzy at first. Don't think of an avatar as representing a user: think of it as representing actions and data available to a user inside your application.

Avatar ID

A string that identifies a specific user, used to get the appropriate Avatar for that user. This is often the login username, but it could be any unique identifier. Examples could be "Joe Smith", "joe@localhost", or "user926344".

Credentials Checker

An object that takes credentials and attempts to verify them. If the credentials correctly identify a user, the credentials checker will return an avatar ID. Credential checker objects implement the interface `twisted.cred.checker.ICredentialsChecker`.

Realm

An object that provides access to all the possible avatars in an application. A realm will take an avatar ID identifying a specific user and return an avatar object that will work on behalf of that user. A realm can support multiple types of avatar, allowing the same user to work with different services provided by the server. Realm objects implement the interface `twisted.cred.portal.IRealm`.

Portal

A `twisted.cred.portal.Portal` object, which unites a realm with a set of credential checkers. Inside a portal, the credential checker objects check incoming credentials, returning an avatar ID if the credentials are valid. The avatar ID is then passed to the realm to create an avatar object that can work on behalf of the user.

Figure 6-1 shows how a portal, realm, and credentials checkers work together.

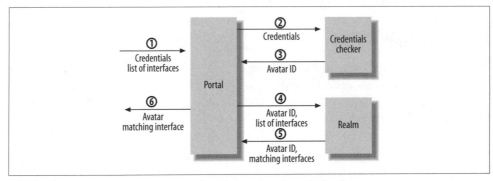

Figure 6-1. Interaction between a portal, realm, and credentials checkers

It might take you a little while to understand all the classes and interfaces in `twisted.cred`, and at first you might wonder why it's necessary to have a system with so many moving parts. The answer is that this system is designed to be extremely flexible. The code that verifies credentials is kept separate from the code that creates Avatar objects, so you can switch your authentication backend from a password file to a database table or LDAP server without having to touch the rest of your application.

If you originally design your system to use plain-text passwords, and later decide to support hashed passwords, all you have to do is plug in a new CredentialsChecker object. If you write a mail server that supports POP3 now, you can later add IMAP4 access, or a web interface, and you won't have to rewrite your authentication code. Your initial investment in understanding twisted.cred now will pay off in flexible, maintainable code later.

In Example 6-1, PasswordDictChecker implements checkers.ICredentialsChecker to check usernames and passwords. The requestAvatarId method will be called when a user tries to log in. requestAvatarId takes a credentials object that implements one of the interfaces listed in credentialsInterfaces, which in this case is limited to credentials.IUsernamePassword. If PasswordDictChecker was capable of accepting credentials other then a plain-text username and password, it would advertise this by including additional interfaces in the credentialsInterfaces list.

If the username and password supplied by the user matches a username and password in the database, requestAvatarId returns a Deferred that will be called back with a value identifying the user, who at that point has been successfully authenticated. Otherwise, it returns a Deferred that fails with a twisted.cred.error. UnauthorizedLogin exception.

The second half of the authentication backend in Example 6-1 is TestRealm, which implements twisted.cred.portal.IRealm. This class does the work of taking the avatar ID of an authenticated user and returning an avatar capable of doing certain tasks on behalf of that user.

TestRealm.requestAvatar takes three or more arguments: avatarID, mind, and one or more interfaces. The first argument, avatarID, is a string identifying the user for whom an avatar should be returned. The second argument, mind, is supposed to represent the actual user on the other end of the connection. In practice, though, mind is used only by Perspective Broker servers. For other applications, you can feel free to ignore it. The interfaces list passed to requestAvatar tell the realm what interface the avatar needs to support. (If there is more than one interface argument, it means that the application calling requestAvatar is capable of working with multiple interfaces. See Example 6-3.) It returns a tuple containing three values: the interface that the avatar supports, the avatar itself, and a logout function that can be called to shut down the avatar when the user is done with the session.

The TestRealm class in Example 6-1 provides access to a single type of avatar, NamedUserAvatar, which implements the interface INamedUser. NamedUserAvatar doesn't do a whole lot: it provides two attributes, username and fullname, that can be used to get some basic information about the user.

TestRealm.requestAvatar first checks to make sure that at least one of the interfaces requested by the client is INamedUser, the only interface which it supports. Then it looks up the full name of the user in its list of users, and uses the full name to construct a NamedUserAvatar object. Then it returns a tuple containing three values: the matching avatar interface (in this case always `INamedUser`), the avatar object itself, and a logout function. As the server in Example 6-1 isn't even keeping track of the current avatars, it doesn't have take any action when a user is logged out. So it uses an anonymous logout function that doesn't do anything.

A `Portal` object combines a realm with credentials checkers to form a complete authentication system. When you initialize a `Portal`, pass it an object that implements `IRealm`. Then call `registerChecker` with an object that implements `credentials.ICredentialsChecker`. You can call `registerChecker` multiple times if you have separate credentials checkers for handling different credentials interfaces.

`Portal` provides a single method, `login`, that encapsulates the whole authentication process. `Portal.login` takes a set of credentials as the first argument, a `mind` object as the second argument (which is rarely used, and usually just the value `None`), and one or more interfaces as the third and following arguments. It looks through its available set of `ICredentialsChecker` objects (which were added with `registerChecker`) and finds one that can handle the provided type of credentials. Then it calls the checker's `requestAvatarId` method to authenticate the user. Next, the `Portal` takes the avatar ID returned by the credentials checker and the list of interfaces passed to `login` and uses them to calls its realm's `requestAvatar` method. The resulting tuple of avatar interface, avatar, and logout function gets called back as the result of `login`.

When you connect to the server in Example 6-1, `LoginTestProtocol` asks for a username and password. When these are provided, it wraps them in a `credentials.UsernamePassword` object and passes it to `self.factory.portal.login` along with `None` (a placeholder for the `mind` argument) and `INamedUserAvatar`, which specifies the kind of avatar `LoginTestProtocol` wants to get back. If `login` is successful, it will call back with a `NamedUserAvatar` object; otherwise, it will errback with an error describing why the login failed.

Authenticating Against a Database Table

The design of `twisted.cred` makes it easy to swap out various parts of your authentication system. This example demonstrates how to replace the dictionaries of usernames and passwords used in Example 6-1 with a SQL database table.

How Do I Do That?

To check usernames and passwords against a database table, write a new class implementing `checkers.ICredentialsChecker`. To create avatars based on database records, write a new class implementing `portal.IRealm`. Example 6-2 demonstrates how to modify the server from Example 6-1 to use a MySQL database for authentication.

Example 6-2. dbcred.py

```python
from twisted.enterprise import adbapi, util as dbutil
from twisted.cred import credentials, portal, checkers, error as credError
from twisted.internet import reactor, defer
from zope.interface import implements
import simplecred

class DbPasswordChecker(object):
    implements(checkers.ICredentialsChecker)
    credentialInterfaces = (credentials.IUsernamePassword,
                            credentials.IUsernameHashedPassword)

    def __init__(self, dbconn):
        self.dbconn = dbconn

    def requestAvatarId(self, credentials):
        query = "select userid, password from user where username = %s" % (
            dbutil.quote(credentials.username, "char"))
        return self.dbconn.runQuery(query).addCallback(
            self._gotQueryResults, credentials)

    def _gotQueryResults(self, rows, userCredentials):
        if rows:
            userid, password = rows[0]
            return defer.maybeDeferred(
                userCredentials.checkPassword, password).addCallback(
                self._checkedPassword, userid)
        else:
            raise credError.UnauthorizedLogin, "No such user"

    def _checkedPassword(self, matched, userid):
        if matched:
            return userid
        else:
            raise credError.UnauthorizedLogin("Bad password")

class DbRealm:
    implements(portal.IRealm)

    def __init__(self, dbconn):
        self.dbconn = dbconn

    def requestAvatar(self, avatarId, mind, *interfaces):
        if simplecred.INamedUserAvatar in interfaces:
            userQuery = """
              select username, firstname, lastname
              from user where userid = %s
            """ % dbutil.quote(avatarId, "int")
            return self.dbconn.runQuery(userQuery).addCallback(
                self._gotQueryResults)
        else:
            raise KeyError("None of the requested interfaces is supported")
```

Example 6-2. dbcred.py (continued)

```python
    def _gotQueryResults(self, rows):
        username, firstname, lastname = rows[0]
        fullname = "%s %s" % (firstname, lastname)
        return (simplecred.INamedUserAvatar,
                simplecred.NamedUserAvatar(username, fullname),

                lambda: None) # null logout function

DB_DRIVER = "MySQLdb"
DB_ARGS = {
    'db': 'your_db',
    'user': 'your_db_username',
    'passwd': 'your_db_password',
    }

if __name__ == "__main__":
    connection = adbapi.ConnectionPool(DB_DRIVER, **DB_ARGS)
    p = portal.Portal(DbRealm(connection))
    p.registerChecker(DbPasswordChecker(connection))
    factory = simplecred.LoginTestFactory(p)
    reactor.listenTCP(2323, factory)
    reactor.run()
```

Before you run *dbcred.py*, create a MySQL database table called user, and insert some records for testing:

```sql
CREATE TABLE user (
    userid int NOT NULL PRIMARY KEY,
    username varchar(20) NOT NULL,
    password varchar(50) NOT NULL,
    firstname varchar(100),
    lastname varchar(100),
);
INSERT INTO user VALUES (1, 'admin', 'aaa', 'Admin', 'User');
INSERT INTO user VALUES (2, 'test1', 'bbb', 'Joe', 'Smith');
INSERT INTO user VALUES (3, 'test2', 'ccc', 'Bob', 'King');
```

dbcred.py works exactly the same way as *simplecred.py* from Example 6-1. It has a new authentication backend, but from the user's, perspective nothing has changed:

```
$ telnet localhost 2323
Trying 127.0.0.1...
Connected to sparky.
Escape character is '^]'.
User Name: admin
Password: aaa
Welcome Admin User!
Connection closed by foreign host.

$ telnet localhost 2323
Trying 127.0.0.1...
Connected to sparky.
Escape character is '^]'.
```

```
User Name: admin
Password: 123
Denied: Bad password.
Connection closed by foreign host.

$ telnet localhost 2323
Trying 127.0.0.1...
Connected to sparky.
Escape character is '^]'.
User Name: someotherguy
Password: pass
Denied: No such user.
Connection closed by foreign host.
```

How Does That Work?

The class DbPasswordChecker in Example 6-2 checks usernames and passwords against a database table. The requestAvatarId function takes the provided username and runs a database query to look for a matching record. The _gotQueryResults function handles the results of the query. If there were no records, it raises a twisted. cred.error.UnauthorizedLogin exception. (Because _gotQueryResults is running as the callback handler of a Deferred that was returned from requestAvatarId, this exception will be caught by that Deferred and eventually passed back to the error handler for Portal.login.)

If there was a matching record in the database, _gotQueryResults checks to see whether the password supplied by the user matches the database password. It does this in an indirect way, calling userCredentials.checkPassword, a method supplied by the credentials.IUsernamePassword interface. checkPassword can return either a Boolean value or a Deferred; wrapping the call in defer.maybeDeferred lets you treat the result as a Deferred in either case.

Using the IUsernamePassword.checkPassword method instead of comparing the passwords yourself gives the server-side protocol that created the credentials object more flexibility: it could use a custom implementation of IUserNamePassword that compared the passwords in a case-insensitive way, or asynchronously. Moreover, using the checkPassword method allows DbPasswordChecker to accept a second credentials interface—IUsernameHashedPassword. If the protocol being used here involved hashed passwords, it wouldn't be possible to do a direct comparison of the hash sent by the user and the plain-text password in our database. The checkPassword method lets the credentials object compare the two using the proper hashing algorithm. This isn't necessary in Example 6-2, since it uses plain-text passwords, but writing your code this way makes it easier to reuse DbPasswordChecker for other services in the future.

The _checkedPassword method handles the Boolean result of checkPassword. If the password matched, it returns the value of the field userid from the database: this is the final result of requestAvatarId. Note that this is a different type of avatar ID than in Example 6-1. In Example 6-1, the avatar ID was equal to the username; this time, it's an integer identifying the database record. This works because the avatar ID is used only by the realm, and Example 6-2 has a new realm as well. DbRealm. requestAvatar takes the avatar ID returned by DbConnector.requestAvatarId and uses it to fetch the full user record from the database. Then it uses the results to construct a NamedUserAvatar object.

Example 6-2 creates a Portal object that uses DbRealm as its realm and registers DbPasswordChecker as a credentials checker. Then the Portal is passed to a LoginTestFactory. This factory and its protocol come directly from the simplecred module in Example 6-1. They are able to function exactly as they did before without any changes, as the Portal hides the implementation details.

Representing Users with Different Capabilities

It can often be useful to authenticate against an external service. You can avoid making users maintain an additional username and password by using a credentials checker that tries to log into a POP mail server, a web application, or some other service where you know your users will already have accounts. However, this approach creates a potential problem. Your realm is going to be asked for avatars after users have been authenticated by the credentials checker. But since the credentials checker is using an external service, rather than a local data source, for authentication, the realm may not have any information about the avatars it's asked for. While you might be able to spontaneously create accounts based on the avatar ID, you will frequently need additional information before users can start using their accounts.

You can handle this scenario by taking advantage of the way twisted.cred supports multiple avatar interfaces. Your realm can use different types of avatars to represent users with different capabilities. One interface can identify users from whom you need additional information, and another interface can identify users who have already provided the necessary information and are ready to use your application.

How Do I Do That?

Write a class implementing portal.IRealm that accepts two different avatar interfaces in requestAvatar. Use one avatar interface for users who need to supply additional information before they can start using your service. This interface should provide a way for users to submit the required information. Use a second avatar interface to provide the normal user actions and data. Example 6-3 demonstrates this technique.

Example 6-3. multiavatar.py

```python
from twisted.cred import portal, checkers, credentials, error as credError
from twisted.protocols import basic
from twisted.internet import protocol, reactor, defer
from zope.interface import Interface, implements

class INamedUserAvatar(Interface):
    "should have attributes username and fullname"

class NamedUserAvatar:
    implements(INamedUserAvatar)
    def __init__(self, username, fullname):
        self.username = username
        self.fullname = fullname

class INewUserAvatar(Interface):
    "should have username attribute only"
    def setName(self, fullname):
        raise NotImplementedError

class NewUserAvatar:
    implements(INewUserAvatar)
    def __init__(self, username, userDb):
        self.username = username
        self.userDb = userDb

    def setName(self, fullname):
        self.userDb[self.username] = fullname
        return NamedUserAvatar(self.username, fullname)

class MultiAvatarRealm:
    implements(portal.IRealm)

    def __init__(self, users):
        self.users = users

    def requestAvatar(self, avatarId, mind, *interfaces):
        logout = lambda: None
        if INamedUserAvatar in interfaces and self.users.has_key(avatarId):
            fullname = self.users[avatarId]
            return (INamedUserAvatar,
                NamedUserAvatar(avatarId, fullname),

                    logout)
        elif INewUserAvatar in interfaces:
            avatar = NewUserAvatar(avatarId, self.users)
            return (INewUserAvatar, avatar, logout)
        else:
            raise KeyError("None of the requested interfaces is supported")

class PasswordDictChecker(object):
    implements(checkers.ICredentialsChecker)
    credentialInterfaces = (credentials.IUsernamePassword,)
```

Example 6-3. multiavatar.py (continued)

```python
    def __init__(self, passwords):
        "passwords: a dict-like object mapping usernames to passwords"
        self.passwords = passwords

    def requestAvatarId(self, credentials):
        username = credentials.username
        if self.passwords.has_key(username):
            if credentials.password == self.passwords[username]:
                return defer.succeed(username)
            else:
                return defer.fail(
                    credError.UnauthorizedLogin("Bad password"))
        else:
            return defer.fail(
                credError.UnauthorizedLogin("No such user"))

class NamedUserLoginProtocol(basic.LineReceiver):
    def lineReceived(self, line):
        cmd = getattr(self, 'handle_' + self.currentCommand)
        cmd(line.strip())

    def connectionMade(self):
        self.transport.write("User Name: ")
        self.currentCommand = 'user'

    def handle_user(self, username):
        self.username = username
        self.transport.write("Password: ")
        self.currentCommand = 'pass'

    def handle_pass(self, password):
        creds = credentials.UsernamePassword(self.username, password)
        avatarInterfaces = (INamedUserAvatar, INewUserAvatar)
        self.factory.portal.login(creds, None, *avatarInterfaces).addCallback(
            self._loginSucceeded).addErrback(
            self._loginFailed)

    def _loginSucceeded(self, avatarInfo):
        avatar, avatarInterface, self.logout = avatarInfo
        if avatarInterface == INewUserAvatar:
            self.transport.write("What's your full name? ")
            self.currentCommand = "fullname"
            self.avatar = avatar
        else:
            self._gotNamedUser(avatar)

    def handle_fullname(self, fullname):
        namedUserAvatar = self.avatar.setName(fullname)
        self._gotNamedUser(namedUserAvatar)
```

Example 6-3. multiavatar.py (continued)

```python
    def _gotNamedUser(self, avatar):
        self.transport.write("Welcome %s!\r\n" % avatar.fullname)
        defer.maybeDeferred(self.logout).addBoth(self._logoutFinished)

    def _logoutFinished(self, result):
        self.transport.loseConnection()

    def _loginFailed(self, failure):
        self.transport.write("Denied: %s.\r\n" % failure.getErrorMessage())
        self.transport.loseConnection()

class NamedUserLoginFactory(protocol.ServerFactory):
    protocol = NamedUserLoginProtocol

    def __init__(self, portal):
        self.portal = portal

users = {
    'admin': 'Admin User',
    }

passwords = {
    'admin': 'aaa',
    'user1': 'bbb',
    'user2': 'ccc'
    }

portal = portal.Portal(MultiAvatarRealm(users))
portal.registerChecker(PasswordDictChecker(passwords))
factory = NamedUserLoginFactory(portal)
reactor.listenTCP(2323, factory)
reactor.run()
```

When you run *multiavatar.py*, it will start up a server on port 2323. This server uses the same simple protocol as the previous examples in this chapter, but with one addition: if you log in as a user who it hasn't seen before, it will ask you for your full name. This information won't be required for subsequent logins, as it will remember the name you entered the first time:

```
$ telnet localhost 2323
Trying 127.0.0.1...
Connected to sparky.
Escape character is '^]'.
User Name: user1
Password: bbb
What's your full name? Abe Fettig
Welcome Abe Fettig!
Connection closed by foreign host.

$ telnet localhost 2323
Trying 127.0.0.1...
Connected to sparky.
```

```
Escape character is '^]'.
User Name: user1
Password: bbb
Welcome Abe Fettig!
Connection closed by foreign host.
```

How Does That Work?

The server protocol and realm in Example 6-3 are both aware that this realm uses two different types of avatar. When the MultiAvatarRealm.requestAvatar method is called, it checks to see whether the avatar is listed in self.users, the dictionary of users it knows about. If it finds the user information, it returns a tuple containing INamedUserAvatar, a NamedUserAvatar object for that user, and a logout function. So far, this is identical to the behavior of TestRealm in Example 6-1 at the beginning of this chapter.

If requestAvatar is called with an unknown avatar ID, though, MultiAvatarRealm returns a different type of avatar. The INewUserAvatar interface and NewUserAvatar class represent the actions available to users from whom the server needs more information. Unlike the regular NamedUserAvatar object, NewUserAvatar doesn't provide a fullname attribute: the server doesn't know this user's name. Instead it provides the setName method, providing a way to store the user's name. As a convenience, setName returns a NamedUserAvatar. This step makes it possible to take a NewUserAvatar object and upgrade to a NamedUserAvatar by supplying the user's full name.

The NamedUserProtocol in Example 6-3 calls portal.login with the user's credentials and two interface arguments, INamedUserAvatar and INewUserAvatar. When it gets the results, it checks the first item in the tuple to see which interface is being used. If it is INewUserAvatar, the server asks the client for his full name, and calls the avatar's setName method. In this case, that's all the information that was missing. The NewUserAvatar stores the user's name for future use, and the server can proceed with the rest of the session (brief as it is).

Using Authentication with Perspective Broker

Example 5-8 in Chapter 5 demonstrated Perspective Broker without any authentication in place. In the real world, though, you probably don't want to give just anyone remote access to objects in your application. You usually need to have an authentication layer in place to control who gets in, and what they're allowed to do.

Perspective Broker lets you perform authentication by integrating with twisted.cred. Adding authentication makes Perspective Broker live up to its name: it can provide different perspectives to different users, hiding or exposing objects and methods depending on the user's permissions.

How Do I Do That?

Create a realm that returns pb.Avatar objects. Each avatar should have methods prefixed with perspective_ that the user of that avatar will be allowed to run. Connect the realm to a Portal, add credentials checkers, and pass the Portal to a pb. PBServerFactory. Example 6-4 demonstrates a Perspective Broker server with authentication.

Example 6-4. pbcred.py

```python
from twisted.spread import pb
from twisted.cred import checkers, portal
from zope.interface import implements

class TodoList:
    def __init__(self):
        self.items = []

    def listItems(self):
        return self.items[:] # return copy of list

    def addItem(self, item):
        self.items.append(item)
        return len(self.items) - 1

    def deleteItem(self, index):
        del(self.items[index])

class UserPerspective(pb.Avatar):
    def __init__(self, todoList):
        self.todoList = todoList

    def perspective_listItems(self):
        return self.todoList.listItems()

class AdminPerspective(UserPerspective):
    def __init__(self, todoList):
        self.todoList = todoList

    def perspective_addItem(self, item):
        return self.todoList.addItem(item)

    def perspective_deleteItem(self, index):
        return self.todoList.deleteItem(index)

class TestRealm(object):
    implements(portal.IRealm)

    def __init__(self, todoList):
        self.todoList = todoList
```

Example 6-4. pbcred.py (continued)

```python
    def requestAvatar(self, avatarId, mind, *interfaces):
        if not pb.IPerspective in interfaces:
            raise NotImplementedError, "No supported avatar interface."
        else:
            if avatarId == 'admin':
                avatar = AdminPerspective(self.todoList)
            else:
                avatar = UserPerspective(self.todoList)
            return pb.IPerspective, avatar, lambda: None

if __name__ == "__main__":
    import sys
    from twisted.internet import reactor
    p = portal.Portal(TestRealm(TodoList()))
    p.registerChecker(
        checkers.InMemoryUsernamePasswordDatabaseDontUse(
        admin='aaa',
        guest='bbb'))
    reactor.listenTCP(8789, pb.PBServerFactory(p))
    reactor.run()
```

To test this server, write a Perspective Broker client that supports authentication. Create a PBClientFactory and call login (instead of getRootObject) with your user's credentials as the only argument. Example 6-5 is a pb client that uses a username and password for authentication.

Example 6-5. pbcred_client.py

```python
from twisted.spread import pb
from twisted.internet import reactor
from twisted.cred import credentials

class PbAuthTester(object):
    def __init__(self, credentials):
        self.credentials = credentials
        self.server = None

    def runTests(self):
        self.connect().addCallback(
            lambda _: self.listItems()).addCallback(
            lambda _: self.addItem()).addErrback(
            self._catchFailure).addCallback(
            lambda _: reactor.stop())

    def connect(self):
        factory = pb.PBClientFactory()
        reactor.connectTCP("localhost", 8789, factory)
        return factory.login(self.credentials).addCallback(self._connected)
```

Example 6-5. pbcred_client.py (continued)

```
    def _connected(self, rootObj):
        self.server = rootObj

    def listItems(self):
        return self.server.callRemote("listItems").addCallback(self._gotList)

    def _gotList(self, list):
        print "%i items in TODO list." % (len(list))

    def addItem(self):
        return self.server.callRemote(
            "addItem", "Buy groceries").addCallback(
            self._addedItem)

    def _addedItem(self, result):
        print "Added 1 item."

    def _catchFailure(self, failure):
        print "Error:", failure.getErrorMessage()

if __name__ == "__main__":
    import sys
    username, password = sys.argv[1:3]
    creds = credentials.UsernamePassword(username, password)
    tester = PbAuthTester(creds)
    tester.runTests()
    reactor.run()
```

Run *pbcred.py* to start the server. *pbcred_client.py* takes a username and password as arguments. Try it with the name and password **admin** and **aaa**. It will list the number of current items on the server, and then add an item:

```
$ python pbcred_client.py admin aaa
Getting item list...
0 items in list.
Adding new item...
Added 1 item.
```

Then try again using the username **guest** and password **bbb**. You'll be able to get the item count, but you'll get an error trying to add an item:

```
$ python pbcred_client.py guest bbb
Getting item list...
1 items in list.
Adding new item...
Error: UserPerspective instance has no attribute 'perspective_addItem'
```

This is because the guest user does not get the same perspective as admin. The guest user's perspective is read-only, and doesn't include methods for adding or deleting items.

How Does That Work?

The server provides the four standard objects needed for Twisted authentication: avatars, a realm, a portal, and credentials checkers. The TestRealm returns either a UserPerspective avatar or a AdminPerspective avatar, depending on the user's name. The admin user will get an AdminPerspective avatar, which includes the additional methods perspective_addItem and perspective_deleteItem. UserPerspective and AdminPerspective both inherit from pb.Avatar, and provide methods prefixed with perspective_. pb.Avatar objects implement the pb.IPerspective interface; the Perspective Broker server will pass this interface to Portal.login to request a pb.Avatar.

For the sake of simplicity, Example 6-5 uses the InMemoryPasswordDatabaseDontUse credentials checker class, which is included in twisted.cred.checkers for use in test programs only. In production, you'd use a real credentials checker that authenticated usernames and passwords against a file, database, or another service.

To use authentication, the client calls PBClient.login instead of calling PBClient.getRootObject directly. The login function attempts to log in using a set of credentials and then returns a reference to a pb.Avatar object on the server representing that user's perspective.

CHAPTER 7

Mail Clients

You're probably reading this chapter because you want to write a mail client, or to extend an existing application to work with email. This is a common desire. In fact, as Jamie Zawinski put it in his Law of Software Envelopment:

> Every program attempts to expand until it can read mail. Those programs which can-not so expand are replaced by ones which can.

That statement was probably made somewhat tongue-in-cheek, but it does make a point about the importance of email. Email is ubiquitous. Reading and writing email is a vital part of many people's communication, both at work and in their personal lives. In addition, users and administrators have come to expect emailing as an inter-face to communicate with their applications. When an application needs to remind users of lost passwords, provide a simple way to update a bug-tracking system, or allow for uploading pictures from mobile phones, email integration becomes a requirement.

Twisted provides support for working with email through all of the standard proto-cols commonly used today: SMTP, POP3, and IMAP.

Downloading Mail from a POP3 Server

One of the most widely used email protocols is the Post Office Protocol version 3 (POP3). POP3 does one thing, and does it well: it allows a user to log into a mail server and download her messages, optionally deleting the copies on the server after-wards. POP3 is a simple enough protocol that you can talk to a server manually, through *Telnet,* as shown in Example 7-1.

Example 7-1. Communicating with a POP3 server using Telnet

```
$ telnet pop.myisp.com 110
Connected to pop.myisp.com.
Escape character is '^]'.
+OK dovecot ready.
user myusername
+OK
```

Example 7-1. Communicating with a POP3 server using Telnet (continued)

```
pass mypassword
+OK Logged in.
list
+OK 2 messages:
1 1385
2 100
.
retr 2
+OK 100 octets
From: somebody@example.com
To: abe@fettig.net
Subject: Hello

How's the weather up there in Maine?
.
quit
+OK Logging out.
Connection closed by foreign host.
```

But even with such a simple protocol, it's nice to be saved the effort of writing your own implementation from scratch. Twisted comes with a `Protocol` class that implements POP3: `twisted.mail.pop3client.POP3Client`. You can use it in your programs to download mail from a POP3 server.

How Do I Do That?

Create a subclass of `POP3Client`. Use the methods `login`, `listSize`, `listUidl`, `retrieve`, and `quit` to send commands to the server and get `Deferred`s that will be called back with the server's response. Example 7-2 demonstrates a POP3 client that logs into a server, retrieves the list of available messages, and then downloads each message to an mbox file.

Example 7-2. pop3download.py

```python
from twisted.mail import pop3client
from twisted.internet import reactor, protocol, defer
from cStringIO import StringIO
import email

class POP3DownloadProtocol(pop3client.POP3Client):
    # permit logging without encryption
    allowInsecureLogin = True

    def serverGreeting(self, greeting):
        pop3client.POP3Client.serverGreeting(self, greeting)
        login = self.login(self.factory.username, self.factory.password)
        login.addCallback(self._loggedIn)
        login.chainDeferred(self.factory.deferred)

    def _loggedIn(self, result):
        return self.listSize().addCallback(self._gotMessageSizes)
```

Example 7-2. pop3download.py (continued)

```python
    def _gotMessageSizes(self, sizes):
        retreivers = []
        for i in range(len(sizes)):
            retreivers.append(self.retrieve(i).addCallback(
                self._gotMessageLines))
        return defer.DeferredList(retreivers).addCallback(
            self._finished)

    def _gotMessageLines(self, messageLines):
        self.factory.handleMessage("\r\n".join(messageLines))

    def _finished(self, downloadResults)
        return self.quit()

class POP3DownloadFactory(protocol.ClientFactory):
    protocol = POP3DownloadProtocol

    def __init__(self, username, password, output):
        self.username = username
        self.password = password
        self.output = output
        self.deferred = defer.Deferred()

    def handleMessage(self, messageData):
        parsedMessage = email.message_from_string(messageData)
        self.output.write(parsedMessage.as_string(unixfrom=True))
        self.output.write('\r\n')

    def clientConnectionFailed(self, connection, reason):
        self.deferred.errback(reason)

import sys, getpass

def handleError(error):
    print error
    print >> sys.stderr, "Error:", error.getErrorMessage()
    reactor.stop()


if __name__ == "__main__":
    if len(sys.argv) != 4:
        print "Usage: %s server username output.mbox" % sys.argv[0]
        sys.exit(1)
    else:
        server, username, outputfile = sys.argv[1:]
        password = getpass.getpass("Password: ")
        f = POP3DownloadFactory(username, password, file(outputfile, 'w+b'))
        f.deferred.addCallback(
            lambda _: reactor.stop()).addErrback(
            handleError)
        reactor.connectTCP(server, 110, f)
        reactor.run()
```

Run *pop3download.py* with three arguments: the server, the login username, and the output filename. It will prompt you for your password, log in to the server, download all the messages, and write them to the output file in the Unix-standard *mbox* format:

```
$ python pop3download.py pop.myisp.com mylogin pop-messages.mbox
Password:
Downloading message 1 of 31
Downloading message 2 of 31
Downloading message 3 of 31
...
Downloading message 30 of 31
Downloading message 31 of 31
```

Note that the contents of your output file will be overwritten every time you run *pop3download.py*—be careful not to clobber any important messages!

How Does That Work?

There are two main classes in *pop3download.py*: POP3DownloadProtocol and POP3DownloadFactory. As a standard factory, a POP3DownloadFactory will create a POP3DownloadProtocol object when a connection to the server is established. The two classes then work together. The POP3DownloadProtocol communicates with the server, and passes each downloaded message to the POP3DownloadFactory by calling self.factory.handleMessage. The POP3DownloadFactory then writes the message data to the output file. The POP3DownloadProtocol will also call either callback or errback on the POP3DownloadFactory's deferred object, to indicate that the process of downloading all messages has completed successfully, or failed with an error.

Example 7-2 uses the POP3Client class from twisted.mail.pop3client. There's another POP3Client in twisted.mail.pop3, but this is an old, deprecated class with a much less friendly API. Use the twisted.mail.pop3client version instead.

POP3Client, which POP3DownloadProtocol inherits from, provides high-level methods for sending POP3 commands, such as login, listSize, listUidl, retrieve, delete, and quit. The action in POP3DownloadProtocol starts in serverGreeting, which is called when the server sends the POP3 WELCOME message. POP3Client.login is an intelligent method that logs in to the server using the best available login technique. If the server supports APOP authentication, which doesn't send the password in plain text, login will use APOP; otherwise, it will log in using the plain-text username and password. POP3DownloadProtocol adds self._loggedIn as the callback handler for login, and then uses chainDeferred to connect the result of logging in to self.factory.deferred.

The self._loggedIn method responds to the successful login by calling POP3Client. listSize. This returns a Deferred that will be called back with a list of message sizes. Notice that _loggedIn returns this Deferred result, which keeps everything happening in the context of the Deferred from self.login, which is chained to self. factory.deferred. Therefore the result of listSize, or any exception that might occur, will be passed up to self.factory.deferred.

The callback handler for listSize, self._gotMessageSizes, requests each message from the server by calling POP3Client.retrieve with the message index number. You can send many retrieve requests at once, as POP3DownloadClient does, and POP3Client will automatically queue them up and send them one at a time. _gotMessageSizes keeps a list of all the calls it's made to retrieve, and then returns a defer. DeferredList wrapping the list. The DeferredList will call back after all the messages have been downloaded. Once again, _gotMessageSizes returns a Deferred, which keeps everything happening inside the callback chain of the original call to self. login.

The _gotMessageLines function is the callback handler used for each call to retrieve. It takes a list of the lines received from the server, joins them into a single string, and passes the message to self.factory.handleMessage.

Note that messages aren't being deleted from the server, which means they will still be available the next time you connect. If you wanted to delete the server's copy of a message, send the POP3 DELETE command by calling self.delete(messageNumber) for each message you want to delete. The POP3 DELETE command doesn't delete messages instantly; it queues up the list of messages to delete and then processes them after you quit. So if you send delete for several messages, and then something happens to your connection before you call quit, the messages will remain on the server.

The POP3DownloadFactory used in Example 7-2 takes three arguments at initialization: the username, the password, and the output file to use for the downloaded messages. Its handleMessage function uses Python's email module to parse the message and write it to the output file in *mbox* format.

 The unixfrom=True argument that you see in *handleMessage*, in the call to *parsedMessage.as_string*, starts the message with a line in the form "From emailaddress timestamp," which the mbox format uses to determine where one message ends and a new message begins. Including that argument is key to generating an mbox file.

What About...

...using SSL (the *Secure Socket Layer*) for encrypted connections? Many POP servers support SSL as a secure alternative to regular TCP connections. By encrypting all the data passing between client and server, SSL keeps your password and email protected from anyone who might be snooping on your network connection.

To use POP3 over SSL, just replace `reactor.connectTCP` with `reactor.connectSSL`, and connect to port 995 instead of 110:

```
from twisted.internet import ssl
reactor.connectSSL(server, 995, factory, ssl.ClientContextFactory())
```

`reactor.connectSSL` takes one additional argument, a `twisted.internet.ssl.ClientContextFactory` object. (The `ClientContextFactory` object can be used for advanced SSL tasks, like using custom certificates, but in most situations you just need to create it and pass it to `reactor.connectSSL`.)

Sending Mail Using SMTP

The standard protocol for sending mail on the Internet is the Simple Mail Transfer Protocol (SMTP). SMTP allows one computer to transfer email messages to another computer using a standard set of commands. Mail clients use SMTP to send outgoing messages, and mail servers use SMTP to forward messages to their final destination. The current specification for SMTP is defined in RFC 2821 (*http://www.faqs.org/rfcs/rfc2821.html*).

Twisted supports SMTP, using the `twisted.protocols.smtp` module. In addition to SMTP Protocol classes, this module has handy functions for sending mail. Combined with the `email` module in the Python standard library, you can create and send messages (even complex MIME messages with attachments) with only a few lines of code.

How Do I Do That?

Create your message using Python's email package. Then use the `twisted.protocols.smtp.sendmail` function to send the message using SMTP, as demonstrated in Example 7-3.

Example 7-3. smtpsend.py

```
from twisted.protocols import smtp
from twisted.internet import reactor, defer
from email.MIMEBase import MIMEBase
from email.MIMEMultipart import MIMEMultipart
from email import Encoders
import sys, mimetypes, os

def buildMessage(fromaddr, toaddr, subject, body, filenames):
    message = MIMEMultipart()
    message['From'] = fromaddr
    message['To'] = toaddr
    message['Subject'] = subject
    textPart = MIMEBase('text', 'plain')
    textPart.set_payload(body)
    message.attach(textPart)
```

Example 7-3. smtpsend.py (continued)

```python
    for filename in filenames:
        # guess the mimetype
        mimetype = mimetypes.guess_type(filename)[0]
        if not mimetype: mimetype = 'application/octet-stream'
        maintype, subtype = mimetype.split('/')
        attachment = MIMEBase(maintype, subtype)
        attachment.set_payload(file(filename).read())
        # base64 encode for safety
        Encoders.encode_base64(attachment)
        # include filename info
        attachment.add_header('Content-Disposition', 'attachment',
                              filename=os.path.split(filename)[1])
        message.attach(attachment)
    return message

def sendComplete(result):
    print "Message sent."
    reactor.stop()

def handleError(error):
    print >> sys.stderr, "Error", error.getErrorMessage()
    reactor.stop()

if __name__ == "__main__":
    if len(sys.argv) < 5:
        print "Usage: %s smtphost fromaddr toaddr file1 [file2, ...]" % (
            sys.argv[0])
        sys.exit(1)

    smtphost = sys.argv[1]
    fromaddr = sys.argv[2]
    toaddr = sys.argv[3]
    filenames = sys.argv[4:]
    subject = raw_input("Subject: ")
    body = raw_input("Message (one line): ")
    message = buildMessage(fromaddr, toaddr, subject, body, filenames)
    messageData = message.as_string(unixfrom=False)
    sending = smtp.sendmail(smtphost, fromaddr, [toaddr], messageData)
    sending.addCallback(sendComplete).addErrback(handleError)
    reactor.run()
```

Run smtpsend.py from the command line with four or more arguments: the name of
your SMTP server, the address the message is from, the address it should be delivered to, and one or more files to attach. It will ask you for a subject line and single-
line message body, and then create and send the email:

```
$ python smtpsend.py smtp.myisp.com me@myisp.com \
> user@otherisp.com logo.png homepage.html
Subject: Project Files
Message (one line): Here are those files I was talking about.
Message sent.
```

How Does That Work?

The `twisted.protocols.smtp.sendmail` function is a simple, handy way to send email using Twisted. It encapsulates all the work of connecting to the STMP server, telling it the address the message is coming from and the address it should be delivered to, and transferring the message data. Call the `sendmail` function with four arguments: the SMTP server hostname, the address the message is coming from, a list of addresses it should be delivered to, and the message data itself (either as a string or a file-like object). It returns a `Deferred` that will call back when the transfer is complete.

There's one potentially tricky thing about `smtp.sendmail` that you should be aware of: if you're sending a message to multiple recipients, a successful callback means that the sever accepted the message for delivery to *at least one* of them. If you're sending the message to more than one address, therefore, be sure to check the return value passed to your callback function. This value will be a tuple in the form (`numberDelivered, addressInfo`), where `numberDelivered` is a count of the number of recipients for which the server accepted the message, and `addressInfo` is a list of tuples in the format (`address, responseCode, responseMessage`). If you're sending a message to a single address, as in Example 7-3, you don't have to check the return value; the callback itself indicates that the message was accepted for the single recipient it was addressed to.

> The `twisted.protocols.smtp` module provides lower-level classes that can be used in SMTP clients, including SMTP-specific `Protocol` and `Factory` objects. But in most cases, the `sendmail` function will do everything you need in one line of code.

Because the `sendmail` function handles all the SMTP work, most of the code in *smtpsend.py* is involved with constructing the email message that will be sent. The Python `email` package contains modules for constructing messages of various types, and the `buildMessage` function uses two of them: `MIMEMultipart`, which creates a message of type `multipart/mixed` (suitable for storing a message body and attachments), and `MIMEBase`, which can hold any type of message data. The `buildMessage` function creates an `email.MIMEMultipart.MIMEMultipart` object called `message`. Then it iterates through the list of filenames and creates a `MIMEBase` object for each one containing the file's data. It uses the Python `mimetypes` module to guess the file type (based on the filename's extension). In addition, it Base64-encodes the attachment contents, which allows binary data to be represented as ASCII text (a requirement for passing through most mail servers).

Once the attachments have been added, the message is ready to be sent. *smtpsend.py* passes the message data to `smtp.sendmail`, along with the hostname of the SMTP server and the sender and recipient addresses. It sets up the callback and errback functions, and it hands off control to the reactor.

Looking Up the SMTP Server for a Domain

Typically, users configure their mail programs to send all mail through a single SMTP server set up by the network administrator. This server is sometimes referred to as a *smart host* because it has the ability to look at an email address, query the Domain Name System (DNS) enough to find out which mail server handles mail for that domain, and then deliver the message.

The server that accepts mail for a domain is sometimes at an obvious location, like *mail.domain.com*, but it can be any server, even one in a different domain. Domain administrators list their mail servers in their public DNS information by adding *MX* (short for Mail Exchange) records that list the SMTP servers that will accept mail addressed to that domain. For example, the DNS records for *oreilly.com* list two MX records, `smtp1.oreilly.com` and `smtp2.oreilly.com`. So when you want to send an email to *somebody@oreilly.com*, it must be delivered to one of those two servers.

Typically, programs that send mail using SMTP are configured to use a smart host. The hostname of the outgoing SMTP server is stored in a configuration file, and all mail, regardless of the domain, is sent through that server. However, there are times when you might want to write a program that doesn't rely on a smart host. For example, you might want your application to be able to move between networks without having to be told where the local SMTP server is. Or you could actually be developing your own mail server. (For much more on mail servers, see Chapter 8.) In these cases, you'll need to query the DNS system to find the appropriate server to use for each address.

How Do I Do That?

Create a `twisted.mail.relaymanager.MXCalculator` object. Use its `getMX` method to look up the appropriate mail server for each address to which you need to deliver mail, as shown in Example 7-4.

Example 7-4. smtplookup.py

```
from twisted.mail import relaymanager

mxCalc = relaymanager.MXCalculator()

def getSMTPServer(emailAddress):
    username, domain = emailAddress.split("@")
    return mxCalc.getMX(domain).addCallback(_gotMXRecord)

def _gotMXRecord(mxRecord):
    return mxRecord.exchange

if __name__ == "__main__":
    from twisted.internet import reactor
```

Example 7-4. smtplookup.py (continued)

```
import sys
address = sys.argv[1]

def printServer(server):
    print server
    reactor.stop()

def handleError(error):
    print >> sys.stderr, error.getErrorMessage()
    reactor.stop()

getSMTPServer(address).addCallback(printServer).addErrback(handleError)
reactor.run()
```

Run smtplookup.py with an email address as its only argument. It will print out the name of a server that accepts mail for the address's domain:

```
$ python smtplookup.py user@oreilly.com
smtp1.oreilly.com
$ python smtplookup.py abe@fettig.net
barclay.textdrive.com
```

How Does That Work?

smtplookup.py creates a twisted.mail.relaymanager.MXCalculator object called mxCalc. Note that it is created at the module level, instead of inside the getSMTPServer function; this will allow for the MXCalculator to use cached results if the same domain is looked up more than once.

The getSMTPServer function extracts the domain from the email address, and then returns the Deferred result of mxCalc.getMX(domain), while adding _gotMXRecord as a callback handler. The _gotMXRecord function does some simple filtering on the result of getMX, taking the result (a twisted.protocols.dns.Record_MX object) and returning just the exchange attribute, which contains the hostname of the mail server. This technique of adding an extra callback handler up front can be quite useful, enabling you to process or transform the result of a deferred function.

Listing Mailboxes on an IMAP Server

The Internet Message Access Protocol (IMAP) was designed to allow for remote access, storage, and management of email messages. This ability to store messages on a central server is useful for a couple of reasons. First, it makes email available in more than one place. If your mail is on an IMAP server, you can switch between your desktop and your laptop and still access your mail. Second, it makes it easier to administer email for workgroups and corporations. Instead of having to track and back up email across hundreds of hard drives, it can be managed in a single, central place.

The specification for the current version of IMAP (Version 4, Revision 1) is defined in RFC 3501 (*http://www.faqs.org/rfcs/rfc3501.html*). IMAP is a powerful but complicated protocol, and the RFC takes up more than 100 pages. It's the kind of protocol that would be a ton of work to implement yourself. Fortunately, the Twisted developers have written an complete IMAP implementation, which provides a nice API for working with IMAP servers. This lab demonstrates how to log in to an IMAP server and get a list of available mailboxes.

How Do I Do That?

Use a subclass of `imap4.IMAP4Client` as your Protocol. In the `serverGreeting` function, call `self.login` with a username and password. Once successfully logged in, call `self.list` to get a list of the available mailboxes (see Example 7-5).

Example 7-5. imapfolders.py

```
from twisted.protocols import imap4
from twisted.internet import protocol, defer

class IMAPFolderListProtocol(imap4.IMAP4Client):

    def serverGreeting(self, capabilities):
        login = self.login(self.factory.username, self.factory.password)
        login.addCallback(self.__loggedIn)
        login.chainDeferred(self.factory.deferred)

    def __loggedIn(self, results):
        return self.list("", "*").addCallback(self.__gotMailboxList)

    def __gotMailboxList(self, list):
        return [boxInfo[2] for boxInfo in list]

    def connectionLost(self, reason):
        if not self.factory.deferred.called:
            # connection was lost unexpectedly!
            self.factory.deferred.errback(reason)

class IMAPFolderListFactory(protocol.ClientFactory):
    protocol = IMAPFolderListProtocol

    def __init__(self, username, password):
        self.username = username
        self.password = password
        self.deferred = defer.Deferred()

    def clientConnectionFailed(self, connection, reason):
        self.deferred.errback(reason)

if __name__ == "__main__":
    from twisted.internet import reactor
    import sys, getpass
```

Example 7-5. imapfolders.py (continued)

```
def printMailboxList(list):
    list.sort( )
    for box in list:
        print box
    reactor.stop( )

def handleError(error):
    print >> sys.stderr, "Error:", error.getErrorMessage( )
    reactor.stop( )

if not len(sys.argv) == 3:
    print "Usage: %s server login" % sys.argv[0]
    sys.exit(1)

server = sys.argv[1]
user = sys.argv[2]
password = getpass.getpass("Password: ")
factory = IMAPFolderListFactory(user, password)
factory.deferred.addCallback(
    printMailboxList).addErrback(
    handleError)
reactor.connectTCP(server, 143, factory)
reactor.run( )
```

Run *imapfolders.py* with two arguments: the IMAP server and your login username.
It will prompt you for your password, log you in to the server, and then download
and print a list of your mailboxes:

```
$ python imapfolders.py imap.myisp.com mylogin
Password:
INBOX
Archive
Drafts
Mailing Lists
Mailing Lists/Twisted
Mailing Lists/Twisted Web
Sent
Spam
Trash
```

How Does That Work?

imapfolders.py uses the familiar pattern of a ClientFactory and Protocol working
together. The Protocol communicates with the server, and the ClientFactory provides a Deferred that the program uses to track the success or failure of the task at
hand.

The IMAPFolderListProtocol class in *imapfolders.py* inherits from IMAP4Client, which
provides a nice Deferred-based interface. Every IMAP command returns a Deferred

that will be called back with the reply received from the server. The use of `Deferreds` makes it easy to run a series of commands, one after the other: have the callback handler for each command run the next command and return its `Deferred`.

There's one `Deferred` method used in *imapfolders.py* that hadn't been used in any of the previous examples: `chainDeferred`. The `chainDeferred` method is used when you want to take the results of one `Deferred` and pass them to another `Deferred`. The line `deferredOne.chainDeferred(deferredTwo)` is equivalent to:

```
deferredOne.addCallback(deferredTwo.callback)
deferredOne.addErrback(deferredTwo.errback)
```

The `IMAPFolderListProtocol` in *imapfolders.py* has its `serverGreeting` method called when the connection to the server is established and the server has indicated that it's ready to accept commands. In response to `serverGreeting`, it calls `self.login`, and sets up a callback to `self._loggedIn`. Then it uses `chainDeferred` to send the eventual results of `self.login` back to `self.factory.deferred`. The order of these steps is important. Because the callback to `self._loggedIn` is added before the call to `chainDeferred`, `self.factory.deferred` won't receive the direct result of `self.login`, but the result returned by `self._loggedIn`. As it turns out, `self._loggedIn` returns another `Deferred`, the result of `self.list`, which will be run through `self._gotMailboxList` to extract the mailbox names from the full response returned by the server. So `self.factory.deferred` is called back with the value that `IMAPFolderListProtocol` is supposed to provide: a list of mailbox names.

One of the most useful things about using `Deferreds` in this way is error handling. Remember how in Example 7-2, the `POP3DownloadProtocol` had to check the results of every command, and call a function to let the factory know there was an error? There's none of that here. Since `self.list` is called as part of the event handler for `self.login`, and `self.login` is chained to `self.factory.deferred`, `self.factory.deferred` will receive any error that occurs in either of these steps.

Downloading Messages from an IMAP Mailbox

This lab demonstrates how to download copies of all the messages in an IMAP mailbox. You can do this using three methods of `IMAP4Client`: `select`, `fetchUID`, and `fetchMessage`.

How Do I Do That?

Create a subclass of `twisted.protocols.imap4.IMAP4Client`. Call `select` to select the mailbox you want to work with. Call `fetchUID` to retrieve the list of message identifiers for the mailbox, and then use `fetchMessage` to download each message, as demonstrated in Example 7-6.

Example 7-6. imapdownload.py

```python
from twisted.protocols import imap4
from twisted.internet import protocol, defer
import email

class IMAPDownloadProtocol(imap4.IMAP4Client):

    def serverGreeting(self, capabilities):
        login = self.login(self.factory.username, self.factory.password)
        login.addCallback(self.__loggedIn)
        login.chainDeferred(self.factory.deferred)

    def __loggedIn(self, result):
        return self.select(self.factory.mailbox).addCallback(
            self.__selectedMailbox)

    def __selectedMailbox(self, result):
        # get a list of all message IDs
        allMessages = imap4.MessageSet(1, None)
        return self.fetchUID(allMessages, True).addCallback(
            self.__gotUIDs)

    def __gotUIDs(self, uidResults):
        self.messageUIDs = [result['UID'] for result in uidResults.values()]
        self.messageCount = len(self.messageUIDs)
        print "%i messages in %s." % (self.messageCount, self.factory.mailbox)
        return self.fetchNextMessage()

    def fetchNextMessage(self):
        if self.messageUIDs:
            nextUID = self.messageUIDs.pop(0)
            messageListToFetch = imap4.MessageSet(nextUID)
            print "Downloading message %i of %i" % (
                self.messageCount-len(self.messageUIDs), self.messageCount)
            return self.fetchMessage(messageListToFetch, True).addCallback(
                self.__gotMessage)
        else:
            # all done!
            return self.logout().addCallback(
                lambda _: self.transport.loseConnection())

    def __gotMessage(self, fetchResults):
        messageData = fetchResults.values()[0]['RFC822']
        self.factory.handleMessage(messageData)
        return self.fetchNextMessage()

    def connectionLost(self, reason):
        if not self.factory.deferred.called:
            # connection was lost unexpectedly!
            self.factory.deferred.errback(reason)
```

Example 7-6. imapdownload.py (continued)

```python
class IMAPDownloadFactory(protocol.ClientFactory):
    protocol = IMAPDownloadProtocol

    def __init__(self, username, password, mailbox, output):
        self.username = username
        self.password = password
        self.mailbox = mailbox
        self.output = output
        self.deferred = defer.Deferred()

    def handleMessage(self, messageData):
        parsedMessage = email.message_from_string(messageData)     ----> filter.
        self.output.write(parsedMessage.as_string(unixfrom=True))
        self.output.write('\r\n')

    def clientConnectionFailed(self, connection, reason):
        self.deferred.errback(reason)

if __name__ == "__main__":
    from twisted.internet import reactor
    import sys, getpass

    def handleError(error):
        print >> sys.stderr, "Error:", error.getErrorMessage()
        reactor.stop()

    if len(sys.argv) != 5:
        usage = "Usage: %s server user mailbox outputfile" % (
            sys.argv[0])
        print >> sys.stderr, usage
        sys.exit(1)

    server = sys.argv[1]
    user = sys.argv[2]
    mailbox = sys.argv[3]
    outputfile = file(sys.argv[4], 'w+b')

    password = getpass.getpass("Password: ")
    factory = IMAPDownloadFactory(user, password, mailbox, outputfile)
    factory.deferred.addCallback(lambda _ : reactor.stop()).addErrback(
        handleError)
    reactor.connectTCP(server, 143, factory)
    reactor.run()
```

Run *imapdownload.py* from the command line with four arguments: the IMAP server, your login, the mailbox from which messages should be downloaded, and the name of the file to which they will be written. It will print out a progress report as it downloads the messages:

```
$ python imapdownload.py imap.myisp.com mylogin Inbox imap-Inbox.mbox
Password:
31 messages in Inbox.
```

```
Downloading message 1 of 31
Downloading message 2 of 31
Downloading message 3 of 31
...
Downloading message 30 of 31
Downloading message 31 of 31
```

How Does That Work?

imapdownload.py retains the basic structure of *imapfolders.py* from the previous lab. A subclass of IMAP4Client communicates with the server, and a subclass of ClientFactory creates the protocol and provides a Deferred for tracking the success or failure of the operation.

The IMAPDownloadProtocol starts by calling self.login to log in. The callback handler for self.login is self.__loggedIn, which calls self.select to select the mailbox and return another Deferred. The callback handler for self.select, self.__selectedMailbox, creates an imap4.MessageSet object, which represents a set of messages. The MessageSet is initialized with the arguments 1 and None, which means that it represents the set of messages from message number 1 to the end of the mailbox. This MessageSet object is then passed to self.fetchUID, instructing the server to return a list of the unique message identifiers in that set of messages.

The callback function for self.fetchUID is self.__gotUIDs, which sets the attributes self.messageUIDs and self.messageCount. Then it returns the deferred result of self.fetchNextMessage, which starts the process of downloading the messages one by one. To download the next available message, fetchNextMessage creates a MessageSet matching only that message's UID. Then the MessageSet is passed to self.fetchMessage, with the uid keyword set to True to tell the server that the MessageSet is referring to messages by UID, not sequence number. The callback for self.fetchMessage is self._gotMessage, which passes the message data to the factory by calling self.factory.handleMessage. _gotMessage then returns another call to self.fetchNextMessage. This process creates a loop where fetchNextMessage will continue to be called until there are no messages left to download, at which point it calls self.logout to log out, and drops the connection.

As shown in IMAPFolderListProtocol in the previous lab, all of the work done in IMAPDownloadProtocol happens in the context of callback handlers for self.login, which is chained to self.factory.deferred. If everything works as expected, self.factory.deferred will be called back with the result of the last function in the chain, self.transport.loseConnection. And if any of the IMAP methods fail, self.factory.deferred will handle the error.

CHAPTER 8

Mail Servers

This chapter is about one of Twisted's greatest strengths: running mail and news servers. Twisted includes modules that you can use to build SMTP, POP3, IMAP, and NNTP servers from scratch, which can be incredibly useful when you have a server application that needs to send, receive, or store email. Server email integration has traditionally required a heavyweight mail server, with a bunch of custom shell scripts to push and pull data between the mail server and your application. But by using Twisted, you can design a mail or news server that does exactly what you need, and that doesn't even require a separate process. This chapter shows you how.

Accepting Mail with SMTP

As described in Chapter 7, SMTP is the Simple Mail Transfer Protocol, the basic means by which email messages are delivered on the Internet. SMTP is the most popular messaging protocol in use today: everyone uses email, and email uses SMTP.

This lab demonstrates how to write a simple SMTP server using Twisted. It shows how to accept SMTP connections, decide what to do with the incoming message based on the email address, and then process the message data.

How Do I Do That?

Write classes to implement the smtp.IMessage and smtp.IMessageDelivery interfaces. Then create a Factory that uses your implementation of IMessageDelivery to initialize the smtp.SMTP protocol. Example 8-1 accepts email for all addresses in a given domain and stores the messages to *maildir* directories.

Example 8-1. smtpserver.py

```
from twisted.mail import smtp, maildir
from zope.interface import implements
from twisted.internet import protocol, reactor, defer
```

Example 8-1. smtpserver.py (continued)

```python
import os
from email.Header import Header

class MaildirMessageWriter(object):
    implements(smtp.IMessage)

    def __init__(self, userDir):
        if not os.path.exists(userDir): os.mkdir(userDir)
        inboxDir = os.path.join(userDir, 'Inbox')
        self.mailbox = maildir.MaildirMailbox(inboxDir)
        self.lines = []

    def lineReceived(self, line):
        self.lines.append(line)

    def eomReceived(self):
        # message is complete, store it
        print "Message data complete."
        self.lines.append('') # add a trailing newline
        messageData = '\n'.join(self.lines)
        return self.mailbox.appendMessage(messageData)

    def connectionLost(self):
        print "Connection lost unexpectedly!"
        # unexpected loss of connection; don't save
        del(self.lines)

class LocalDelivery(object):
    implements(smtp.IMessageDelivery)

    def __init__(self, baseDir, validDomains):
        if not os.path.isdir(baseDir):
            raise ValueError, "'%s' is not a directory" % baseDir
        self.baseDir = baseDir
        self.validDomains = validDomains

    def receivedHeader(self, helo, origin, recipients):
        myHostname, clientIP = helo
        headerValue = "by %s from %s with ESMTP ; %s" % (
            myHostname, clientIP, smtp.rfc822date())
        # email.Header.Header used for automatic wrapping of long lines
        return "Received: %s" % Header(headerValue)

    def validateTo(self, user):
        if not user.dest.domain in self.validDomains:
            raise smtp.SMTPBadRcpt(user)
        print "Accepting mail for %s..." % user.dest
        return lambda: MaildirMessageWriter(
            self._getAddressDir(str(user.dest)))
```

Example 8-1. smtpserver.py (continued)

```
    def _getAddressDir(self, address):
        return os.path.join(self.baseDir, "%s" % address)

    def validateFrom(self, helo, originAddress):
        # accept mail from anywhere. To reject an address, raise
        # smtp.SMTPBadSender here.
        return originAddress

class SMTPFactory(protocol.ServerFactory):
    def __init__(self, baseDir, validDomains):
        self.baseDir = baseDir
        self.validDomains = validDomains

    def buildProtocol(self, addr):
        delivery = LocalDelivery(self.baseDir, self.validDomains)
        smtpProtocol = smtp.SMTP(delivery)
        smtpProtocol.factory = self
        return smtpProtocol

if __name__ == "__main__":
    import sys
    mailboxDir = sys.argv[1]
    domains = sys.argv[2].split(",")
    reactor.listenTCP(25, SMTPFactory(mailboxDir, domains))
    from twisted.internet import ssl
    # SSL stuff here... and certificates...
    reactor.run()
```

This example uses the SMTP standard TCP port 25, so it can receive mail from other servers. If you're already running another SMTP server, you'll need to stop it before you run *smtpserver.py*, to make port 25 available. Also, most operating systems don't give ordinary users the right to run services on TCP ports below 1024, which are reserved for system services. So you'll have to run *smtpserver.py* as root or from an administrator account.

Run *smtpserver.py* with two arguments: the directory to use for storing messages and a comma-delimited list of domains for which to accept mail. You can tell it to handle mail for as many domains as you like, but for the purposes of this example, make one of them *localhost*:

```
$ python smtpserver.py mail_storage localhost,example.com
```

Now that the server is running, you can try sending some mail. In the real world, you'd run your SMTP server on an Internet-connected computer with a public IP address, where all the the other SMTP servers in the world (including your ISP's SMTP server, which your regular email client is configured to use for outgoing mail) could connect to it. However, let's assume that you're running *smtpserver.py*, and the other examples in this chapter, on a computer that's behind the firewall on your local network. In this case, it's best to use an email client configured to send mail through *localhost*.

 Mozilla Thunderbird (*http://mozilla.org/thunderbird*) is a great email client to use for testing your servers. Thunderbird is free, open source, and runs on all popular operating systems. It also supports multiple profiles, so you can keep your test settings and messages separate from your real email. To set up multiple profiles, run Thunderbird with the *–ProfileManager* flag.

Try sending a message to *test@localhost*, as shown in Figure 8-1.

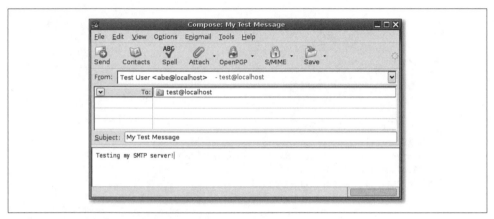

Figure 8-1. Sending a test email to a local SMTP server

Your server should print a couple of lines showing that it received the message:

```
Accepting mail for test@localhost...
Message data complete.
```

You can then take a look at the message file that was created. *smtpserver.py* writes messages in maildir format, where each mailbox is a directory with the subdirectories *new*, *cur*, and *tmp*, and each message is a file with a unique name. Message files in a maildir directory are initially stored in *new*, and then moved to *cur* to indicate that they've been read. If you told *smtpserver.py* to use *mail_storage* as the base directory for storing email, the message you sent should have a unique filename in the directory *mail_storage/test@localhost/Inbox/new*. The contents of that file will be the message you sent:

```
$ cd mail_storage
$ ls
test@localhost
$ cd test@localhost
$ ls Inbox/new
1115584078.M4515569P19924Q4.sparky
$ cat Inbox/new/1115584078.M4515569P19924Q4.sparky
```

```
Received: by [127.0.0.1] from 127.0.0.1 with ESMTP ; Sun, 08 May 2005 16:27:58 -0400
Message-ID: <427E764E.1000900@localhost>
Date: Sun, 08 May 2005 16:27:58 -0400
From: Test User <abe@localhost>
User-Agent: Mozilla Thunderbird 1.0.2 (X11/20050404)
To:  test@localhost
Subject: My Test Message

Testing my SMTP server!
```

How Does That Work?

The smtp.SMTP Protocol class provides a very clean, high-level interface. Instead of asking you respond directly to the commands coming from the client, smtp.SMTP asks you to give it an object implementing the smtp.IMessageDelivery interface. smtp. IMessageDelivery requires three methods: receivedHeader, validateTo, and validateFrom.

The receivedHeader method is used to generate a Received: header that will be added to an incoming email message. SMTP servers are responsible for adding a Received header when they accept a message; these headers can be used later to see the path the message took en route to being delivered. receivedHeader takes three arguments. The first, helo, is a tuple containing two strings: the server name by which the the client addressed the server when it said HELO, and the client's IP address. The second argument, origin, is an smtp.Address object identifying who the message is coming from. The third argument, recipients, is a list of smtp.Address objects identifying who the message is being delivered to. From all that information, receivedHeader is asked to return a simple response: a string containing a valid SMTP Received header.

According to RFC 821, the Received header should be in the following form:

    Received: FROM domain BY domain [VIA link] [WITH protocol] [ID id] [FOR path] ;
    timestamp

The VIA, WITH, ID, and FOR parts are optional. The LocalDelivery object used in Example 8-1 has a basic implementation of receivedHeader that generates a valid header string.

> Email headers may look simple, but it's a mistake to naively assume you can just return a string in the form HeaderName: value. What about long value strings that need to be properly wrapped? What about Unicode characters? If you haven't planned for these, you could end up generating corrupt emails. Fortunately, there's a class in the Python standard library, *email.Header.Header,* that will do all the work of generating proper headers for you. Don't forget to use it!

The next method required by smtp.IMessageDelivery is validateFrom. This method gives your server a chance to accept or reject messages based on the address it's coming from. For example, if you had an application that allowed users to post to their weblogs through email, you might use validateFrom to make sure the message was coming from the email address of a user who had permission to post. (Keep in mind, though, that this isn't a bulletproof security mechanism; it's trivially easy to forge the sending address on an email message.) validateFrom takes two arguments: a tuple with the hostname used in by the client when it said HELO and the client's IP address, and an smtp.Address object identifying the sender. In Example 8-1, the LocalDelivery object has a validateFrom method that always returns the sender's address, indicating that it's willing to accept mail from that sender. To reject a sender, you'd raise an smtp.SMTPBadSender exception instead.

The third method of smtp.IMessageDelivery is the most important. validateTo takes a single smtp.User object (which contains the address of the recipient and information about where the message came from) as an argument. It then either raises an smtp.SMTPBadRecipient exception, or returns a function that returns an object implementing smtp.IMessage.

That's a little confusing, and worth repeating: validateTo should return a *function* that will return an object implementing smtp.IMessage when it is called (with no arguments). The easy way to handle this quirk of the IMessageDelivery API is to return lambda: myObject instead of myObject, as demonstrated in Example 8-1.

The SMTP server in Example 8-1 is a little different from the typical email server. It doesn't have a fixed list of users, but will accept mail for any address within one of its domains. As long as the domain is valid, it assigns that user a directory in the form baseDir/user@domain, and passes the directory to a MaildirMessageWriter object, which implements smtp.IMessage.

smtp.IMessage defines an interface for receiving an email message. There are three functions in smtp.IMessage. The first, lineReceived, will be called once for each line of the incoming email message, with the line data (which does not include the trailing newline) as an argument. The second method, eomReceived, is called after the entire message has been received. Return a Deferred result from eomReceived to let the client know when the message has been processed successfully. The third method, connectionLost, is called only if the connection is broken while message data is being received, and indicates that your class should discard whatever incomplete data has been received so far.

In Example 8-1, MaildirMessageWriter uses the maildir.MaildirMailbox class provided by twisted.mail to write to write to the *Inbox* maildir in each user's directory. It isn't necessary to check whether the *Inbox* directory exists; maildir. MaildirMailbox will create it automatically.

Using SMTP as a User Interface

SMTP is more than just a protocol for routing messages between people; it can also be used for communications in which the recipient is a computer program. Many server applications use SMTP to allow people to publish information via email. By sending mail to a special address, users can post to their weblogs, add a page to a Wiki, or import image files into their photo sharing services. Offering an SMTP interface to your application makes getting data in and out as easy as sending and receiving email. This lets people use your application as part of their existing email workflow, which makes it more likely that they're actually going to use that program you worked so hard to write. SMTP is also supported by many mobile phones, so it can be an easy way to enable mobile access to your applications.

How Do I Do That?

Example 8-2 shows how you might offer an SMTP interface to an application. *smtpgoogle.py* is an SMTP server that takes email as input and uses it to run a Google "I'm Feeling Lucky" search. Then it sends a reply containing the search result. The code is similar to the basic SMTP server in Example 8-1, but with application-specific classes implementing `smtp.IMessage` and `smtp.ImessageDelivery`.

Example 8-2. smtpgoogle.py

```python
from twisted.mail import smtp
from twisted.web import google, client
from zope.interface import implements
from twisted.internet import protocol, reactor, defer
import os, email, email.Utils
from email import Header, MIMEBase, MIMEMultipart, MIMEText

class GoogleQueryPageFetcher(object):
    def fetchFirstResult(self, query):
        """
        Given a query, finds the first Google result, and
        downloads that page. Returns a Deferred, which will
        be called back with a tuple containing
        (firstMatchUrl, firstMatchPageData)
        """
        # the twisted.web.google.checkGoogle function does an
        # "I'm feeling lucky" search on Google
        return google.checkGoogle(query).addCallback(
            self._gotUrlFromGoogle)

    def _gotUrlFromGoogle(self, url):
        # grab the page
        return client.getPage(url).addCallback(
            self._downloadedPage, url)
```

Example 8-2. smtpgoogle.py (continued)

```
    def _downloadedPage(self, pageContents, url):
        # return a tuple containing both the url and page data
        return (url, pageContents)

class ReplyFromGoogle(object):
    implements(smtp.IMessage)

    def __init__(self, address, upstreamServer):
        self.address = address
        self.lines = []
        self.upstreamServer = upstreamServer

    def lineReceived(self, line):
        self.lines.append(line)

    def eomReceived(self):
        message = email.message_from_string("\n".join(self.lines))
        fromAddr = email.Utils.parseaddr(message['From'])[1]
        query = message['Subject']
        searcher = GoogleQueryPageFetcher()
        return searcher.fetchFirstResult(query).addCallback(
            self._sendPageToEmailAddress, query, fromAddr)

    def _sendPageToEmailAddress(self, pageData, query, destAddress):
        pageUrl, pageContents = pageData
        msg = MIMEMultipart.MIMEMultipart()
        msg['From'] = self.address
        msg['To'] = destAddress
        msg['Subject'] = "First Google result for '%s'" % query
        body = MIMEText.MIMEText(
            "The first Google result for '%s' is:\n\n%s" % (
            query, pageUrl))
        # create a text/html attachment with the page data
        attachment = MIMEBase.MIMEBase("text", "html")
        attachment['Content-Location'] = pageUrl
        attachment.set_payload(pageContents)
        msg.attach(body)
        msg.attach(attachment)

        return smtp.sendmail(
            self.upstreamServer, self.address, destAddress, msg)

    def connectionLost(self):
        pass

class GoogleMessageDelivery(object):
    implements(smtp.IMessageDelivery)

    def __init__(self, googleSearchAddress, upstreamSMTPServer):
        self.googleSearchAddress = googleSearchAddress
        self.upstreamServer = upstreamSMTPServer
```

Example 8-2. smtpgoogle.py (continued)

```
    def receivedHeader(self, helo, origin, recipients):
        myHostname, clientIP = helo
        headerValue = "by %s from %s with ESMTP ; %s" % (
            myHostname, clientIP, smtp.rfc822date())
        # email.Header.Header used for automatic wrapping of long lines
        return "Received: %s" % Header.Header(headerValue)

    def validateTo(self, user):
        if not str(user.dest).lower() == self.googleSearchAddress:
            raise smtp.SMTPBadRcpt(user.dest)
        else:
            return lambda: ReplyFromGoogle(self.googleSearchAddress,
                                           self.upstreamServer)

    def validateFrom(self, helo, originAddress):
        # accept mail from anywhere. To reject an address, raise
        # smtp.SMTPBadSender here.
        return originAddress

class SMTPServerFactory(protocol.ServerFactory):
    def __init__(self, googleSearchAddress, upstreamSMTPServer):
        self.googleSearchAddress = googleSearchAddress
        self.upstreamSMTPServer = upstreamSMTPServer

    def buildProtocol(self, addr):
        delivery = GoogleMessageDelivery(self.googleSearchAddress,
                                         self.upstreamSMTPServer)
        smtpProtocol = smtp.SMTP(delivery)
        smtpProtocol.factory = self
        return smtpProtocol

if __name__ == "__main__":
    import sys
    googleSearchAddress = sys.argv[1]
    upstreamSMTPServer = sys.argv[2]
    reactor.listenTCP(
        25, SMTPServerFactory(googleSearchAddress, upstreamSMTPServer))
    reactor.run()
```

Run *smtpgoogle.py* from the command line with two arguments. The first is the email address you want to use for Google searches: you'll send mail to this address to search Google, and you'll get a reply from this address with the result. The second argument is the upstream SMTP server you want to use for sending the reply emails; typically this is your ISP's mail server:

```
$ python smtpgoogle.py google@myhostname.mydomain smtp.myisp.com
```

If you're running this command behind a firewall, you might have to fake the address you use for Google searches in order to send the reply emails. The address *google@localhost*, for example, might be rejected by your upstream mail server as an invalid sender address. As long as you're using a mail client configured to send all mail through localhost, you should be able to use any address; *smtpgoogle.py* will use that address for Google searches, and refuse to accept mail for any other address.

Once the server is running, try sending an email to the address you specified. The subject of the email should be the query you want to send to Google. Figure 8-2 shows a query email being sent.

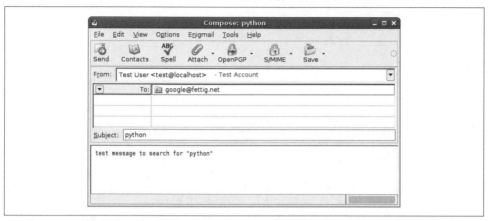

Figure 8-2. Sending a query to the smtpgoogle.py search service

smtpgoogle.py should process your query and send a reply to whatever From: address you used when sending the email. Check your mail, and you should get an email similar to that in Figure 8-3 with the first Google result.

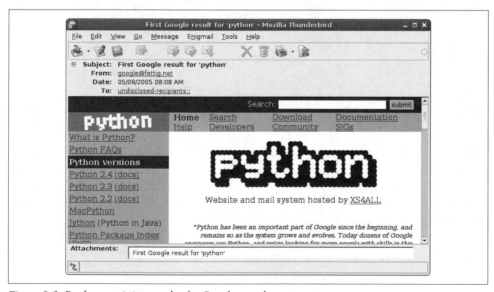

Figure 8-3. Reply containing result of a Google search

How Does That Work?

Example 8-2 defines the `GoogleQueryPageFetcher` class, which does the work of finding the first Google result for a query and then downloading that page. The function `fetchFirstResult` returns a `Deferred` object that will be called back with a tuple containing the URL and contents of the first matching page.

The `ReplyFromGoogle` class takes this feature and makes it available to SMTP by implementing `smtp.IMessage`. The key is the `eomReceived` function, which is called once the entire message has been received. The `smtp.IMessage` interface says that `eomReceived` should return a `Deferred`. Because of this, `ReplyFromGoogle` is free to run a series of asynchronous operations while processing the email, as long as it eventually returns a successful value or raises an exception. Rather than just writing the message data to disk, `ReplyFromGoogle.eomReceived` runs the Google search and sets up a callback to take the search result and send it out by email. It constructs a message using classes in Python's `email` module, and sends it back to the address that the query came from.

This technique of doing all the work in the context of `eomReceived` is a good approach to use when you expect that it won't take more than a second or two to process the incoming message. At other times, you might need to do something that's going to take a while. In this case, you don't want to leave the SMTP client hanging there waiting for a response, especially because it will eventually get tired of waiting and time out. So you might choose to add the incoming message to a queue for processing, and to immediately return a successful result for `eomReceived`. If something goes wrong later, you can always send an email back to the sender informing them of what happened.

Providing POP3 Access to Mailboxes

The POP3 protocol allows mail clients to periodically download new mail from a server. POP3 support is a requirement for most applications that store mail. It's also the easiest way to let people pull their messages out of your application and store them on their computer.

How Do I Do That?

To make a Twisted POP3 server, first write a class to represent a user's Inbox. This class should implement `twisted.mail.pop3.IMailbox`, which defines methods for reading and deleting messages from a mailbox. Then set up a `Portal` that checks each user's login credentials and gives them access to their Inbox. Example 8-3 offers POP access to the maildir mailboxes created by the SMTP server in Example 8-1.

Example 8-3. pop3server.py

```python
from twisted.mail import pop3, maildir
from twisted.cred import portal, checkers, credentials, error as credError
from twisted.internet import protocol, reactor, defer
from zope.interface import implements
import os

class UserInbox(maildir.MaildirMailbox):
    """
    maildir.MaildirMailbox already implements the pop3.IMailbox
    interface, so methods need to be defined only to
    override the default behavior. For non-maildir mailboxes,
    you'd have to implement all of pop3.IMailbox:
    """
    def __init__(self, userdir):
        inboxDir = os.path.join(userdir, 'Inbox')
        maildir.MaildirMailbox.__init__(self, inboxDir)

class POP3Protocol(pop3.POP3):
    debug = True

    def sendLine(self, line):
        if self.debug: print "POP3 SERVER:", line
        pop3.POP3.sendLine(self, line)

    def lineReceived(self, line):
        if self.debug: print "POP3 CLIENT:", line
        pop3.POP3.lineReceived(self, line)

class POP3Factory(protocol.Factory):
    protocol = POP3Protocol
    portal = None

    def buildProtocol(self, address):
        p = self.protocol()
        p.portal = self.portal
        p.factory = self
        return p

class MailUserRealm(object):
    implements(portal.IRealm)
    avatarInterfaces = {
        pop3.IMailbox: UserInbox,
        }

    def __init__(self, baseDir):
        self.baseDir = baseDir

    def requestAvatar(self, avatarId, mind, *interfaces):
        for requestedInterface in interfaces:
            if self.avatarInterfaces.has_key(requestedInterface):
                # make sure the user dir exists
                userDir = os.path.join(self.baseDir, username)
```

Example 8-3. pop3server.py (continued)

```
                if not os.path.exists(userDir):
                    os.mkdir(userDir)
                # return an instance of the correct class
                avatarClass = self.avatarInterfaces[requestedInterface]
                avatar = avatarClass(userDir)
                # null logout function (FIXME: explain why)
                logout = lambda: None
                return defer.succeed(requestedInterface, avatar, logout)

        # none of the requested interfaces was supported
        raise KeyError("None of the requested interfaces is supported")

class CredentialsChecker(object):
    implements(checkers.ICredentialsChecker)
    credentialInterfaces = (credentials.IUsernamePassword,
                            credentials.IUsernameHashedPassword)

    def __init__(self, passwords):
        "passwords: a dict-like object mapping usernames to passwords"
        self.passwords = passwords

    def requestAvatarId(self, credentials):
        username = credentials.username
        if self.passwords.has_key(username):
            realPassword = self.passwords[username]
            checking = defer.maybeDeferred(
                credentials.checkPassword, realPassword)
            # pass result of checkPassword, and the username that was
            # being authenticated, to self._checkedPassword
            checking.addCallback(self._checkedPassword, username)
            return checking
        else:
            raise credError.UnauthorizedLogin("No such user")

    def _checkedPassword(self, matched, username):
        if matched:
            # password was correct
            return username
        else:
            raise credError.UnauthorizedLogin("Bad password")

def passwordFileToDict(filename):
    passwords = {}
    for line in file(filename):
        if line and line.count(':'):
            username, password = line.strip().split(':')
            passwords[username] = password
    return passwords

if __name__ == "__main__":
    import sys
    dataDir = sys.argv[1]
```

Example 8-3. pop3server.py (continued)

```
factory = POP3Factory( )
factory.portal = portal.Portal(MailUserRealm(dataDir))
passwordFile = os.path.join(dataDir, 'passwords.txt')
passwords = passwordFileToDict(passwordFile)
passwordChecker = CredentialsChecker(passwords)
factory.portal.registerChecker(passwordChecker)
reactor.listenTCP(110, factory)
reactor.run( )
```

This example, *pop3server.py*, uses the directory structure created by *smtpserver.py* in Example 8-1, and illustrated in Figure 8-4. A base directory called *mail_storage* has directories for each email address, each of which contains a *maildir* directory called Inbox.

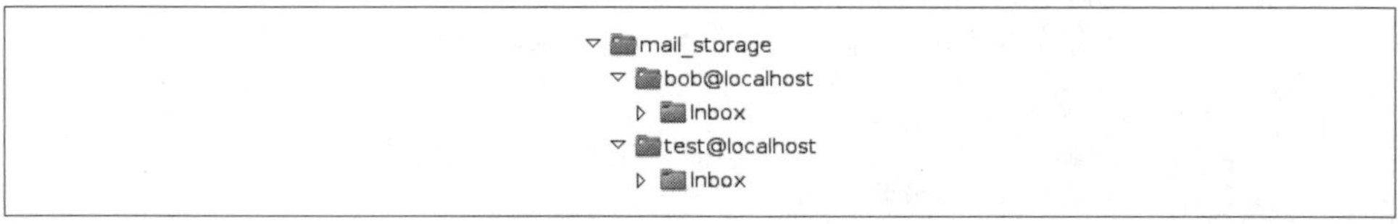

Figure 8-4. The mail directory structure

Before you run *pop3server.py*, create a file called *passwords.txt* in your base *mail_storage* directory. This file should contain a list of usernames and passwords, separated by colons:

```
testuser@localhost:password
bob@localhost:password
```

Run *pop3server.py* with the name of the base mail directory as the only argument:

```
$ python pop3server.py mail_storage
```

Now configure your mail client to download mail from *localhost* using POP3. Use a full email address as the username, and the corresponding password. Then you should be able to download all the messages you sent to that email address while running *smtpserver.py* from Example 8-1. Figure 8-5 illustrates the process.

How Does That Work?

There are two major pieces that pop3.POP3Protocol requires to create a working POP3 server. First, you need to have a class implementing pop3.IMailbox, which gives the server methods for reading and deleting messages in a user's mailbox. Second, you need to have a twisted.cred.portal.Portal object that will take a username and password, make sure they are valid, and then return the mailbox object for that user.

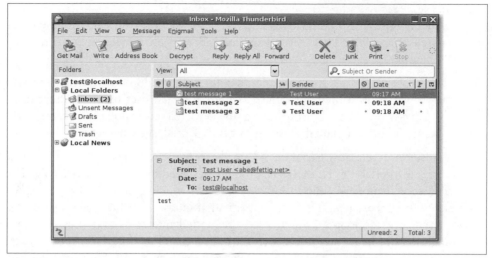

Figure 8-5. Downloading messages from the POP3 server

In Example 8-3, each user's mail is kept in a *maildir* directory. The `maildir.`
`MaildirMailbox` class helpfully implements `pop3.IMailbox` already, so it isn't necessary to write a special class. If you were serving mail that wasn't in a *maildir* directory, you'd have to implement `pop3.IMailbox` yourself, by providing the following
methods:

def listMessages(self, index=None):
> Return a list of integers representing the sizes of all the messages in this mail-
> box, in bytes. If `index` is not `None`, return an integer representing the size of that
> message.

def getMessage(self, index):
> Return a file-like object containing the message at `index`.

def getUidl(self, index):
> Return a unique identifier string for the message at `index`. This value will be used
> by POP3 clients to determine whether they've seen a message before. `getUidl`
> should never return the same value for different messages, and it should consis-
> tently return the same value for a specific message.

def deleteMessage(self, index):
> Mark the message at `index` for deletion. The number of messages in the mailbox
> should not change, and the message shouldn't actually be deleted until the sync
> method is called.

def undeleteMessages(self):
> Cancel pending deletions. Any messages that have been marked for deletion
> using `deleteMessage` should be restored to their previous state.

```
def sync(self):
```
> Delete any messages that have been marked for deletion, and perform any other housecleaning tasks. This method will be called when a POP3 client sends the QUIT command.

Once you've set up a pop3.IMailbox interface for your mailboxes, you need to give the server a way to load the appropriate mailbox for each user based on their username and password. This is done using the Twisted authentication framework, twisted.cred. (For a complete discussion of twisted.cred, see Chapter 6.)

The MailUserRealm class in Example 8-3 needs to work with pop3.POP3 only, so it offers just one interface: pop3.IMailbox. Still, it's designed in a fairly generic way. The class defines a dictionary called avatarInterfaces, which maps the pop3.IMailbox interface to UserInbox, a class that implements that interface. When requestAvatar is called, MailUserRealm loops through list of requested interfaces and tries to find a matching interface in avatarInterfaces. If it finds a matching interface, it constructs an avatar based on the interface and the requested avatarID. In this case, the avatarID is the email address whose mailbox should be opened. The MailUserRealm checks to make sure that mailbox exists, creates it if needed, and then creates the avatar by passing the user's mailbox directory to the class whose interface matched the requested interface, which in this case will always be UserInbox. Finally, it returns a tuple containing three values: the interface that matched, the avatar (which implements that interface), and a function to clean up the avatar when the user is done with his session. In this case, there isn't anything to do at logout, so MailUserRealm uses an anonymous function that doesn't actually do anything.

The requestAvatarId method takes a credentials object that implements one of the interfaces listed in credentialsInterfaces; in this case, either credentials. IUsernamePassword or credentials.IUsernameHashedPassword. Both of these interfaces have a checkPassword method that returns a Deferred Boolean value saying whether the password matched. Using checkPassword lets your code work with both plaintext passwords and encrypted password hashes. In the specific case of a POP3 server, accepting credentials that implement credentials.IUsernameHashedPassword allows the server to accept MD5 passwords.

Once you've defined classes for your implementations of pop3.IMailbox, portal. IRealm and credentials.ICredentialsChecker, it doesn't take much code to put them together into a working POP3 server. In Example 8-3, POP3Factory has a custom buildProtocol method that creates a POP3Protocol object and sets its portal attribute. POP3Protocol is a simple class that inherits from pop3.POP3 and adds an optional debugging mode: when debug is true, it will print all the commands received from the client and the replies sent back from the server. This technique can be very useful when you want to see exactly what a protocol is doing.

Providing IMAP Access to Mailboxes

IMAP is a powerful and full-featured protocol for mail management. But its many features are both a blessing and a curse. IMAP is a great protocol to use: it provides all the necessary tools to store, organize, and mail on a central server. But IMAP's complexity makes it an intimidating protocol to implement: the base IMAP protocol spec in RFC 2060 runs to more than 80 dense pages. IMAP also puts a lot of burden on the mail server. IMAP servers have to support message parsing (to allow the client to download only selected parts of a message), message searching (using a special query language), and the ability to reference messages using two completely different sets of numeric identifiers (message sequence numbers and unique IDs).

This complexity has historically caused all but the most dedicated developers to steer clear of IMAP, settling for the simpler but less capable POP3. So the fact that twisted.mail includes IMAP support is a great opportunity for developers. It makes it possible for you to write your own custom IMAP server, but without having to deal with all the nasty details of the IMAP protocol.

How Do I Do That?

To make an IMAP server, write classes to implement the IAccount, IMailbox, IMessage, and IMessagePart interfaces defined in twisted.mail.imap4. Then set up a realm that makes your IAccount implementation available as an avatar. Wrap the realm in a Portal, and set up a Factory that will pass the Portal to an imap4. IMAP4Server Protocol. Example 8-4 demonstrates a complete IMAP server.

Example 8-4. imapserver.py

```
from twisted.mail import imap4, maildir
from twisted.internet import reactor, defer, protocol
from twisted.cred import portal, checkers, credentials
from twisted.cred import error as credError
from twisted.python import filepath
from zope.interface import implements
import time, os, random, pickle

MAILBOXDELIMITER = "."

class IMAPUserAccount(object):
  implements(imap4.IAccount)

  def __init__(self, userDir):
    self.dir = userDir
    self.mailboxCache = {}
    # make sure Inbox exists
    inbox = self._getMailbox("Inbox", create=True)
```

Example 8-4. imapserver.py (continued)

```python
def listMailboxes(self, ref, wildcard):
    for box in os.listdir(self.dir):
        yield box, self._getMailbox(box)

def select(self, path, rw=True):
    "return an object implementing IMailbox for the given path"
    return self._getMailbox(path)

def _getMailbox(self, path, create=False):
    """
    Helper function to get a mailbox object at the given
    path, optionally creating it if it doesn't already exist.
    """
    # According to the IMAP spec, Inbox is case-insensitive
    pathParts = path.split(MAILBOXDELIMITER)
    if pathParts[0].lower() == 'inbox': pathParts[0] = 'Inbox'
    path = MAILBOXDELIMITER.join(pathParts)

    if not self.mailboxCache.has_key(path):
        fullPath = os.path.join(self.dir, path)
        if not os.path.exists(fullPath):
            if create:
                maildir.initializeMaildir(fullPath)
            else:
                raise KeyError, "No such mailbox"
        self.mailboxCache[path] = IMAPMailbox(fullPath)
    return self.mailboxCache[path]

def create(self, path):
    "create a mailbox at path and return it"
    self._getMailbox(path, create=True)

def delete(self, path):
    "delete the mailbox at path"
    raise imap4.MailboxException("Permission denied.")

def rename(self, oldname, newname):
    "rename a mailbox"
    oldPath = os.path.join(self.dir, oldname)
    newPath = os.path.join(self.dir, newname)
    os.rename(oldPath, newPath)

def isSubscribed(self, path):
    "return a true value if user is subscribed to the mailbox"
    return self._getMailbox(path).metadata.get('subscribed', False)

def subscribe(self, path):
    "mark a mailbox as subscribed"
    box = self._getMailbox(path)
    box.metadata['subscribed'] = True
    box.saveMetadata()
    return True
```

Example 8-4. imapserver.py (continued)

```python
    def unsubscribe(self, path):
        "mark a mailbox as unsubscribed"
        box = self._getMailbox(path)
        box.metadata['subscribed'] = False
        box.saveMetadata()
        return True

class ExtendedMaildir(maildir.MaildirMailbox):
    """
    Extends maildir.MaildirMailbox to expose more
    of the underlying filename data
    """
    def __iter__(self):
        "iterates through the full paths of all messages in the maildir"
        return iter(self.list)

    def __len__(self):
        return len(self.list)

    def __getitem__(self, i):
        return self.list[i]

    def deleteMessage(self, filename):
        index = self.list.index(filename)
        os.remove(filename)
        del(self.list[index])

class IMAPMailbox(object):
    implements(imap4.IMailbox)

    def __init__(self, path):
        self.maildir = ExtendedMaildir(path)
        self.metadataFile = os.path.join(path, '.imap-metadata.pickle')
        if os.path.exists(self.metadataFile):
            self.metadata = pickle.load(file(self.metadataFile, 'r+b'))
        else:
            self.metadata = {}
        self.initMetadata()
        self.listeners = []
        self._assignUIDs()

    def initMetadata(self):
        if not self.metadata.has_key('flags'):
            self.metadata['flags'] = {} # dict of message IDs to flags
        if not self.metadata.has_key('uidvalidity'):
            # create a unique integer ID to identify this version of
            # the mailbox, so the client could tell if it was deleted
            # and replaced by a different mailbox with the same name
            self.metadata['uidvalidity'] = random.randint(1000000, 9999999)
        if not self.metadata.has_key('uids'):
            self.metadata['uids'] = {}
```

Example 8-4. imapserver.py (continued)

```python
    if not self.metadata.has_key('uidnext'):
      self.metadata['uidnext'] = 1 # next UID to be assigned

  def saveMetadata(self):
    pickle.dump(self.metadata, file(self.metadataFile, 'w+b'))

  def _assignUIDs(self):
    # make sure every message has a uid
    for messagePath in self.maildir:
      messageFile = os.path.basename(messagePath)
      if not self.metadata['uids'].has_key(messageFile):
        self.metadata['uids'][messageFile] =
self.metadata['uidnext']
        self.metadata['uidnext'] += 1
    self.saveMetadata()

  def getHierarchicalDelimiter(self):
    return MAILBOXDELIMITER

  def getFlags(self):
    "return list of flags supported by this mailbox"
    return [r'\Seen', r'\Unseen', r'Deleted',
        r'\Flagged', r'\Answered', r'\Recent']

  def getMessageCount(self):
    return len(self.maildir)

  def getRecentCount(self):
    return 0

  def getUnseenCount(self):
    def messageIsUnseen(filename):
      filename = os.path.basename(filename)
      uid = self.metadata['uids'].get(filename)
      flags = self.metadata['flags'].get(uid, [])
      if not r'\Seen' in flags:
        return True
    return len(filter(messageIsUnseen, self.maildir))

  def isWriteable(self):
    return True

  def getUIDValidity(self):
    return self.metadata['uidvalidity']

  def getUID(self, messageNum):
    filename = os.path.basename(self.maildir[messageNum-1])
    return self.metadata['uids'][filename]

  def getUIDNext(self):
    return self.folder.metadata['uidnext']
```

Example 8-4. imapserver.py (continued)

```python
def _uidMessageSetToSeqDict(self, messageSet):
    """
    take a MessageSet object containing UIDs, and return
    a dictionary mapping sequence numbers to filenames
    """
    # if messageSet.last is None, it means 'the end', and needs to
    # be set to a sane high number before attempting to iterate
    # through the MessageSet
    if not messageSet.last:
        messageSet.last = self.metadata['uidnext']
    allUIDs = []
    for filename in self.maildir:
        shortFilename = os.path.basename(filename)
        allUIDs.append(self.metadata['uids'][shortFilename])
    allUIDs.sort()
    seqMap = {}
    for uid in messageSet:
        # the message set covers a span of UIDs. not all of them
        # will necessarily exist, so check each one for validity
        if uid in allUIDs:
            sequence = allUIDs.index(uid)+1
            seqMap[sequence] = self.maildir[sequence-1]
    return seqMap

def _seqMessageSetToSeqDict(self, messageSet):
    """
    take a MessageSet object containing message sequence numbers,
    and return a dictionary mapping sequence number to filenames
    """
    # if messageSet.last is None, it means 'the end', and needs to
    # be set to a sane high number before attempting to iterate
    # through the MessageSet
    if not messageSet.last: messageSet.last = len(self.maildir)-1
    seqMap = {}
    for messageNo in messageSet:
        seqMap[messageNo] = self.maildir[messageNo-1]
    return seqMap

def fetch(self, messages, uid):
    if uid:
        messagesToFetch = self._uidMessageSetToSeqDict(messages)
    else:
        messagesToFetch = self._seqMessageSetToSeqDict(messages)
    for seq, filename in messagesToFetch.items():
        uid = self.getUID(seq)
        flags = self.metadata['flags'].get(uid, [])
        yield seq, MaildirMessage(file(filename).read(), uid, flags)

def addListener(self, listener):
    self.listeners.append(listener)
    return True
```

Example 8-4. imapserver.py (continued)

```python
  def removeListener(self, listener):
    self.listeners.remove(listener)
    return True

  def requestStatus(self, path):
    return imap4.statusRequestHelper(self, path)

  def addMessage(self, msg, flags=None, date=None):
    if flags is None: flags = []
    return self.maildir.appendMessage(msg).addCallback(
      self._addedMessage, flags)

  def _addedMessage(self, _, flags):
    # the first argument is the value returned from
    # MaildirMailbox.appendMessage. It doesn't contain any meaningful
    # information and can be discarded. Using the name "_" is a Twisted
    # idiom for unimportant return values.
    self._assignUIDs()
    messageFile = os.path.basename(self.maildir[-1])
    messageID = self.metadata['uids'][messageFile]
    self.metadata['flags'][messageID] = flags
    self.saveMetadata()

  def store(self, messageSet, flags, mode, uid):
    if uid:
      messages = self._uidMessageSetToSeqDict(messageSet)
    else:
      messages = self._seqMessageSetToSeqDict(messageSet)
    setFlags = {}
    for seq, filename in messages.items():
      uid = self.getUID(seq)
      if mode == 0: # replace flags
        messageFlags = self.metadata['flags'][uid] = flags
      else:
        messageFlags = self.metadata['flags'].setdefault(uid, [])
        for flag in flags:
          # mode 1 is append, mode -1 is delete
          if mode == 1 and not messageFlags.count(flag):
            messageFlags.append(flag)
          elif mode == -1 and messageFlags.count(flag):
            messageFlags.remove(flag)
      setFlags[seq] = messageFlags
    self.saveMetadata()
    return setFlags

  def expunge(self):
    "remove all messages marked for deletion"
    removed = []
    for filename in self.maildir:
      uid = self.metadata['uids'].get(os.path.basename(filename))
      if r"Deleted" in self.metadata['flags'].get(uid, []):
        self.maildir.deleteMessage(filename)
```

Example 8-4. imapserver.py (continued)

```
            # you could also throw away the metadata here
            removed.append(uid)
        return removed

    def destroy(self):
        "complete remove the mailbox and all its contents"
        raise imap4.MailboxException("Permission denied.")

from cStringIO import StringIO
import email

class MaildirMessagePart(object):
    implements(imap4.IMessagePart)

    def __init__(self, mimeMessage):
        self.message = mimeMessage
        self.data = str(self.message)

    def getHeaders(self, negate, *names):
        """
        Return a dict mapping header name to header value. If *names
        is empty, match all headers; if negate is true, return only
        headers _not_ listed in *names.
        """
        if not names: names = self.message.keys()
        headers = {}
        if negate:
            for header in self.message.keys():
                if header.upper() not in names:
                    headers[header.lower()] = self.message.get(header, '')
        else:
            for name in names:
                headers[name.lower()] = self.message.get(name, '')
        return headers

    def getBodyFile(self):
        "return a file-like object containing this message's body"
        bodyData = str(self.message.get_payload())
        return StringIO(bodyData)

    def getSize(self):
        return len(self.data)

    def getInternalDate(self):
        return self.message.get('Date', '')

    def isMultipart(self):
        return self.message.is_multipart()

    def getSubPart(self, partNo):
        return MaildirMessagePart(self.message.get_payload(partNo))
```

Example 8-4. imapserver.py (continued)

```
class MaildirMessage(MaildirMessagePart):
  implements(imap4.IMessage)

  def __init__(self, messageData, uid, flags):
    self.data = messageData
    self.message = email.message_from_string(self.data)
    self.uid = uid
    self.flags = flags

  def getUID(self):
    return self.uid

  def getFlags(self):
    return self.flags

class MailUserRealm(object):
  implements(portal.IRealm)
  avatarInterfaces = {
    imap4.IAccount: IMAPUserAccount,
    }

  def __init__(self, baseDir):
    self.baseDir = baseDir

  def requestAvatar(self, avatarId, mind, *interfaces):
    for requestedInterface in interfaces:
      if self.avatarInterfaces.has_key(requestedInterface):
        # make sure the user dir exists (avatarId is username)
        userDir = os.path.join(self.baseDir, avatarId)
        if not os.path.exists(userDir):
          os.mkdir(userDir)
        # return an instance of the correct class
        avatarClass = self.avatarInterfaces[requestedInterface]
        avatar = avatarClass(userDir)
        # null logout function: take no arguments and do nothing
        logout = lambda: None
        return defer.succeed((requestedInterface, avatar, logout))

    # none of the requested interfaces was supported
    raise KeyError("None of the requested interfaces is supported")

def passwordFileToDict(filename):
  passwords = {}
  for line in file(filename):
    if line and line.count(':'):
      username, password = line.strip().split(':')
      passwords[username] = password
  return passwords

class CredentialsChecker(object):
  implements(checkers.ICredentialsChecker)
```

Example 8-4. imapserver.py (continued)

```
  credentialInterfaces = (credentials.IUsernamePassword,
            credentials.IUsernameHashedPassword)

  def __init__(self, passwords):
    "passwords: a dict-like object mapping usernames to passwords"
    self.passwords = passwords

  def requestAvatarId(self, credentials):
    """
    check to see if the supplied credentials authenticate.
    if so, return an 'avatar id', in this case the name of
    the IMAP user.
    The supplied credentials will implement one of the classes
    in self.credentialInterfaces. In this case both
    IUsernamePassword and IUsernameHashedPassword have a
    checkPassword method that takes the real password and checks
    it against the supplied password.
    """
    username = credentials.username
    if self.passwords.has_key(username):
      realPassword = self.passwords[username]
      checking = defer.maybeDeferred(
        credentials.checkPassword, realPassword)
      # pass result of checkPassword, and the username that was
      # being authenticated, to self._checkedPassword
      checking.addCallback(self._checkedPassword, username)
      return checking
    else:
      raise credError.UnauthorizedLogin("No such user")

  def _checkedPassword(self, matched, username):
    if matched:
      # password was correct
      return username
    else:
      raise credError.UnauthorizedLogin("Bad password")

class IMAPServerProtocol(imap4.IMAP4Server):
  "Subclass of imap4.IMAP4Server that adds debugging."
  debug = True

  def lineReceived(self, line):
    if self.debug:
      print "CLIENT:", line
    imap4.IMAP4Server.lineReceived(self, line)

  def sendLine(self, line):
    imap4.IMAP4Server.sendLine(self, line)
    if self.debug:
      print "SERVER:", line
```

Example 8-4. imapserver.py (continued)

```
class IMAPFactory(protocol.Factory):
  protocol = IMAPServerProtocol
  portal = None # placeholder

  def buildProtocol(self, address):
    p = self.protocol()
    p.portal = self.portal
    p.factory = self
    return p

if __name__ == "__main__":
  import sys
  dataDir = sys.argv[1]

  portal = portal.Portal(MailUserRealm(dataDir))
  passwordFile = os.path.join(dataDir, 'passwords.txt')
  passwords = passwordFileToDict(passwordFile)
  passwordChecker = CredentialsChecker(passwords)
  portal.registerChecker(passwordChecker)

  factory = IMAPFactory()
  factory.portal = portal

  reactor.listenTCP(143, factory)
  reactor.run()
```

Run *imapserver.py* from the command line with the name of the base mail directory as the only argument. This should be the same directory you used for the SMTP and POP3 servers in Examples 8-1 and 8-3:

```
$ python imapserver.py mail_storage
```

Once the server is running, set up your mail client to connect to *localhost* using IMAP. You should be able to see the Inbox folder, create folders and subfolders, subscribe to folders, view messages, mark messages as read or unread, and move messages between folders, as shown in Figure 8-6.

How Does That Work?

Compared to the other examples in this chapter, there's a lot of code required to make an IMAP server. But don't let that intimidate you. Most of the code in Example 8-4 is in the classes IMAPUserAccount, IMAPMaildir, MaildirMessagePart, and MaildirMessage, which respectively implement the interfaces imap4.IAccount, imap4. IMailbox, imap4.IMessagePart, and imap4.IMessage. These interfaces have a lot of methods, because the IMAP server needs to be able to do a lot of different things. However, most of the methods themselves are pretty simple, taking just a few lines of code. The following subsections go through the interfaces one at a time, to look at how they're used in Example 8-4.

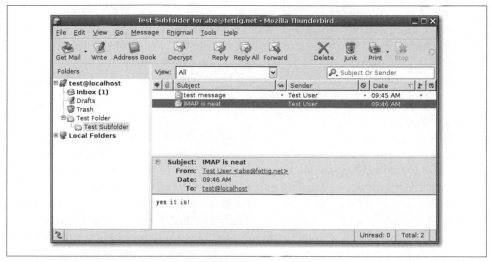

Figure 8-6. Working with messages on the IMAP server

IAccount

The imap4.IAccount interface defines a user account, and provides access to the user's mailboxes. imap4.IAccount defines methods for listing, creating, deleting, renaming, and subscribing to mailboxes. Mailboxes are hierarchal, with a server-defined delimiter character. In Example 8-4, the delimiter character is a period, so the folder MailingLists.Twisted would be considered a subfolder of MailingLists. In this case, the user's mailboxes are a set of maildir directories kept within a single parent directory. The use of a period as a delimiter makes it easier to keep all the maildirs in a single flat directory structure while still keeping track of their hierarchy. You could feel free to use another delmiter character, such as a forward slash (/), if it were more convenient for your needs.

According to RFC 2060, each IMAP user will have a folder called Inbox available in her account at all times. The name Inbox is case-insensitive, however, so different mail clients may ask for INBOX, Inbox, or inbox. Make sure you account for this in your code.

The select and create methods of IAccount return objects implementing IMailbox. The list method returns an iterable of tuples, with each tuple containing a path and an object implementing IMailbox.

IMailbox

The imap4.IMailbox interface represents a single mailbox on the IMAP server. It has methods for getting information about the mailbox, reading and writing messages, and storing metadata. There are a couple of considerations to keep in mind when you write a class to implement IMailbox. First, note that an IMAP mailbox is more than just a collection of messages. It also is responsible for managing metadata about those messages and the mailbox itself. In Example 8-4, the IMAPMaildir class keeps metadata in a dictionary, which is pickled and stored in a hidden file in the maildir directory for persistence between sessions. These are some of the specific kinds of metadata you'll need to track:

Message UIDs

Every message in an IMAP mailbox has a permanent unique identifier. These are sequential, and are maintained over the life of the mailbox. The first ever message in a mailbox will have a UID of 1, the second a UID of 2, etc. These are different from simple sequence numbers in that they continue to build over the lifetime of a mailbox. For example, if you added 1000 messages to a new IMAP mailbox, they would be assigned the UIDs 1–1001. If you then deleted all those messages and added a single new message, it would be given a UID of 1002, even though there wouldn't be any other messages in the mailbox. UIDs are used by the client for caching purposes, to avoid repeatedly downloading the same message. In IMailbox, the getUID function returns the UID of a message, given its sequence number. The getUIDNext function returns the UID number that will be assigned to the next message added to the mailbox.

Message flags

Every message in the mailbox can have an arbitrary number of flags associated with it. The flags are set by the client to keep track of metadata about that message, such as whether it's been read, replied to, or flagged. RFC 2060 defines a set of system flags that all IMAP clients should use the same way: \Seen, \Answered, \Flagged, \Deleted, \Draft, and \Recent. The IMailbox getFlags methods returns the list of flags supported by the mailbox. The store method sets the flags on a group of messages.

The mailbox UID validity identifier

There can be times when a mailbox keeps the same name, but changes its list of UIDs. The most common example of this is when a mailbox is deleted and a new mailbox with the same name is created. This could cause confusion for a mail client, since it may have a cached copy of the message with UID 1, which is now different from the message on the server with UID 1. To prevent this, IMAP has the concept of a UID validity identifier. Each mailbox has a unique number associated with it. As long as this number remains the same, the client can be confident that its UID numbers are still valid. If this number changes, the client knows to forget all its cached UID information. You should assign a UID validity identifier number for each mailbox, and return it as the result of getUIDValidity.

The mailbox subscription status

IMAP clients may not want or need to display all the mailboxes that actually exist on the server. The client can tell the server which mailboxes it is interested in by subscribing to those mailboxes. Subscribing doesn't do anything special other than toggling a subscribed bit on the mailbox. The subscription status of each mailbox is stored on the server, so that it can be maintained from session to session and between different clients.

The second thing to be aware of when implementing IMailbox is that there are two different numbering schemes that clients may use to refer to messages. The first is UIDs, persistent unique identifiers. The second is sequence numbers, which are a simple list of numbers from 1 to the number of messages in the mailbox. The fetch and store methods of IMailbox take an imap4.MessageSet object along with a Boolean uid argument. The MessageSet is an iterable list of numbers, but you have to check the uid argument to determine whether it's a list of UIDs or a list of sequence numbers. The IMAPMaildir class in Example 8-4 uses two methods, _uidMessageSetToSeqDict and _seqMessageSetToSeqDict, to take either type of MessageSet and normalize it into a dictionary mapping sequence numbers to the filenames it uses internally to identify messages. Note that the lists returned by fetch and store always use sequence numbers, whether or not the uid argument was true.

The last property of a MessageSet may be set to None, which means that the MessageSet covers all messages from its start to the end of the mailbox. You can't actually iterate through a MessageSet in this state, though, so you should set last to a value just beyond the last message in the mailbox before you attempt to use the MessageSet.

The IMAP protocol includes support for server-to-client notification. A client will generally keep an open connection to the IMAP server, so rather than having the client periodically ask the server if there are any new messages, the server can send a message to the client to alert it as soon as messages have arrived. The IMailbox interface includes methods for managing these notifications. The addListener method registers an object implementing imap4.IMailboxListener. If you keep track of this object, you can use it later to notify the client when a new message arrives. The IMAPMaildir class in Example 8-4 keeps track of listeners, but doesn't actually use them. Example 8-5 shows how you might use listeners to notify the client of new messages.

Example 8-5. Using listener objects for notification

```
# run this code to let the client know when a new message
# appears in the mailbox
for listener in self.listeners:
    listener.newMessages(self.getMessageCount(), self.getRecentCount())
```

IMessagePart and IMessage

In IMAP, an email message is not just a blob of data: it has a structure that can be accessed one part at a time. In its simplest form, a message is a group of headers and a body. More complex messages can have a multi-part body, with alternative versions of the body content (such as HTML and plain text) and attachments (which may themselves be other messages with their own structure).

The IMessagePart interface provides methods for investigating the structure of one part of a multi-part message. IMessage inherits from IMessagePart and adds the getUID and getFlags methods for retrieving metadata about the message. Implementing IMessagePart would be a chore if not for the excellent email module in the Python standard library, which contains a complete set of classes for parsing and working with email messages. In Example 8-4, the MaildirMessage class uses the email.message_from_string function to parse the message data into an email.Message.Message object. MaildirMessagePart takes an email.Message.Message object and wraps it in the IMessagePart interface.

Putting It All Together

Once you've implemented IAccount, IMailbox, IMessagePart, and IMessage, just tie the pieces together to get a working IMAP server. Example 8-4 uses the same classes, MailUserRealm and CredentialsChecker, as the POP3 server in Example 8-3, except that the realm is set up to return IMAPMaildir avatars when the imap4.IMailbox interface is requested. The IMAPFactory object creates IMAPServerProtocol objects and sets their portal attribute to a Portal wrapping the realm and credentials checkers. The IMAPServerProtocol class is another example of how you can inherit from a Twisted Protocol class and add some print statements for debugging.

CHAPTER 9

NNTP Clients and Servers

Usenet is a long-standing network of servers used for public discussion on the Internet. Each discussion forum in Usenet is called a *newsgroup*, and each Usenet server can host any number of newsgroups. Messages in a Usenet newsgroup are referred to as *articles*. Usenet servers communicate with each other to keep their copies of each newsgroup up-to-date, so that an article posted to a newsgroup on one server will eventually propagate to all the servers that host that newsgroup. This setup allows many people to participate in Usenet discussions without putting the load on any one central server.

The Usenet system dates back to before the Internet and TCP/IP had become widely accepted. Originally, computers participating in Usenet would connect to each other directly using dial-up modem connections, and then push articles back and forth using UUCP, the Unix-to-Unix Copy Protocol. After TCP/IP became the standard way to transfer data between computers, a new protocol was developed for Usenet communications. This Network News Transfer Protocol, or NNTP, is defined in RFC 977 (*http://www.faqs.org/rfc/rfc977.txt*). NNTP is used by Usenet clients for reading and posting articles to servers, as well as for server-to-server article transfers.

Support for NNTP in Twisted is provided by the `twisted.news` package. This chapter demonstrates how to use `twisted.news` to build Usenet clients and servers.

Listing the Newsgroups on a Server

This lab demonstrates how to use the `twisted.news.nntp` module to perform one of the most common tasks in Usenet: retrieving a list of the available newsgroups on a server.

How Do I Do That?

Use a subclass of `twisted.news.nntp.NNTPClient` as your Protocol. `NNTPClient` is one of the older protocol implementations in Twisted, and it's starting to show its age. It was developed before the best practices for writing Twisted client protocols had really been understood. In particular, you'll notice that it doesn't make use of Deferreds. Instead, `NNTPClient` has an API that provides methods for sending commands to the server, and you write handler methods for receiving the server's reply.

To get the list of newsgroups from the server, call the `fetchGroups` method of `NNTPClient`. Use the `gotAllGroups` method as shown in Example 9-1 to handle the result, and `getAllGroupsFailed` to handle an error.

Example 9-1. nntplist.py

```python
from twisted.news import nntp
from twisted.internet import protocol, defer

class NNTPGroupListerProtocol(nntp.NNTPClient):

    def connectionMade(self):
        nntp.NNTPClient.connectionMade(self)
        self.fetchGroups()

    def gotAllGroups(self, groups):
        groupnames = [groupInfo[0] for groupInfo in groups]
        self.factory.deferred.callback(groupnames)
        self.quit()

    def getAllGroupsFailed(self, error):
        self.factory.deferred.errback(error)

    def connectionLost(self, error):
        if not self.factory.deferred.called:
            self.factory.deferred.errback(error)

class NNTPGroupListerFactory(protocol.ClientFactory):
    protocol = NNTPGroupListerProtocol

    def __init__(self):
        self.deferred = defer.Deferred()

if __name__ == "__main__":
    from twisted.internet import reactor

    def printGroups(groups):
        for group in groups:
            print group
        reactor.stop()

    def handleError(error):
        print >> sys.stderr, error.getErrorMessage()
        reactor.stop()
```

Example 9-1. nntplist.py (continued)

```
factory = NNTPGroupListerFactory()
factory.deferred.addCallback(printGroups).addErrback(handleError)

reactor.connectTCP('news-server.maine.rr.com', 119, factory)
reactor.run()
```

Run *nntplist.py* with the hostname of an NNTP server as the only argument. It will download and print the list of available newsgroups:

```
$ python nntplist.py freetext.usenetserver.com
aaaustin.jobs
aacc.general
aapg.general
ab.agriculture
...
zipworld.help
zoom.cheesedog
zoomnet.general
zz.unity.chat
zz.unity.netlink
zzz.3
```

How Does That Work?

NNTP doesn't require authentication, so `NNTPGroupListerProtocol` only has to call one method: `self.fetchGroups()`. When the server responds with a list of newsgroups, the `gotAllGroups` method is called, with the newsgroup list as an argument. This list is a set of tuples in the form (`groupName`, `articleCount`). `NNTPGroupListerProtocol`'s `gotAllGroups` method extracts the group names and uses them to call back the Factory's `Deferred` object.

The `getAllGroupsFailed` method is the error handler for `fetchGroups`. If an error occurs, it will be passed to the factory's `Deferred`.

Downloading Usenet Articles

The core of Usenet, of course, is downloading and reading articles. This lab shows how to learn which articles are available in a group, and then download the most recent ones.

How Do I Do That?

Call `NNTPClient`'s `fetchGroup` method to get the article count and first and last message numbers for a newsgroup. Then call `fetchArticle` to download each article. Example 9-2 demonstrates the technique.

Example 9-2. nntpdownload.py

```python
from twisted.news import nntp
from twisted.internet import protocol, defer
import time, email

class NNTPGroupDownloadProtocol(nntp.NNTPClient):

    def connectionMade(self):
        nntp.NNTPClient.connectionMade(self)
        self.fetchGroup(self.factory.newsgroup)

    def gotGroup(self, groupInfo):
        articleCount, first, last, groupName = groupInfo
        first = int(first)
        last = int(last)
        start = max(first, last-self.factory.articleCount)
        self.articlesToFetch = range(start+1, last+1)
        self.articleCount = len(self.articlesToFetch)
        self.fetchNextArticle( )

    def fetchNextArticle(self):
        if self.articlesToFetch:
            nextArticleIdx = self.articlesToFetch.pop(0)
            print "Fetching article %i of %i..." % (
                self.articleCount-len(self.articlesToFetch),
                self.articleCount),
            self.fetchArticle(nextArticleIdx)
        else:
            # all done
            self.quit( )
            self.factory.deferred.callback(0)

    def gotArticle(self, article):
        print "OK"
        self.factory.handleArticle(article)
        self.fetchNextArticle( )

    def getArticleFailed(self, errorMessage):
        print errorMessage
        self.fetchNextArticle( )

    def getGroupFailed(self, errorMessage):
        self.factory.deferred.errback(Exception(errorMessage))
        self.quit( )
        self.transport.loseConnection( )

    def connectionLost(self, error):
        if not self.factory.deferred.called:
            self.factory.deferred.errback(error)
```

Example 9-2. nntpdownload.py (continued)

```
class NNTPGroupDownloadFactory(protocol.ClientFactory):
    protocol = NNTPGroupDownloadProtocol

    def __init__(self, newsgroup, outputfile, articleCount=10):
        self.newsgroup = newsgroup
        self.articleCount = articleCount
        self.output = outputfile
        self.deferred = defer.Deferred()

    def handleArticle(self, articleData):
        parsedMessage = email.message_from_string(articleData)
        self.output.write(parsedMessage.as_string(unixfrom=True))
        self.output.write('\r\n\r\n')

if __name__ == "__main__":
    from twisted.internet import reactor
    import sys

    def handleError(error):
        print >> sys.stderr, error.getErrorMessage()
        reactor.stop()

    if len(sys.argv) != 4:
        print >> sys.stderr, "Usage: %s nntpserver newsgroup outputfile"
        sys.exit(1)

    server, newsgroup, outfile = sys.argv[1:4]
    factory = NNTPGroupDownloadFactory(newsgroup, file(outfile, 'w+b'))
    factory.deferred.addCallback(
        lambda _: reactor.stop()).addErrback(
        handleError)
    reactor.connectTCP(server, 119, factory)
    reactor.run()
```

Run *nntpdownload.py* with the name of an NNTP server, a newsgroup, and the file-name to which the messages should be written. It will connect to the server, download the most recent 10 messages from that newsgroup, and then quit:

```
$ python nntpdownload.py freetext.usenetserver.com comp.lang.python \
> comp.lang.python-latest.mbox
Fetching article 1 of 10... OK
Fetching article 2 of 10... OK
Fetching article 3 of 10... OK
Fetching article 4 of 10... OK
Fetching article 5 of 10... OK
Fetching article 6 of 10... OK
Fetching article 7 of 10... OK
Fetching article 8 of 10... OK
Fetching article 9 of 10... OK
Fetching article 10 of 10... OK
```

How Does That Work?

The `NNTPGroupDownloadProtocol` class, a subclass of `nntp.NNTPClient`, does most of the work in *nntpdownload.py*. The `self.fetchGroup` method asks the server for information about the newsgroup. When the server responds, `gotGroup` is called with the returned information: the total number of articles in the group, the index of the first article, the index of the last article, and the group name. `NNTPGroupDownloadProtocol` then goes back the number of articles specified by `self.factory.articleCount` (unless there aren't that many messages, in which case it just goes back to the first available article) and uses Python's `range` function to create a list of every number from the starting message index to the ending message index. Then it calls `fetchNextArticle` to begin downloading the set of messages.

`fetchNextArticle` takes the remaining list of article indexes and downloads the first one with a call to `self.fetchArticle`. The `gotArticle` method, called when the article has been successfully downloaded, passes the article data to `self.factory.handleArticle`, and then calls `self.fetchArticle` again. If an article download fails, the `gotArticleFailed` method will be called. `gotArticleFailed` prints an error message, but doesn't abort the entire operation; instead, it simply goes on to the next message.

 An alternative to the approach used here is to use the *fetchNewNews* method, which takes a date and returns a list of all the articles posted since. Unfortunately, the underlying *NEWNEWS* command is not supported by many servers.

Because Usenet articles are in the same format as email, they can be stored in the same Unix *mbox* format used by the mail client examples shown in Chapter 7. The `NNTPGroupDownloadFactory`'s `handleArticle` method parses the message using the `email` module and writes it to the output file in *mbox* format, followed by two blank lines to ensure that it will be clearly delimited from the next article in the file.

Posting a Message to an NNTP Server

While you're connected to an NNTP server, you can post messages to Usenet. Usenet articles are in the same basic format as email, but with some slightly stricter rules about required headers. You can read the full article format specification in RFC 1036 (*http://www.faqs.org/rfc/rfc1036.txt*). After you post an article through NNTP, your local NNTP server will pass it on to the other servers it knows about. From there, the article will continue to be passed from server to server until it's available throughout the Usenet network.

How Do I Do That?

Construct an article using the email.Message module (see Example 9-3). Select the newsgroup to which you'll be posting, and then post the article.

Example 9-3. nntppost.py

```
from twisted.news import nntp
from twisted.internet import protocol, defer
import time, email

class NNTPPostProtocol(nntp.NNTPClient):

    def connectionMade(self):
        nntp.NNTPClient.connectionMade(self)
        self.fetchGroup(self.factory.newsgroup)

    def gotGroup(self, groupInfo):
        # post the article to the current newsgroup
        self.postArticle(self.factory.articleData)

    def postedOk(self):
        self.factory.deferred.callback(None)

    def postFailed(self, errorMessage):
        self.factory.deferred.errback(Exception(errorMessage))

    def connectionLost(self, error):
        if not self.factory.deferred.called:
            self.factory.deferred.errback(error)

class NNTPPostFactory(protocol.ClientFactory):
    protocol = NNTPPostProtocol

    def __init__(self, newsgroup, articleData):
        self.newsgroup = newsgroup
        self.articleData = articleData
        self.deferred = defer.Deferred()

from email.Message import Message
from email.Utils import make_msgid

def makeArticle(sender, newsgroup, subject, body):
    article = Message()
    article["From"] = sender
    article["Newsgroups"] = newsgroup
    article["Subject"] = subject
    article["Message-Id"] = make_msgid()
    article.set_payload(body)
    return article.as_string(unixfrom=False)
```

Example 9-3. nntppost.py (continued)

```python
if __name__ == "__main__":
    from twisted.internet import reactor
    import sys

    def handleError(error):
        print >> sys.stderr, error.getErrorMessage()
        reactor.stop()

    if len(sys.argv) != 3:
        print >> sys.stderr, "Usage: %s server newsgroup" % sys.argv[0]
        sys.exit(1)

    server, newsgroup = sys.argv[1:3]
    sender = raw_input("From: ")
    subject = raw_input("Subject: ")
    bodyLines = []
    while True:
        line = raw_input()
        if line == ".": break
        bodyLines.append(line)
    body = "\n".join(bodyLines)
    articleData = makeArticle(sender, newsgroup, subject, body)
    print articleData
    factory = NNTPPostFactory(newsgroup, articleData)
    factory.deferred.addCallback(
        lambda _: reactor.stop()).addErrback(
        handleError)
    reactor.connectTCP(server, 119, factory)
    reactor.run()
```

Run *nntppost.py* with two arguments: the newsgroup and the NNTP server. It will prompt you to enter your article, connect to the server, and post your article to the newsgroup:

```
$ python nntppost.py alt.local.test localhost
From: abe@fettig.net
Subject: Test Message
Enter article body below, followed by a single period:
Hello Usenet World!
.
Posting message.... done!
```

 Don't post test messages to public newsgroups, except for alt.test, which is set aside specifically for testing purposes. If you want to run a private NNTP server so you can post test messages without disturbing anyone, see "Running a Basic NNTP Server," later in this chapter.

How Does That Work?

In Example 9-3, the `makeArticle` function uses the `email.Message.Message` class to create an article in the proper format for posting to Usenet. It sets the following headers:

From

> The email address of the person posting the article. This header is the same as in an email message.

Newsgroups

> The list of newsgroups to which the article is being posted. If the message is being posted to multiple newsgroups, they should be separated by commas.

Subject

> The subject, just like in an email message.

Message-Id

> A globally unique identifier for this article, in the form `<uniqueid@sending.host>`. This is the same as the `Message-Id` header in an email message. It's important to use something truly unique, as the message ID will be used to identify this specific article as it moves from server to server in Usenet. The `email.Utils` module provides the helpful function `make_msgid` for generating unique message IDs.

Date

> The date and time the article was created. This header is the same as in an email message. The function `formatdate` in `email.Utils` will take the floating-point number returned from `time.time` or `time.gmtime` and return a string in the proper format. If called with no arguments, as in Example 9-3, it returns the formatted current time.

The body of the article is a standard text message, which you add to the `Message` object using `set_payload`.

The `NNTPPostProtocol` class in Example 9-3 posts an article to the server using the `postArticle` method of `nntp.NNTPClient`. The `postedOK` method will be called if the article is posted successfully; the `postFailed` method will be called if it fails. Note that `postArticle` doesn't take the name of the newsgroup as an argument: the article will be posted to whatever newsgroups are listed in the `Newsgroups` header.

Running a Basic NNTP Server

The `twisted.news` package includes classes for building NNTP servers. The server architecture is designed in two layers: the Factory and Protocol, which communicate with clients; and the news storage interface, which is responsible for reading and storing articles. `twisted.news` comes with working examples of the news storage interface, which you can use to create a functional NNTP server in just a few lines of code.

How Do I Do That?

Create a `database.NewsShelf` object, which implements the `database.INewsStorage` interface. Pass the `NewsShelf` object to a `news.NNTPFactory` object, and listen on port 119. As Example 9-4 shows, this is very easy to do.

Example 9-4. tinynntpserver.py

```
from twisted.internet import reactor
from twisted.news import database, news, nntp

GROUPS = [
    'local.programming',
    'local.programming.python',
    'local.knitting',
    ]
SMTP_SERVER = 'upstream-server.com'
STORAGE_DIR = 'storage'

newsStorage = database.NewsShelf(SMTP_SERVER, STORAGE_DIR)
for group in GROUPS:
    newsStorage.addGroup(group, [])
factory = news.NNTPFactory(newsStorage)
reactor.listenTCP(119, factory)
reactor.run( )
```

Run this example from the command line, without any arguments:

```
$ python tinynntpserver.py
```

Then connect to *localhost* using a newsreader application. You should be able to see the list of available newsgroups, as in Figure 9-1.

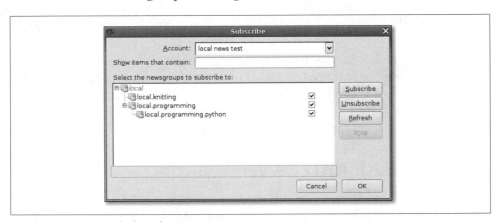

Figure 9-1. Browsing the list of newsgroups

Subscribe to the newsgroups, and you should be able to read and post articles. If you connect with multiple clients, you'll be able to start discussions and reply to each other's articles, as shown in Figure 9-2.

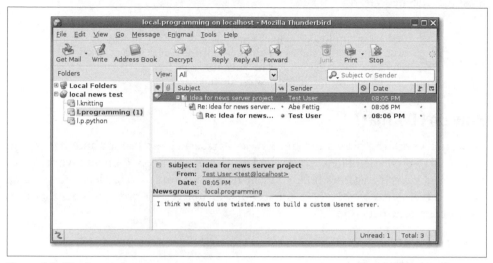

Figure 9-2. Reading and posting messages

How Does That Work?

The database.NewsShelf class is an implementation of database.INewsStorage that stores articles using a twisted.persisted.dirdbm.Shelf. dirdbm.Shelf is a useful class that works like a dictionary, but writes its data to a directory so that it can persist after the program exists. The NewsShelf class is initialized with two arguments: the hostname of an SMTP server (which it will use for sending notification messages to the server administrator) and the directory where it should store article data.

Once you've created a NewsShelf object, all you have to do is pass it to a news. NNTPFactory object. This factory uses nntp.NNTPServer for a protocol, which is designed to work with any implementation of database.INewsStorage.

Using NNTP as a User Interface

NNTP was designed to be a protocol for working with Usenet. But this doesn't prevent it from being used to access other kinds of messaging systems. Like the email protocols discussed in Chapter 7, you can use NNTP as an interface, a way to let users interact with your application's data. For example, you could provide an NNTP interface to a web discussion board. This would allow users familiar with Usenet to participate in the discussion board using their Usenet client, taking advantage of features like offline message reading, message threading, and spellcheck.

NNTP is a good protocol to use any time you want to offer a public (nonauthenti-cated) means of reading and writing messages. This example demonstrates how you could use `twisted.news` to provide an NNTP interface to a popular type of public message: RSS news feeds.

 RSS (short for Really Simple Syndication) is an XML format that many web sites use to publish a summary of their most recent articles or changes. By periodically checking the RSS feed, a client can see whether there is anything new on the site.

How Do I Do That?

Write a class that implements `twisted.news.database.INewsStorage` and makes your data available as a set of newsgroups and articles. If you need to do an asynchronous task in an `INewsStorage` method, you can return a `Deferred`. This lets you write an NNTP server, such as that in Example 9-5, which acts as a proxy to data that lives elsewhere on the network.

Example 9-5. rss2nntp.py

```
from twisted.internet import reactor, defer
from twisted.news import database, news, nntp
from twisted.web import client, microdom
from zope.interface import implements
from cStringIO import StringIO
from email.Message import Message
import email.Utils
import socket, time, md5

GROUPS = {
    "rss.slashdot": "http://www.slashdot.org/slashdot.rdf",
    "rss.abefettig": "http://fettig.net/xml/rss2.xml",
    }

class RssFeed(object):
    refreshRate = 60*60 # hourly refresh

    def __init__(self, groupName, feedUrl):
        self.title = ""
        self.groupName = groupName
        self.feedUrl = feedUrl
        self.articles = []
        self.articlesById = {}
        self.lastRefreshTime = 0
        self.refreshing = None

    def refreshIfNeeded(self):
        timeSinceRefresh = time.time() - self.lastRefreshTime
        if timeSinceRefresh > self.refreshRate:
```

Example 9-5. rss2nntp.py (continued)

```python
        if not self.refreshing:
            self.refreshing = client.getPage(self.feedUrl).addCallback(
                self._gotFeedData).addErrback(
                self._getDataFailed)
        d = defer.Deferred( )
        self.refreshing.chainDeferred(d)
        return d
    else:
        return defer.succeed(None)

def _gotFeedData(self, data):
    print "Loaded feed data from %s" % self.feedUrl
    self.refreshing = None
    self.lastRefreshTime = time.time( )

    # this is a naive and brittle way to parse RSS feeds.
    # It should work for most well-formed feeds, but will choke
    # if the feed has a structure that doesn't meet its
    # expectations. In the real world, you'd want to use a
    # more robust means of parsing feeds, such as FeedParser
    # (http://feedparser.org) or Yarn (http://yarnproject.org).

    xml = microdom.parseString(data)
    self.title = xml.documentElement.getElementsByTagName(
        'title')[0].childNodes[0].data
    items = xml.documentElement.getElementsByTagName('item')
    for item in items:
        rssData = {}
        for field in 'title', 'link', 'description':
            nodes = item.getElementsByTagName(field)
            if nodes:
                rssData[field] = nodes[0].childNodes[0].data
            else:
                rssData[field] = ''
        guid = md5.md5(
            rssData['title'] + rssData['link']).hexdigest( )
        articleId = "<%s@%s>" % (guid, socket.getfqdn( ))
        if not self.articlesById.has_key(articleId):
            article = Message( )
            article['From'] = self.title
            article['Newsgroups'] = self.groupName
            article['Message-Id'] = articleId
            article['Subject'] = rssData['title']
            article['Date'] = email.Utils.formatdate( )
            body = "%s\r\n\r\n%s" % (
                rssData['description'], rssData['link'])
            article.set_payload(body)
            self.articles.append(article)
            self.articlesById[articleId] = article
```

Example 9-5. rss2nntp.py (continued)

```python
    def _getDataFailed(self, failure):
        print "Failed to load RSS data from %s: %s" % (
            self.feedUrl, failure.getErrorMessage())
        self.refreshing = None
        return failure

    def _refreshComplete(self, _):
        # schedule another refresh
        reactor.callLater(self.refreshRate, self.refresh)

class RssFeedStorage(object):
    "keeps articles in memory, loses them when the process exits"
    implements(database.INewsStorage)

    def __init__(self, feeds):
        "feeds is a dict of {groupName:url}"
        self.feeds = {}
        for groupName, url in feeds.items():
            self.feeds[groupName] = RssFeed(groupName, url)

    def refreshAllFeeds(self):
        refreshes = [feed.refreshIfNeeded() for feed in self.feeds.values()]
        return defer.DeferredList(refreshes)

    def _refreshAllFeedsAndCall(self, func, *args, **kwargs):
        "refresh all feeds and then return the results of calling func"
        return self.refreshAllFeeds().addCallback(
            lambda _: func(*args, **kwargs))

    def _refreshFeedAndCall(self, groupName, func, *args, **kwargs):
        "refresh one feed and then return the results of calling func"
        if self.feeds.has_key(groupName):
            feed = self.feeds[groupName]
            return feed.refreshIfNeeded().addCallback(
                lambda _: func(*args, **kwargs))
        else:
            return defer.fail(KeyError(groupName))

    def listRequest(self):
        """
        List information about the newsgroups on this server.
        Returns a Deferred which will call back with a list of tuples
        in the form
        (groupname, messageCount, firstMessage, postingAllowed)
        """
        return self._refreshAllFeedsAndCall(self._listRequest)

    def _listRequest(self):
        groupInfo = []
        for feed in self.feeds.values():
            # set to 'y' to indicate that posting is allowed
            postingAllowed = 'n'
```

Example 9-5. rss2nntp.py (continued)

```python
        groupInfo.append(
            (feed.groupName, len(feed.articles), 0, postingAllowed))
    return groupInfo

def listGroupRequest(self, groupname):
    "return the list of message indexes for the group"
    return self._refreshFeedAndCall(groupname, self._listGroupRequest,
                                    groupname)

def _listGroupRequest(self, groupname):
    feed = self.feeds[groupname]
    return range(len(feed.articles))

def subscriptionRequest(self):
    "return the list of groups the server recommends to new users"
    return defer.succeed(self.feeds.keys())

def overviewRequest(self):
    """
    Return a list of headers that will be used for giving
    an overview of a message. twisted.news.database.OVERVIEW_FMT
    is such a list.
    """
    return defer.succeed(database.OVERVIEW_FMT)

def groupRequest(self, groupName):
    """
    Return a tuple of information about the group:
    (groupName, articleCount, startIndex, endIndex, flags)
    """
    return self._refreshFeedAndCall(groupName,
                                    self._groupRequest,
                                    groupName)

def _groupRequest(self, groupName):
    feed = self.feeds[groupName]
    groupInfo = (groupName,
                 len(feed.articles),
                 len(feed.articles),
                 0,
                 {})
    return defer.succeed(groupInfo)

def xoverRequest(self, groupName, low, high):
    """
    Return a list of tuples, once for each article between low and high.
    Each tuple contains the article's values of the headers that
    were returned by self.overviewRequest.
    """
    return self._refreshFeedAndCall(groupName,
                                    self._processXOver,
                                    groupName, low, high,
                                    database.OVERVIEW_FMT)
```

Example 9-5. rss2nntp.py (continued)

```
def xhdrRequest(self, groupName, low, high, header):
    """
    Like xoverRequest, except that instead of returning all the
    header values, it should return only the value of a single header.
    """
    return self._refreshFeedAndCall(groupName,
                                    self._processXOver,
                                    groupName, low, high,
                                    [header])


def _processXOver(self, groupName, low, high, headerNames):
    feed = self.feeds[groupName]
    if low is None: low = 0
    if high is None: high = len(feed.articles)-1
    results = []
    for i in range(low, high+1):
        article = feed.articles[i]
        articleData = article.as_string(unixfrom=False)
        headerValues = [i]
        for header in headerNames:
            # check for special headers
            if header == 'Byte-Count':
                headerValues.append(len(articleData))
            elif header == 'Line-Count':
                headerValues.append(len(articleData.split('\n')))
            else:
                headerValues.append(article.get(header, ''))
        results.append(headerValues)
    return defer.succeed(results)

def articleExistsRequest(self, groupName, id):
    feed = self.feeds[groupName]
    return defer.succeed(feed.articlesById.has_key(id))

def articleRequest(self, groupName, index, messageId=None):
    """
    Return the contents of the article specified by either
    index or message ID
    """
    feed = self.feeds[groupName]
    if messageId:
        message = feeds.articlesById(messageId)
        # look up the index
        index = feed.articles.index(message)
    else:
        message = feed.articles[index]
        # look up the message ID
        for mId, m in feed.articlesById.items():
            if m == message:
                messageId = mId
                break
```

Example 9-5. rss2nntp.py (continued)

```
        messageData = message.as_string(unixfrom=False)
        return defer.succeed((index, id, (StringIO(messageData))))

    def headRequest(self, groupName, index):
        "return the headers of them message at index"
        group = self.groups[groupName]
        article = group.articles[index]
        return defer.succeed(article.getHeaders())

    def bodyRequest(self, groupName, index):
        "return the body of the message at index"
        group = self.groups[groupName]
        article = group.articles[index]
        return defer.succeed(article.body)

    def postRequest(self, message):
        "post the message."
        return defer.fail(Exception("RSS feeds are read-only."))

class DebuggingNNTPProtocol(nntp.NNTPServer):
    debug = True

    def lineReceived(self, line):
        if self.debug:
            print "CLIENT:", line
        nntp.NNTPServer.lineReceived(self, line)

    def sendLine(self, line):
        nntp.NNTPServer.sendLine(self, line)
        if self.debug:
            print "SERVER:", line

class DebuggingNNTPFactory(news.NNTPFactory):
    protocol = DebuggingNNTPProtocol

if __name__ == "__main__":
    factory = DebuggingNNTPFactory(RssFeedStorage(GROUPS))
    reactor.listenTCP(119, factory)
    reactor.run()
```

Run *rss2nntp.py* without any arguments:

```
$ python rss2nntp.py
```

Then connect to localhost using a news reader. The DebuggingNNTPProtocol class in *rss2nntp.py* causes the server to print a log of all the commands and replies sent between the client and server, so you'll be able to see what's going on behind the scenes. Figure 9-3 shows how the server will download RSS feeds on demand and present the contents of the feeds through NNTP.

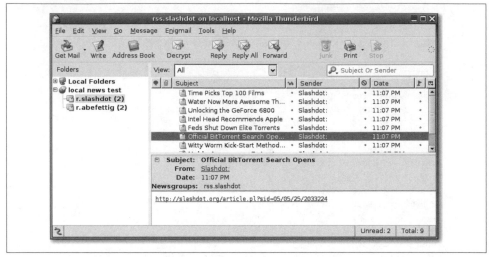

Figure 9-3. Reading an RSS feed through NNTP

How Does That Work?

Although it has a lot more code, the *rss2nntp.py* program in Example 9-5 follows the same design as the minimal NNTP server in Example 9-4. The difference is that this time the program includes its own implementation of database.InewsStorage, instead of using one of the storage backends that come with twisted.news.

The RssFeedStorage class has all the methods required by INewsStorage. You can identify these messages because they end with Request. The RssFeedStorage object keeps a collection of RssFeed objects in a list called feeds. Each RssFeed object loads messages from the RSS feed at a certain URL.

RSS feeds have to be periodically polled for new messages. The RssFeed object has a method called refreshIfNecessary that will compare self.lastRefreshTime to self. refreshRate and decide whether the feed needs to be refreshed. If it does, refreshIfNecessary will return a Deferred that issues a callback after the feed has been downloaded and checked for new messages. Otherwise, it will return a Deferred that calls back immediately. If you want to make sure that the feed is up-to-date before you run a certain function, you can call refreshIfNecessary and assign the function as a callback handler:

```
myfeed.refreshIfNecessary().addCallback(
    lambda _: myFunctionThatNeedsFreshData)
```

The RssFeedStorage class in Example 9-5 has a method called _refreshFeedAndCall that sets up a function to be the callback handler for refreshIfNecessary. The method _refreshAllFeedsAndCall works the same way, but uses a DeferredList to manage calling refreshIfNecessary on all available feeds. These methods are used in places where RssFeedStorage wants to make sure it has up-to-date feed data before it returns a result.

When implementing a complex interface like INewsStorage, there are bound to be bugs. You might return data in the wrong format, confusing the NNTP client on the other end. To make it easier to debug problems during development, Example 9-5 includes the DebuggingNTTPProtocol class, which inherits from nntp.NNTPProtocol and adds print statements, so you can view the commands and replies sent between the client and server.

CHAPTER 10

SSH

SSH, the *Secure SHell*, is an essential tool for many developers and administrators. SSH provides a way to establish encrypted, authenticated connections. The most common use of an SSH connection is to get a remote shell, but it's possible to do many other things through SSH as well, including transferring files and tunneling other connections.

The `twisted.conch` package adds SSH support to Twisted. This chapter shows how you can use the modules in `twisted.conch` to build SSH servers and clients.

Setting Up a Custom SSH Server

The command line is an incredibly efficient interface for certain tasks. System administrators love the ability to manage applications by typing commands without having to click through a graphical user interface. An SSH shell is even better, as it's accessible from anywhere on the Internet.

You can use `twisted.conch` to create an SSH server that provides access to a custom shell with commands you define. This shell will even support some extra features like command history, so that you can scroll through the commands you've already typed.

How Do I Do That?

Write a subclass of `twisted.conch.recvline.HistoricRecvLine` that implements your shell protocol. `HistoricRecvLine` is similar to `twisted.protocols.basic.LineReceiver`, but with higher-level features for controlling the terminal.

To make your shell available through SSH, you need to implement a few different classes that `twisted.conch` needs to build an SSH server. First, you need the `twisted.cred` authentication classes: a portal, credentials checkers, and a realm that returns avatars. Use `twisted.conch.avatar.ConchUser` as the base class for your avatar. Your avatar class should also implement twisted.conch.interfaces.ISession, which includes an openShell method in which you create a Protocol to manage the user's interactive session. Finally, create a twisted.conch.ssh.factory.SSHFactory object and set its portal attribute to an instance of your portal.

Example 10-1 demonstrates a custom SSH server that authenticates users by their username and password. It gives each user a shell that provides several commands.

Example 10-1. sshserver.py

```python
from twisted.cred import portal, checkers, credentials
from twisted.conch import error, avatar, recvline, interfaces as conchinterfaces
from twisted.conch.ssh import factory, userauth, connection, keys, session, common
from twisted.conch.insults import insults
from twisted.application import service, internet
from zope.interface import implements
import os

class SSHDemoProtocol(recvline.HistoricRecvLine):
    def __init__(self, user):
        self.user = user

    def connectionMade(self):
        recvline.HistoricRecvLine.connectionMade(self)
        self.terminal.write("Welcome to my test SSH server.")
        self.terminal.nextLine()
        self.do_help()
        self.showPrompt()

    def showPrompt(self):
        self.terminal.write("$ ")

    def getCommandFunc(self, cmd):
        return getattr(self, 'do_' + cmd, None)

    def lineReceived(self, line):
        line = line.strip()
        if line:
            cmdAndArgs = line.split()
            cmd = cmdAndArgs[0]
            args = cmdAndArgs[1:]
            func = self.getCommandFunc(cmd)
            if func:
                try:
                    func(*args)
                except Exception, e:
                    self.terminal.write("Error: %s" % e)
                    self.terminal.nextLine()
            else:
                self.terminal.write("No such command.")
                self.terminal.nextLine()
        self.showPrompt()
```

Example 10-1. sshserver.py (continued)

```python
    def do_help(self, cmd=''):
        "Get help on a command. Usage: help command"
        if cmd:
            func = self.getCommandFunc(cmd)
            if func:
                self.terminal.write(func.__doc__)
                self.terminal.nextLine()
                return

        publicMethods = filter(
            lambda funcname: funcname.startswith('do_'), dir(self))
        commands = [cmd.replace('do_', '', 1) for cmd in publicMethods]
        self.terminal.write("Commands: " + " ".join(commands))
        self.terminal.nextLine()

    def do_echo(self, *args):
        "Echo a string. Usage: echo my line of text"
        self.terminal.write(" ".join(args))
        self.terminal.nextLine()

    def do_whoami(self):
        "Prints your user name. Usage: whoami"
        self.terminal.write(self.user.username)
        self.terminal.nextLine()

    def do_quit(self):
        "Ends your session. Usage: quit"
        self.terminal.write("Thanks for playing!")
        self.terminal.nextLine()
        self.terminal.loseConnection()

    def do_clear(self):
        "Clears the screen. Usage: clear"
        self.terminal.reset()

class SSHDemoAvatar(avatar.ConchUser):
    implements(conchinterfaces.ISession)

    def __init__(self, username):
        avatar.ConchUser.__init__(self)
        self.username = username
        self.channelLookup.update({'session':session.SSHSession})

    def openShell(self, protocol):
        serverProtocol = insults.ServerProtocol(SSHDemoProtocol, self)
        serverProtocol.makeConnection(protocol)
        protocol.makeConnection(session.wrapProtocol(serverProtocol))

    def getPty(self, terminal, windowSize, attrs):
        return None
```

Example 10-1. sshserver.py (continued)

```
    def execCommand(self, protocol, cmd):
        raise NotImplementedError

    def closed(self):
        pass

class SSHDemoRealm:
    implements(portal.IRealm)

    def requestAvatar(self, avatarId, mind, *interfaces):
        if conchinterfaces.IConchUser in interfaces:
            return interfaces[0], SSHDemoAvatar(avatarId), lambda: None
        else:
            raise Exception, "No supported interfaces found."

def getRSAKeys():
    if not (os.path.exists('public.key') and os.path.exists('private.key')):
        # generate a RSA keypair
        print "Generating RSA keypair..."
        from Crypto.PublicKey import RSA
        KEY_LENGTH = 1024
        rsaKey = RSA.generate(KEY_LENGTH, common.entropy.get_bytes)
        publicKeyString = keys.makePublicKeyString(rsaKey)
        privateKeyString = keys.makePrivateKeyString(rsaKey)
        # save keys for next time
        file('public.key', 'w+b').write(publicKeyString)
        file('private.key', 'w+b').write(privateKeyString)
        print "done."
    else:
        publicKeyString = file('public.key').read()
        privateKeyString = file('private.key').read()
    return publicKeyString, privateKeyString

if __name__ == "__main__":
    sshFactory = factory.SSHFactory()
    sshFactory.portal = portal.Portal(SSHDemoRealm())
    users = {'admin': 'aaa', 'guest': 'bbb'}
    sshFactory.portal.registerChecker(
        checkers.InMemoryUsernamePasswordDatabaseDontUse(**users))

    pubKeyString, privKeyString = getRSAKeys()
    sshFactory.publicKeys = {
        'ssh-rsa': keys.getPublicKeyString(data=pubKeyString)}
    sshFactory.privateKeys = {
        'ssh-rsa': keys.getPrivateKeyObject(data=privKeyString)}

    from twisted.internet import reactor
    reactor.listenTCP(2222, sshFactory)
    reactor.run()
```

sshserver.py will run an SSH server on port 2222. Connect to this server with an SSH client using the username **admin** and password **aaa**, and try typing some commands:

```
$ ssh admin@localhost -p 2222
admin@localhost's password: aaa

>>> Welcome to my test SSH server.
Commands: clear echo help quit whoami
$ whoami
admin
$ help echo
Echo a string. Usage: echo my line of text
$ echo hello SSH world!
hello SSH world!
$ quit

Connection to localhost closed.
```

 If you've already been using an SSH server on your local machine, you might get an error when you try to connect to the server in this example. You'll get a message saying something like "Remote host identification has changed" or "Host key verification failed," and your SSH client will refuse to connect.

The reason you get this error message is that your SSH client is remembering the public key used by your regular *localhost* SSH server. The server in Example 10-1 has its own key, and when the client sees that the keys are different, it gets suspicious that this new server may be an impostor pretending to be your regular *localhost* SSH server. To fix this problem, edit your *~/.ssh/known_hosts* file (or wherever your SSH client keeps its list of recognized servers) and remove the *localhost* entry.

How Does That Work?

The SSHDemoProtocol class in Example 10-1 inherits from twisted.conch.recvline. HistoricRecvline. HistoricRecvLine is a protocol with built-in features for building command-line shells. It gives your shell features that most people take for granted in a modern shell, including backspacing, the ability to use the arrow keys to move the cursor forwards and backwards on the current line, and a command history that can be accessed using the up and down arrows. twisted.conch.recvline also provides a plain RecvLine class that works the same way, but without the command history.

The lineReceived method in HistoricRecvLine is called whenever a user enters a line. Example 10-1 shows how you might override this method to parse and execute commands. There are a couple of differences between HistoricRecvLine and a regular Protocol, which come from the fact that with HistoricRecvLine you're actually manipulating the current contents of a user's terminal window, rather than just printing out text. To print a line of output, use self.terminal.write; to go to the next line, use self.nextLine.

The `twisted.conch.avatar.ConchUser` class represents the actions available to an authenticated SSH user. By default, `ConchUser` doesn't allow the client to do anything. To make it possible for the user to get a shell, make his avatar implement `twisted.conch.interfaces.ISession`. The `SSHDemoAvatar` class in Example 10-1 doesn't actually implement all of `ISession`; it only implements enough for the user to get a shell. The `openShell` method will be called with a `twisted.conch.ssh.session.SSHSessionProcessProtocol` object that represents the encrypted client's end of the encrypted channel. You have to perform a few steps to connect the client's protocol to your shell protocol so they can communicate with each other. First, wrap your protocol class in a `twisted.conch.insults.insults.ServerProtocol` object. You can pass extra arguments to `insults.ServerProtocol`, and it will use them to initialize your protocol object. This sets up your protocol to use a virtual terminal. Then use `makeConnection` to connect the two protocols to each other. The client's protocol actually expects `makeConnection` to be called with a an object implementing the lower-level `twisted.internet.interfaces.ITransport` interface, not a `Protocol`; the `twisted.conch.session.wrapProtocol` function wraps a `Protocol` in a minimal `ITransport` interface.

 The library traditionally used for manipulating a Unix terminal is called *curses*. So the Twisted developers, never willing to pass up the chance to use a pun in a module name, chose the name *insults* for this library of classes for terminal programming.

To make a realm for your SSH server, write a class that has a `requestAvatar` method. The SSH server will call `requestAvatar` with the username as `avatarId` and `twisted.conch.interfaces.IAvatar` as one of the interfaces. Return your subclass of `twisted.conch.avatar.ConchUser`.

There's only one more thing you'll need to have a complete SSH server: a unique set of public and private keys. Example 10-1 demonstrates how you can use the `Crypto.PublicKey.RSA` module to generate these keys. `RSA.generate` takes a key length as the first argument and an entropy-generating function as the second argument; the `twisted.conch.ssh.common` module provides the `entropy.get_bytes` function for this purpose. `RSA.generate` returns a `Crypto.PublicKey.RSA.RSAobj` object. You extract public and private key strings from the `RSAobj` by passing it to the `getPublicKeyString` and `getPrivateKeyString` functions from the `twisted.conch.ssh.keys` module. Example 10-1 saves its keys to disk after generating them the first time it runs: you need to keep these keys preserved between clients so clients can identify and trust your sever.

 Note that you wouldn't want to call `RSA.generate` after your program has entered the Twisted event loop. `RSA.generate` is a blocking function that can take quite some time to complete.

To run the SSH server, create a `twisted.conch.ssh.factory.SSHFactory` object. Set its `portal` attribute to a portal using your realm, and register a credentials checker that can handle `twisted.cred.credentials.IUsernamePassword` credentials. Set the `SSHFactory`'s `publicKeys` attribute to a dictionary that matches encryption algorithms to key string objects. To get the RSA key string object, pass your public key as the `data` keyword to `keys.getPublicKeyString`. Then set the `privateKeys` attribute to a dictionary that matches protocols to key objects. To get the RSA private key object, pass your private key as the `data` keyword to `keys.getPrivateKey`. Both `getPublicKeyString` and `getPrivateKey` can take a filename keyword instead, to load a key directly from a file. Once the `SSHFactory` has the keys, it's ready to go. Call `reactor.listenTCP` to have it start listening on a port and you've got an SSH server.

Using Public Keys for Authentication

The SSH server in Example 10-1 used usernames and passwords for authentication. But heavy SSH users will tell you that one of the nicest features of SSH is its support for key-based authentication. With key-based authentication, the server is given a copy of a user's private key. When the user tries to log in, the server asks her to prove her identity by signing some data with her private key. The server then checks the signed data against its copy of the user's public key.

In practice, using public keys for authentication is nice, because it saves the user from having to manage a lot of passwords. A user can use the same key for multiple servers. She can choose to password-protect her key for extra security, or she can use a key with no password for a completely transparent login process.

This lab shows you how to set up a Twisted SSH server to use public key authentication. It uses the same server code as Example 10-1, but with a new authentication backend.

How Do I Do That?

Store a public key for each user. Write a credentials checker that accepts credentials implementing `twisted.conch.credentials.ISSHPrivateKey`. Verify the user's credentials by checking to make sure that his public key matches the key you have stored, and that his signature proves that the user possesses the matching private key. Example 10-2 shows how to do this.

Example 10-2. pubkeyssh.py

```
from sshserver import SSHDemoRealm, getRSAKeys
from twisted.conch import credentials, error
from twisted.conch.ssh import keys, factory
from twisted.cred import checkers, portal
from twisted.python import failure
from zope.interface import implements
import base64
```

Example 10-2. pubkeyssh.py (continued)

```
class PublicKeyCredentialsChecker:
    implements(checkers.ICredentialsChecker)
    credentialInterfaces = (credentials.ISSHPrivateKey,)

    def __init__(self, authorizedKeys):
        self.authorizedKeys = authorizedKeys

    def requestAvatarId(self, credentials):
        if self.authorizedKeys.has_key(credentials.username):
            userKey = self.authorizedKeys[credentials.username]
            if not credentials.blob == base64.decodestring(userKey):
                raise failure.failure(
                    error.ConchError("I don't recognize that key"))
            if not credentials.signature:
                return failure.Failure(error.ValidPublicKey())
            pubKey = keys.getPublicKeyObject(data=credentials.blob)
            if keys.verifySignature(pubKey, credentials.signature,
                                    credentials.sigData):
                return credentials.username
            else:
                return failure.Failure(
                    error.ConchError("Incorrect signature"))
        else:
            return failure.Failure(error.ConchError("No such user"))

if __name__ == "__main__":
    sshFactory = factory.SSHFactory()
    sshFactory.portal = portal.Portal(SSHDemoRealm())
    authorizedKeys = {
    "admin":
"AAAAB3NzaC1yc2EAAAABIwAAAIEAxIfv4ICpuKFaGA/r2cJsQjUZsZ4VAsA1c9TXPYEc2Ue1lp78lqOrm/
nQTlK9lg+YEbRxCPcgymaz6OcjGspqqoQ35qPiwJ4xgVUeYKfxs+ZSl3YGIODVfsqLYxLl33b6yCnEObfBjEPmb9P
OkL2TA1owlBfTL2+t+Hbx+clDCwE="
    }
    sshFactory.portal.registerChecker(
        PublicKeyCredentialsChecker(authorizedKeys))

    pubKeyString, privKeyString = getRSAKeys()
    sshFactory.publicKeys = {
        'ssh-rsa': keys.getPublicKeyString(data=pubKeyString)}
    sshFactory.privateKeys = {
        'ssh-rsa': keys.getPrivateKeyObject(data=privKeyString)}

    from twisted.internet import reactor
    reactor.listenTCP(2222, sshFactory)
    reactor.run()
```

To test this example, you'll need to generate a public key, if you don't have one already. The *OpenSSH* SSH implementation that comes with most Linux distributions (and also with Mac OS X) includes a command-line utility named *ssh-keygen* that you can use to generate a new private/public key pair:

```
$ ssh-keygen -t rsa
Generating public/private rsa key pair.
Enter file in which to save the key (/home/abe/.ssh/id_rsa):
Enter passphrase (empty for no passphrase):
Enter same passphrase again:
Your identification has been saved in /home/abe/.ssh/id_rsa.
Your public key has been saved in /home/abe/.ssh/id_rsa.pub.
The key fingerprint is:
6b:13:3a:6e:c3:76:50:c7:39:c2:e0:8b:06:68:b4:11 abe@sparky
```

 Windows users can generate keys with PuTTYgen, which is distrib-
uted along with the popular free PuTTY SSH client (*http://www.
chiark.greenend.org.uk/~sgtatham/putty/download.html*).

Once you've generated a key, you can get the public key from the file *~/.ssh/id_rsa.pub*.
Edit Example 10-2 to use your public key for the admin user in the authorizedKeys
dictionary. Then run *pubkeyssh.py* to start the server on port 2222. You should log
right in without being prompted for a password:

```
$ ssh admin@localhost -p 2222

>>> Welcome to my test SSH server.
Commands: clear echo help quit whoami
$
```

If you try to log in as a user who doesn't possess the matching private key, you'll be
denied access:

```
$ ssh admin@localhost -p 2222
Permission denied (publickey).
```

How Does That Work?

Example 10-2 reuses most of the SSH server classes from Example 10-1. To support
public key authentication, it uses a new credentials checker class named
PublicKeyCredentialsChecker. PublicKeyCredentialsChecker accepts credentials implementing ISSHPrivateKey, which have the attributes username, blob, signature, and
sigData. To verify the key, PublicKeyCredentialsChecker goes through three tests.
First, it makes sure it has a public key on file for the user username. Next, it verifies
that the public key provided in blob matches the public key it has on file for that
user.

It's possible that the user may have provided just the public key at this point, but not
a signed token. If the public key was valid, but no signature was provided,
PublicKeyCredentialsChecker.requestAvatar raises the special exception twisted.
conch.error.ValidPublicKey. The SSH server will understand the meaning of this
exception and ask the client for the missing signature.

Finally, the `PublicKeyCredentialsChecker` uses the function `twisted.conch.ssh.keys.verifySignature` to check whether the data in `signature` really is the data in `sigData` signed with the user's private key. If `verifySignature` returns a true value, authentication is successful, and `requestAvatarId` returns `username` as the avatar ID.

 You can support both username/password and key-based authentication in an SSH server. Just register both credentials checkers with your portal.

Providing an Administrative Python Shell

Example 10-1 demonstrated how to provide an interactive shell through SSH. That example implemented its own language with a small set of commands. But there's another kind of shell that you can run over SSH: the same interactive Python prompt you know and love from the command line.

How Do I Do That?

The `twisted.conch.manhole` and `twisted.conch.manhole_ssh` modules have classes designed to provide a remote interactive Python shell inside your running server. Create a `manhole_ssh.TerminalRealm` object and set its `chainedProtocolFactory.protocolFactory` attribute to a function that will return `manhole.Manhole` objects. Example 10-3 demonstrates a web server that can be modified on the fly using SSH and `twisted.conch.manhole`.

Example 10-3. manholeserver.py

```
from twisted.internet import reactor
from twisted.web import server, resource
from twisted.cred import portal, checkers
from twisted.conch import manhole, manhole_ssh

class LinksPage(resource.Resource):
    isLeaf = 1

    def __init__(self, links):
        resource.Resource.__init__(self)
        self.links = links

    def render(self, request):
        return "<ul>" + "".join([
            "<li><a href='%s'>%s</a></li>" % (link, title)
            for title, link in self.links.items()]) + "</ul>"

links = {'Twisted': 'http://twistedmatrix.com/',
         'Python': 'http://python.org'}
site = server.Site(LinksPage(links))
reactor.listenTCP(8000, site)
```

Example 10-3. manholeserver.py (continued)

```
def getManholeFactory(namespace, **passwords):
    realm = manhole_ssh.TerminalRealm( )
    def getManhole(_): return manhole.Manhole(namespace)
    realm.chainedProtocolFactory.protocolFactory = getManhole
    p = portal.Portal(realm)
    p.registerChecker(
        checkers.InMemoryUsernamePasswordDatabaseDontUse(**passwords))
    f = manhole_ssh.ConchFactory(p)
    return f

reactor.listenTCP(2222, getManholeFactory(globals( ), admin='aaa'))
reactor.run( )
```

manholeserver.py will start up a web server on port 8000 and an SSH server on port 2222. Figure 10-1 shows what the home page looks like when the server starts.

Figure 10-1. The default manholeserver.py web page

Now log in using SSH. You'll get a Python prompt, with full access to all the objects in the server. Try modifying the links dictionary:

```
$ ssh admin@localhost -p 2222
admin@localhost's password: aaa

>>> dir( )
['LinksPage', '__builtins__', '__doc__', '__file__', '__name__', 'checkers',
'getManholeFactory', 'links', 'manhole', 'manhole_ssh', 'portal', 'reactor',
'resource', 'server', 'site']
>>> links
{'Python': 'http://python.org', 'Twisted': 'http://twistedmatrix.com/'}
>>> links["Abe Fettig"] = "http://fettig.net"
>>> links["O'Reilly"] = "http://oreilly.com"
>>> links
{'Python': 'http://python.org', "O'Reilly": 'http://oreilly.com', 'Twisted': 'http://
twistedmatrix.com/', 'Abe Fettig': 'http://fettig.net'}
>>>
```

Then refresh the home page of the web server. Figure 10-2 shows how your changes will be reflected on the web site.

Figure 10-2. The modified manholeserver.py web page

How Does That Work?

Example 10-3 defines a function called getManholeFactory that makes running a manhole SSH server trivially easy. getManholeFactory takes an argument called namespace, which is a dictionary defining which Python objects to make available, and then a number of keyword arguments representing usernames and passwords. It constructs a manhole_ssh.TerminalRealm and sets its chainedProtocolFactory. protocolFactory attribute to an anonymous function that returns manhole.Manhole objects for the requested namespace. It then sets up a portal using the realm and a dictionary of usernames and passwords, attaches the portal to a manhole_ssh. ConchFactory, and returns the factory.

Like its name implies, manhole provides a portal to something that is off-limits to the she is allowed in, she can do anything she wants. You can pass a dictionary of Python objects as namespace only for the sake of convenience (to limit the set of objects the user has to look through), not for security. Only administrative users should have permission to use the manhole server.

Example 10-3 creates a manhole factory using the built-in globals() function, which returns a dictionary of all the objects in the current global namespace. When you log in through SSH, you can see all the global objects in *manholeserver.py*, including the links dictionary. Because this dictionary is also being used to generate the home page of the web site, any changes you make through SSH are instantly reflected on the Web.

> The manhole_ssh.ConchFactory class includes its own default public/private key pair. For your own projects you shouldn't rely on these built-in keys. Instead, generate your own and set the publicKeys and privateKeys attributes of the ConchFactory. See Example 10-1, earlier in this chapter, for an example of how to do this.

Running Commands on a Remote Server

This lab demonstrates how to write an SSH client. You can use `twisted.conch` to communicate with a server using SSH: logging in, executing commands, and capturing the output.

How Do I Do That?

There are several classes that work together to make up a `twisted.conch.ssh` SSH client. The `transport.SSHClientTransport` class sets up the connection and verifies the identity of the server. The `userauth.SSHUserAuthClient` logs in using your authentication credentials. The `connection.SSHConnection` class takes over once you've logged in, and creates one or more `channel.SSHChannel` objects, which you then use to communicate with the server over a secure channel. Example 10-4 shows how you can use these classes to make an SSH client that logs into a server, runs a command, and prints the output.

Example 10-4. sshclient.py

```
from twisted.conch import error
from twisted.conch.ssh import transport, connection, keys, userauth, channel, common
from twisted.internet import defer, protocol, reactor

class ClientCommandTransport(transport.SSHClientTransport):
    def __init__(self, username, password, command):
        self.username = username
        self.password = password
        self.command = command

    def verifyHostKey(self, pubKey, fingerprint):
        # in a real app, you should verify that the fingerprint matches
        # the one you expected to get from this server
        return defer.succeed(True)

    def connectionSecure(self):
        self.requestService(
            PasswordAuth(self.username, self.password,
                        ClientConnection(self.command)))

class PasswordAuth(userauth.SSHUserAuthClient):
    def __init__(self, user, password, connection):
        userauth.SSHUserAuthClient.__init__(self, user, connection)
        self.password = password

    def getPassword(self, prompt=None):
        return defer.succeed(self.password)
```

Example 10-4. sshclient.py (continued)

```python
class ClientConnection(connection.SSHConnection):
    def __init__(self, cmd, *args, **kwargs):
        connection.SSHConnection.__init__(self)
        self.command = cmd

    def serviceStarted(self):
        self.openChannel(CommandChannel(self.command, conn=self))

class CommandChannel(channel.SSHChannel):
    name = 'session'

    def __init__(self, command, *args, **kwargs):
        channel.SSHChannel.__init__(self, *args, **kwargs)
        self.command = command

    def channelOpen(self, data):
        self.conn.sendRequest(
            self, 'exec', common.NS(self.command), wantReply=True).addCallback(
            self._gotResponse)

    def _gotResponse(self, _):
        self.conn.sendEOF(self)

    def dataReceived(self, data):
        print data

    def closed(self):
        reactor.stop()

class ClientCommandFactory(protocol.ClientFactory):
    def __init__(self, username, password, command):
        self.username = username
        self.password = password
        self.command = command

    def buildProtocol(self, addr):
        protocol = ClientCommandTransport(
            self.username, self.password, self.command)
        return protocol

if __name__ == "__main__":
    import sys, getpass
    server = sys.argv[1]
    command = sys.argv[2]
    username = raw_input("Username: ")
    password = getpass.getpass("Password: ")
    factory = ClientCommandFactory(username, password, command)
    reactor.connectTCP(server, 22, factory)
    reactor.run()
```

Run *sshclient.py* with two arguments: a hostname and a command. It will ask for your username and password, log into the server, execute the command, and print the output. For example, you could run the *who* command to get a list of who's currently logged in to the server:

```
$ python sshclient.py myserver.example.com who
Username: abe
Password: password
root     pts/0        Jun 11 21:35 (192.168.0.13)
phil     pts/2        Jun 22 13:58 (192.168.0.1)
phil     pts/3        Jun 22 13:58 (192.168.0.1)
```

How Does That Work?

The `ClientCommandTransport` in Example 10-4 handles the initial connection to the SSH server. Its `verifyHostKey` method checks to make sure the server's public key matches your expectations. Typically, you'd remember each server the first time you connected, and then check on subsequent connections to make sure that another server wasn't maliciously trying to pass itself off as the server you expected. Here, it just returns a `True` value without bothering to check the key. The `connectionSecure` method is called as soon as the initial encrypted connection has been established. This is the appropriate time to send your login credentials, by passing a `userauth.SSHUserAuthClient` to `self.requestService`, along with a `connection.SSHConnection` object that should manage the connection after authentication succeeds.

The `PasswordAuth` inherits from `userauth.SSHUserAuthClient`. It has to implement only a single method, `getPassword`, which returns the password it will use to log in. If you wanted to use public key authentication, you'd implement the methods `getPublicKey` and `getPrivateKey` instead, returning the appropriate key as a string in each case.

The `ClientConnection` class in Example 10-4 will have its `serviceStarted` method called as soon as the client has successfully logged in. It calls `self.openChannel` with a `CommandChannel` object, which is a subclass of `channel.SSHChannel`. This object is used to work with an authenticated channel to the SSH server. Its `channelOpen` method is called when the channel is ready. At this point, you can call `self.conn.sendRequest` to send a command to the server. You have to encode data sent over SSH as a specially formatted *network string*; to get a string in this format, pass it to the `twisted.conch.common.NS` function. Set the keyword argument `wantReply` to `True` if you're interested in getting a response from the command; this setting will cause `sendRequest` to return a `Deferred` that will be called back when the command is completed. (If you don't set `wantReply` to `True`, `sendRequest` will return `None`.) As data is received from the server, it will be passed to `dataReceived`. Once you're done using the channel, close it by calling `self.conn.sendEOF`. The `closed` method will be called to let you know when the channel has been successfully closed.

CHAPTER 11

Services, Processes, and Logging

Once you've built an application that behaves the way you want, the next step is to think about how you're going to deploy it. How will you start and stop the process? Under which user account should it run? How will you keep track of what's going on? Twisted provides a number of tools that you can use to manage how your application behaves in these areas. You can run your application in a background process, and limit its permissions by having it run as a specific user. You can run multiple services in the same process. And you can use logging to record errors and track your program's usage.

Running a Twisted Application as a Daemon

Just as servers are different from regular applications, server processes are different from regular processes. A server needs to be available all the time, to all users, so it can't be tied to one user's session. Server processes run in the background and are usually started and stopped automatically by the operating system. In Unix and Unix-like operating systems, such long-running background processes are traditionally knows as *daemons*.

Twisted comes with a program called *twistd* that you can use to run your application as a background process. *twistd* can also help your program to do other things you'd expect from a well-behaved server: write log messages to the system log, run in a chrooted environment where it has limited directory access, and run with the permissions of an unprivileged user.

 For more information on using *twistd* to limit your program's file access and permissions, see Example 11-3.

How Do I Do That?

First, encapsulate each logical service in your application in a class implementing `twisted.application.service.IService`. Example 11-1 shows how easy this is to do for a typical server based on a Protocol and Factory.

Example 11-1. reverse.py

```
from twisted.application import service, internet
from twisted.internet import protocol, reactor
from twisted.protocols import basic

def reverse(string):
    return string[::-1]

class ReverserProtocol(basic.LineReceiver):
    def lineReceived(self, line):
        if hasattr(self, 'handle_' + line):
            getattr(self, 'handle_' + line)()
        else:
            self.sendLine(reverse(line))

    def handle_quit(self):
        self.transport.loseConnection()

class ReverserFactory(protocol.ServerFactory):
    protocol = ReverserProtocol

class ReverserService(internet.TCPServer):
    def __init__(self):
        internet.TCPServer.__init__(self, 2323, ReverserFactory())
```

Next, write a Python script that defines a variable named application pointing to an object created by calling `twisted.application.service.Application`. Add your service to the application, and run the script using the command **twistd -y *yourappname***. Example 11-2 does this for the service from Example 11-1.

Example 11-2. reverse_app.py

```
from twisted.application import service
import reverse

application = service.Application("Reverser")
reverserService = reverse.ReverserService()
reverserService.setServiceParent(application)
```

Run this application using *twistd*. It will start the process in the background, and immediately return:

```
$ twistd -y reverse_app.py
$
```

At this point, the server is running as a background process. It runs a tiny protocol that sends back a reversed copy of every line it receives, unless that line is **quit**, in which case it closes the connection. You can connect to the server on port 2323 using Telnet:

```
$ telnet localhost 2323
Trying 127.0.0.1...
Connected to sparky.
Escape character is '^]'.
hello world!
!dlrow olleh
quit
Connection closed by foreign host.
```

twistd creates in the current directory a file called *twistd.pid*, which contains the process ID of the daemon process. To stop the application, kill this process. You can do this easily on Unix-like operating systems by running the command **kill `cat twistd.pid`**. *twistd* also creates a logfile called *twistd.log*, which you can use to monitor the activity of your server while it's running.

How Does That Work?

The `twisted.application.service` module provides the interface `IService`, which represents part of an application that provides a specific service. `IService` objects have `startService` and `stopService` methods that can be used to control the service. Services can be grouped together into a hierarchy, so that each service manages a set of child services. An application is made up of one or more services.

Example 11-1 defines a protocol and factory, `ReverserProtocol` and `ReverserFactory`. Instead of starting the factory directly by calling `reactor.listenTCP`, it creates a subclass of `twisted.application.internet.TCPServer`. The `TCPServer` class lets you define a service that sets up a factory to listen on a port. Initialize a `TCPServer` with the same arguments you'd pass to `reactor.connectTCP`. The `TCPServer` won't start the factory immediately, however; it will wait until its `startService` method is called. `TCPServer` also provides a `stopService` method that stops listening on the port.

Example 11-2 takes the `ReverserService` from Example 11-1 and makes it into an application suitable for running with *twistd*. To create an application object, call `twisted.application.service.Application` with a string representing the name of your application. `service.Application` is actually not a class, but a function that creates a `twisted.python.components.Componentized` object. `Componentized` objects are multifaceted: internally, they contain multiple objects, which they can expose in order to implement different interfaces. The application object returned by `service.Application` is three objects in one. First, it's a `twisted.application.service.MultiService` object, which is a service that contains other services. When this service is started or stopped, all its child services will be started or stopped along with it.

Second, the application is a `twisted.application.service.Process` object, meaning that it will be the top-level object in a process whose permissions can be managed by the operating system. And third, it's a `twisted.persisted.sob.Persistent` object, which means that its state can be preserved between sessions by writing it to disk.

Attach a service to an application by calling `service.setServiceParent(application)`. This step registers the service as a child of the application, so it will be started and stopped automatically when the application is run with *twistd*.

The -y flag tells *twistd* that you're passing it a Python file with your application in the application variable. *twistd* is capable of loading applications from other formats, including Python pickle files and XML files, but using -y and a Python script is the most straightforward. You can think of the script you pass to *twistd* as being the configuration file for your application. It's best to define your application's services elsewhere, and then use a minimal script to tie it together into an application object for *twistd*.

An interesting thing that *twistd* does by default is save a pickled version of your application object at shutdown in a file called *YourAppName-shutdown.tap*. Although it's in a different format than your Python script, this file can also be used to run your application with *twistd*. After running Example 11-2, you should have a file named *Reverser-shutdown.tap* in the directory where you started *twistd*. You could run your application from this file by passing it to *twistd* with the -f flag:

```
$ twistd -f Reverser-shutdown.tap
```

The potentially useful thing about this feature is that the *.tap* file contains the state of the application object just before shutdown, including any configuration changes made while the program was running. This information could be useful if you want your program to include its own configuration interface, perhaps allowing the administrator to change the port your server will listen on. In practice, however, this knowledge is rarely needed. If you're not planning to use this feature, and don't want *.tap* files cluttering up your filesystem, disable it by passing the -o flag to *twistd*.

Another useful *twistd* flag is -n, which tells the application not to run as a background process. This option is useful for testing purposes. It will run in the foreground and print log messages to stdout.

Setting Limits on an Application's Permissions

Most operating systems reserve ports below 1024 for system-wide servers. To enforce this reservation, only users with root permissions are allowed to run programs that bind to these ports. But running a server with root permissions tends to greatly magnify security issues. Security breaches happen when a malicious user tricks your application into doing something you didn't intend. This problem is never desirable, but the possibility for damage is especially high if your application has access to every file on the computer.

To limit the potential for damage, a well-behaved Unix server will run under a privileged account for just long enough to listen on the necessary ports, and then switch its identity to that of another user with minimal permissions. *twistd* makes it easy to use this technique for running your application.

 This example is specific to Unix-like operating systems, such as Linux and Mac OS X. Twisted doesn't provide a way to switch user IDs on Windows.

How Do I Do That?

Pass uid and gid keyword arguments when you call twisted.application.service. Application. Once your application has started listening on the ports it needs, *twistd* will change your application's user and group to those you specified. Example 11-3 creates a server that runs on the reserved Telnet port, 23, and reads the contents of files from disk. By running it with a set user ID and group ID, it's limited to reading files that are available to its user and group.

Example 11-3. catserver.py

```
from twisted.application import service, internet
from twisted.internet import protocol, reactor
from twisted.protocols import basic
import os

class FileDumpProtocol(basic.LineReceiver):
    def lineReceived(self, line):
        if hasattr(self, 'handle_' + line):
            getattr(self, 'handle_' + line)()
        else:
            self.listDir(line)

    def listDir(self, filename):
        try:
            f = open(filename)
            for line in f:
                self.transport.write(line)
        except Exception, e:
            self.sendLine("ERROR: %s" % e)

    def handle_quit(self):
        self.transport.loseConnection()

class FileDumpFactory(protocol.ServerFactory):
    protocol = FileDumpProtocol

UID = 1000
GID = 1000
```

Example 11-3. catserver.py (continued)

```
fileDumpService = internet.TCPServer(23, FileDumpFactory())
application = service.Application('Cat Server', uid=UID, gid=GID)
fileDumpService.setServiceParent(application)
```

Modify the UID and GID values in Example 11-3 to match a valid user and group on your system. Start *catserver.py* as root using *twistd* with the -n option to keep it in the foreground. It will start a server on port 23. (If you're already running a Telnet server on port 23, modify Example 11-3 to use a different port.) You'll see a log message informing you that *twistd* has switched to your user and group:

```
$ twistd -noy catserver.py
2005/06/25 17:32 EDT [-] Log opened.
2005/06/25 17:32 EDT [-] twistd 2.0.0 (/usr/bin/python2.3 2.3.5) starting up
2005/06/25 17:32 EDT [-] reactor class: twisted.internet.selectreactor.SelectReactor
2005/06/25 17:32 EDT [-] Loading catserver.py...
2005/06/25 17:32 EDT [-] Loaded.
2005/06/25 17:32 EDT [-] __builtin__.FileDumpFactory starting on 2323
2005/06/25 17:32 EDT [-] Starting factory <__builtin__.FileDumpFactory instance at
0xb7b2cd2c>
2005/06/25 17:32 EDT [-] set uid/gid 1000/1000
```

Telnet to localhost and enter some filenames. You will be able to access only files that your application's user has the right to read:

```
$ telnet localhost
Trying 127.0.0.1...
Connected to sparky.
Escape character is '^]'.
/etc/passwd
root:x:0:0:root:/root:/bin/bash
daemon:x:1:1:daemon:/usr/sbin:/bin/sh
bin:x:2:2:bin:/bin:/bin/sh
sys:x:3:3:sys:/dev:/bin/sh
...
sshd:x:110:65534::/var/run/sshd:/bin/false
bind:x:112:117::/var/cache/bind:/bin/false
/etc/shadow
ERROR: [Errno 13] Permission denied: '/etc/shadow'
quit
Connection closed by foreign host.
```

How Does That Work?

Example 11-3 calls twisted.application.service.Application with uid and gid keyword arguments. *twistd* uses these values to set the process owner of the application after it has opened the ports. Behind the scenes, this process works by using the privilegedStartService method of IService. If a service provides the method privilegedStartService, it will be called at startup before the application switches users. After it switches to the unprivileged user, the application calls the Service's regular `startService` method. In the `twisted.application.internet.TCPServer` class, the code for listening on a port is in the `privilegedStartService` method, so it's able to bind to the port as *root* before the process switches to an unprivileged user.

Typically, you wouldn't design a protocol like `FileDumpProtocol` in Example 11-3, which lets any anonymous user dump the contents of any file on your system. But it's possible that you'd accidentally create a security hole in your application that would let a malicious user trick it into reading arbitrary files. By running it as an unprivileged user, you prevent such a security hole from revealing sensitive files on your system, such as */etc/shadow*, which contains user/password hashes.

 Example 11-3 defines the application classes and builds the application object in the same file. This is OK for short examples like this one, but the best practice is to set up your `application` object in a separate, minimal file.

What About...

...running the application in a *chroot* environment? An alternative way to limit the potential damage of a security flaw in your application is to run it in a chroot "jail," where the operating system makes it impossible for the process to see or access any files outside of one specific directory. *twistd* has built-in support for this: just run it with the flag `--chroot` *directory*.

Managing Multiple Services

One of the most powerful features of Twisted is its ability to run multiple services in a single process. You can write an application that shares objects and data with many different protocols at the same time. You can also manage the different services in an application at runtime, starting and stopping them individually without having to restart your application.

How Do I Do That?

Add more than one service to an application object and run the application using *twistd*. You can iterate through the current services in your application by wrapping the application object in the `service.IServiceCollection` interface. Call `startService` and `stopService` to start or stop one of the services. Example 11-4 creates an application that offers both web and Telnet interfaces to the same data, and a web administration interface that lets you selectively start and stop services.

Example 11-4. multiservice.py

```python
from twisted.application import service, internet
from twisted.internet import protocol, reactor, defer
from twisted.protocols import basic
from twisted.web import resource, server as webserver

class Reverser:
    def __init__(self):
        self.history = []

    def reverse(self, string):
        self.history.append(string)
        reversed = string[::-1]
        return reversed

class ReverserLineProtocol(basic.LineReceiver):
    def lineReceived(self, line):
        if hasattr(self, 'handle_' + line):
            getattr(self, 'handle_' + line)()
        else:
            self.sendLine(self.factory.reverser.reverse(line))

    def handle_quit(self):
        self.transport.loseConnection()

class ReverserLineFactory(protocol.ServerFactory):
    protocol = ReverserLineProtocol

    def __init__(self, reverser):
        self.reverser = reverser

class ReverserPage(resource.Resource):
    def __init__(self, reverser):
        self.reverser = reverser

    def render(self, request):
        if request.args.has_key("string"):
            string = request.args["string"][0]
            reversed = self.reverser.reverse(string)
        else:
            reversed = ""

        return """
        <html><body><form>
        <input type='text' name='string' value='%s' />
        <input type='submit' value='Go' />
        <h2>Previous Strings</h2>
        <ul>
        %s
        </ul>
        </form></body></html>
        """ % (reversed,
               "\n".join(["<li>%s</li>" % s for s in self.reverser.history]))
```

Example 11-4. multiservice.py (continued)

```python
class ServiceAdminResource(resource.Resource):
    def __init__(self, app):
        self.app = app

    def render_GET(self, request):
        request.write("""
        <html><body>
        <h1>Current Services</h1>
        <form method='post'>
        <ul>
        """)
        for srv in service.IServiceCollection(self.app):
            if srv.running:
                checked = "checked='checked'"
            else:
                checked = ""
            request.write("""
            <input type='checkbox' %s name='service' value='%s'>%s<br />
            """ % (checked, srv.name, srv.name))
        request.write("""
        <input type='submit' value='Go' />
        </form>
        </body></html>
        """)
        return ''

    def render_POST(self, request):
        actions = []
        serviceList = request.args.get('service', [])
        for srv in service.IServiceCollection(self.app):
            if srv.running and not srv.name in serviceList:
                stopping = defer.maybeDeferred(srv.stopService)
                actions.append(stopping)
            elif not srv.running and srv.name in serviceList:
                # wouldn't work if this program were using reserved ports
                # and running under an unprivileged user id
                starting = defer.maybeDeferred(srv.startService)
                actions.append(starting)
        defer.DeferredList(actions).addCallback(
            self._finishedActions, request)
        return webserver.NOT_DONE_YET

    def _finishedActions(self, results, request):
        request.redirect('/')
        request.finish()

application = service.Application("Reverser")
reverser = Reverser()

lineService = internet.TCPServer(2323, ReverserLineFactory(reverser))
lineService.setName("Telnet")
lineService.setServiceParent(application)
```

Example 11-4. multiservice.py (continued)

```python
webRoot = resource.Resource( )
webRoot.putChild('', ReverserPage(reverser))
webService = internet.TCPServer(8000, webserver.Site(webRoot))
webService.setName("Web")
webService.setServiceParent(application)

webAdminRoot = resource.Resource( )
webAdminRoot.putChild('', ServiceAdminPage(application))
webAdminService = internet.TCPServer(8001, webserver.Site(webAdminRoot))
webAdminService.setName("WebAdmin")
webAdminService.setServiceParent(application)
```

Run *multiservice.py* using *twistd*. It will start a server that offers two different interfaces to a Reverser object, which reverses strings. You can connect to the server using telnet on port 2323:

```
$ telnet localhost 2323
Trying 127.0.0.1...
Connected to sparky.
Escape character is '^]'.
this is a test
tset a si siht
another test
tset rehtona
quit
Connection closed by foreign host.
```

You can also access the server using a web browser on port 8000. Figure 11-1 shows how the history data is shared between the Telnet service and the web service.

Figure 11-1. The multiservice.py web interface

Example 11-4 also runs a second web server on port 8001. This server provides the interface shown in Figure 11-2 for starting and stopping services.

Now, if you try to telnet to port 2323, you find that the service is no longer available:

```
$ telnet localhost 2323
Trying 127.0.0.1...
telnet: Unable to connect to remote host: Connection refused
```

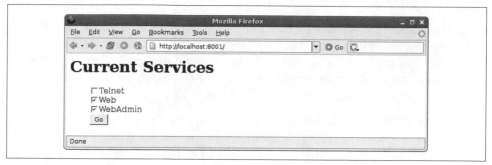

Figure 11-2. Stopping the Telnet service through the web administration interface

How Does That Work?

Example 11-4 creates three Resource objects: lineService, webService, and webAdminService. It uses setServiceParent to register each of them as a child of application. The ReverserLineFactory used by lineService is initialized with a Reverser object; this same object is passed to the ReverserPage that webService uses to handle web requests. Since both services are using the same object, they're able to transparently share data.

The webAdminService in Example 11-4 uses a ServiceAdminPage object to provide a web interface for starting and stopping resources. ServiceAdminPage is initialized with the application object so that it can access all available services. As a twisted. python.components.Componentized object, there's not much you can do with the application directly. Instead, you expose one of its internal objects by wrapping it in the interface you want to use. To loop through all the services, the ServiceAdminPage class uses the service.IServiceCollection interface, which returns an iterable object. ServiceAdminPage renders a form with an input checkbox for each service. When you submit this form, ServiceAdminPage loops through the services again and compares their current state with the checkbox value. If the service is running, but the box wasn't checked, it stops the service; if the service wasn't running, but the box was checked, it starts the service.

The web administration service in Example 11-4 even lets you stop it. That's probably not something you want to allow in a real application!

Logging Events and Errors

Server logfiles provide an important way to keep track of what's going on in your application. Logfiles let you see how many users your application has, how frequently it's being used, and what it's being used for. Logfiles also collect errors and debugging information, making it much easier to track down problems.

As Example 11-2 demonstrated, *twistd* creates a logfile named *twistd.log* automatically. By default, this logfile will capture several useful kinds of information. First, it will store anything that your application normally writes to stdout, including print statements. Second, it will record tracebacks for any uncaught exceptions. Third, it will capture log messages generated by twisted modules; many of the modules in Twisted automatically log events that you're likely to be interested in.

It's nice that *twistd* does all this for you, but sometimes you need more control. For example, you might have code in your application that catches exceptions and reports them to the user. *twistd* won't log these exceptions for you, but you might want to capture the tracebacks for debugging. It can also be a chore to wade through a giant logfile containing a mix of usage reporting, debug messages, and errors. This is especially true for error messages: if everything is in the same file, the only way to tell whether your application is generating errors is to search through the file. It's much better to divert error messages to their own log: that way you can just glance at the file to see whether it has any contents and you'll know immediately whether your application is generating errors.

Twisted included a framework for logging that you can use to generate your own log messages. Using the Twisted logging framework also gives you more control over how log events and logfiles are managed, so you can do things like keep separate logfiles for different types of events.

How Do I Do That?

Use the `twisted.python.log` module to generate log messages. Use the `twisted.python.logfile` module to write logfiles to disk and rotate logfiles. Example 11-5 demonstrates a `Protocol` that logs user activity and exceptions, and shows how to log errors to a separate file.

Example 11-5. logger.py

```
from twisted.internet import protocol
from twisted.protocols import basic
from twisted.application import service, internet
from twisted.python import log, logfile
import time

class ChatProtocol(basic.LineReceiver):
    def lineReceived(self, line):
        log.msg("Got command:", line)

        parts = line.split()
        cmd = parts[0]
        args = parts[1:]
```

Example 11-5. logger.py (continued)

```
        if hasattr(self, 'do_'+cmd):
            try:
                getattr(self, 'do_'+cmd)(*args)
            except Exception, e:
                log.err(e)
                self.sendLine("Error: %s" % e)
        else:
            log.msg("User sent invalid command", cmd, args)
            self.sendLine("Invalid command '%s'" % cmd)

    def do_time(self):
        self.sendLine(str(time.strftime("%x %X")))

    def do_echo(self, *strings):
        self.sendLine(" ".join(strings))

    def do_quit(self):
        self.transport.loseConnection()

class ErrorLog(log.FileLogObserver):
    def emit(self, logEntryDict):
        if not logEntryDict.get('isError'): return
        log.FileLogObserver.emit(self, logEntryDict)

class ErrLogService(service.Service):
    def __init__(self, logName, logDir):
        self.logName = logName
        self.logDir = logDir
        self.maxLogSize = 1000000

    def startService(self):
        # logfile is a file-like object that supports rotation
        self.logFile = logfile.LogFile(
            self.logName, self.logDir, rotateLength=self.maxLogSize)
        self.logFile.rotate() # force rotation each time restarted
        self.errlog = ErrorLog(self.logFile)
        self.errlog.start()

    def stopService(self):
        self.errlog.stop()
        self.logFile.close()
        del(self.logFile)

application = service.Application("LogDemo")

# quick and dirty way to create a service from a protocol
chatFactory = protocol.ServerFactory()
chatFactory.protocol = ChatProtocol
chatService = internet.TCPServer(2323, chatFactory)
chatService.setServiceParent(application)
```

Example 11-5. logger.py (continued)

```
ERR_LOG_DIR = "." # use an absolute path for real apps
ERR_LOG_NAME = "chaterrors.log"

ErrLogService(ERR_LOG_NAME, ERR_LOG_DIR).setServiceParent(application)
```

Run the logger.py application in Example 11-5 using *twistd*:

```
$ twistd -noy logger.py
2005/06/23 15:27 PDT [-] Log opened.
2005/06/23 15:27 PDT [-] twistd 2.0.0 (/usr/bin/python2.3 2.3.5) starting up
2005/06/23 15:27 PDT [-] reactor class: twisted.internet.selectreactor.SelectReactor
2005/06/23 15:27 PDT [-] Loading logger.py...
2005/06/23 15:27 PDT [-] Loaded.
2005/06/23 15:27 PDT [-] twisted.internet.protocol.ServerFactory starting on 2323
2005/06/23 15:27 PDT [-] Starting factory <twisted.internet.protocol.ServerFactory
instance at 0xb7921ccc>
```

It will start a server on port 2323. You can connect to this server using Telnet and issue the commands time, echo, and quit. If you attempt to call a command with the wrong syntax, the server will raise an exception, and you'll get an error message:

```
$ telnet localhost 2323
Trying 127.0.0.1...
Connected to sparky.
Escape character is '^]'.
time
06/23/05 15:22:41
echo hello
hello
time time
Error: do_time( ) takes exactly 1 argument (2 given)
quit
Connection closed by foreign host.
```

Meanwhile, the server will be printing its log to *stdout* for you to see:

```
2005/06/23 15:27 PDT [ChatProtocol,0,127.0.0.1] Got command: time
2005/06/23 15:27 PDT [ChatProtocol,0,127.0.0.1] Got command: echo hello
2005/06/23 15:27 PDT [ChatProtocol,0,127.0.0.1] Got command: time time
2005/06/23 15:27 PDT [ChatProtocol,0,127.0.0.1] Traceback (most recent call last):
        Failure: exceptions.TypeError: do_time( ) takes exactly 1 argument (2 given)

2005/06/23 15:27 PDT [ChatProtocol,0,127.0.0.1] Got command: quit
```

Shut down the server, and there should be a file in the same directory named *chaterrors.log*. This file will contain only the exceptions that were logged:

```
$ cat chaterrors.log
2005/06/23 15:25 PDT [ChatProtocol,0,127.0.0.1] Traceback (most recent call last):
        Failure: exceptions.TypeError: do_time( ) takes exactly 1 argument (2 given)
```

How Does That Work?

The ChatProtocol class in Example 11-5 uses the functions twisted.python.log.msg and twisted.python.log.err. These are used to write log messages to the default log. log.msg takes a series of strings and writes them on a single line; log.err takes an Exception or twisted.python.Failure object and writes the traceback.

 Behind the scenes, the twisted.python.log module creates exactly one global LogPublisher object. The LogPublisher is in charge of routing log messages to LogObserver objects, which then write the messages to a file or do something else useful with them.

The lineReceived method of chatProtocol tries to perform a method call based on the command sent from the client. If this method call raises an exception, it sends an error message to the client. But it also calls log.err with the exception. This step creates a record in the logfile containing the exception and a full traceback.

The ErrorLog class in Example 11-5 is a subclass of log.FileLogObserver. FileLogObserver is an object that observes log events and writes them to a file. The emit method is called with a dictionary containing information about the log message. If the log message is an error, it will have a true value for the key isError. ErrorLog uses the isError key to filter out log messages that aren't errors.

 You can pass extra information to log observers by adding keyword arguments when you call *log.msg*. For example, you could say:

    log.msg('test', debugLevel=1)

which could cause the dictionary passed to LogObserver.emit to have a key named 'debugLevel' with a value of 1.

The ErrLogService class implements a service that uses the ErrorLog class to get any errors being logged and write them to a separate file. Instead of just passing an open file handle to ErrorLog, ErrorLogService passes a twisted.python.logfile.LogFile object. A LogFile object represents a rotating logfile. When the logfile reaches a certain size, or when you call LogFile.rotate, LogFile moves the current logfile to a file named *filename.1*, and starts using a fresh file. If *filename.1* exists, the current *filename.1* will be renamed *filename.2*, and so on. You initialize a LogFile object with two arguments: the directory where the logfiles should be stored and the name of the logfile. You can also pass an optional rotateLength keyword argument to set the size at which the logfile should be rotated.

Index

Symbols

/ (slash), trailing slashes in URIs, 51

A

addCallback function, 16, 25
addErrback function, 16, 25
addListener method (IMailbox), 151
anonymous functions, 34
answers to questions from Twisted
        community, 8
asynchronous results, 15–19
asynchronous, event-based framework, xiii
authentication, 88–106
    against a database table, 94–98
    HTTP Authorization header, 27, 29
    Perspective Broker, 102–106
    POP3 server, 138
    SSH server
        username and password, 173
        using public keys, 178–181
    in Twisted server, 88–94
    twisted.cred classes, 172
    users with different capabilities, 98–102
    web pages requiring, 27–29
avatar IDs, 92, 98
    requesting, 93
    requesting with database query, 97
Avatar objects, 91
    IMAP server, 152
    multiple, for users with different
        capabilities, 98–102
    Perspective Broker, 103
    requesting, 93
    separation from credential verification, 92
    SSH server, 177
    twisted.conch.avatar.ConchUser, 172,
        177
avatarInterfaces dictionary, 138

B

background processes (daemons), running
        Twisted applications as, 187–190
BasicClientFactory class, 15
Binary object (xmlrpc), 76
BSD variants
    Twisted, PyOpenSSL, and PyCrypto,
        prepackaged, 2
buildMessage function, 114

C

CallbackAndDisconnectProtocol.connection
        Made method, 17
callRemote method (soap.Proxy), 81, 83
callRemote method (xmlrpc.Proxy), 76, 78
chainDeferred method, 110, 119
channel.SSHChannel class, 184, 186
_checkedPassword method, 98
checkHTTPError function, 28
checkPassword method
    IUsernameHashedPassword, 138
    IUsernamePassword, 97, 138
checkStatus function, 34

We'd like to hear your suggestions for improving our indexes. Send email to *index@oreilly.com*.

About the Author

Abe Fettig is a software developer specializing in Internet applications. He currently works as a software enginner for JotSpot, Inc. His open source projects include Yarn, a Python library that uses Twisted to transfer information between RSS, email, weblogs, and web services. Abe lives in Portland, Maine with his wife, Hannah.

Colophon

Our look is the result of reader comments, our own experimentation, and feedback from distribution channels. Distinctive covers complement our distinctive approach to technical topics, breathing personality and life into potentially dry subjects.

The image on the cover of *Twisted Network Programming Essentials* shows a ball of snakes. When the ground begins to thaw in spring, things heat up for some species of snakes. Males emerge from their hibernation dens cold, hungry, and randy! An estimated 50,000 male snakes can fill a location such as a limestone quarry, waiting patiently for nearby females to emerge. When they do, the mating frenzy begins, and it can last up to three weeks.

As many as 100 to 1,000 males will compete to mate with a single female, sometimes surrounding her before she can fully emerge from her den. The males wrap around the female, becoming a living ball that can grow to be two feet high. The constant writhing of the snakes can even propel the ball over rocks and tree roots.

In some cases, the size of the snake ball will crush the female to death. However, this does not always deter the males, who may continue to mate with her.

A female will normally mate with only one male in the ball; once a male has successfully copulated with her, he releases a pheromone that temporarily makes all other males in the ball impotent. When the female selects her partner, the ball unravels and the unsuccessful males go in search of another female.

Since it is difficult for snakes to determine the gender of their potential partner, males detect the female by using their flicking tongues to sense the female's pheromones, which stimulate the males to mate. The male rubs his chin against the grain of the female's scales to squeeze out her pheromones. It is believed that the male can also determine the position of the female by detecting the direction of her pheromones and then aligning himself with her body accordingly.

One interesting phenomenon that is still not completely understood is that of the "she-male" snake—a male that gives off female pheromones when it emerges from the ground. One theory is that weaker male snakes emerging from the cold ground may do this so that other males will surround them in a ball to warm them up and protect them from predators. Studies have shown that "she-males" in this situation will return to being normal males after about three hours. Another theory is that "she-males" use their pheromones to confuse other males, who will try to mate with the "she-male' rather than vying for the true female.

Marlowe Shaeffer was the production editor for *Twisted Network Programming Essentials*. Nancy Kotary was the copyeditor, and Sada Preisch was the proofreader. Marlowe Shaeffer and Claire Cloutier provided quality control. Ellen Troutman Zaig wrote the index.

Karen Montgomery designed the cover of this book, based on a series design by Edie Freedman. The cover image is a 19th-century engraving from the Dover Pictorial Archive. Karen Montgomery produced the cover layout with Adobe InDesign CS using Adobe's ITC Garamond font.

David Futato designed the interior layout. This book was converted by Keith Fahlgren to FrameMaker 5.5.6. The text font is Linotype Birka; the heading font is Adobe Myriad Condensed; and the code font is LucasFont's TheSans Mono Condensed. The illustrations that appear in the book were produced by Robert Romano, Jessamyn Read, and Lesley Borash using Macromedia FreeHand MX and Adobe Photoshop CS. The tip and warning icons were drawn by Christopher Bing. This colophon was written by Jansen Fernald.

Related Titles from O'Reilly

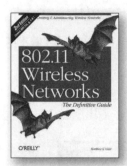

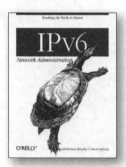

Networking

802.11 Security

802.11 Wireless Networks: The Definitive Guide, *2nd Edition*

Asterisk: The Future of Telephony

BGP

Building Wireless Community Networks, *2nd Edition*

Cisco Cookbook

Cisco IOS Access Lists

Cisco IOS in a Nutshell, *2nd Edition*

DNS & BIND Cookbook

DNS & BIND, 4th Edition

Essential SNMP, *2nd Edition*

IP Routing

IPv6 Essentials

IPv6 Network Administration

LDAP System Administration

Managing NFS and NIS, *2nd Edition*

Network Troubleshooting Tools

RADIUS

sendmail 8.13 Companion

sendmail, *3rd Edition*

sendmail Cookbook

SpamAssassin

Switching to VOIP

TCP/IP Network Administration, *3rd Edition*

Unix Backup and Recovery

Using Samba, *2nd Edition*

Using SANs and NAS

Windows Server 2003 Network Administration

Our books are available at most retail and online bookstores.

To order direct: 1-800-998-9938 • *order@oreilly.com* • *www.oreilly.com*

Online editions of most O'Reilly titles are available by subscription at *safari.oreilly.com*

Keep in touch with O'Reilly

Download examples from our books

To find example files from a book, go to: *www.oreilly.com/catalog* select the book, and follow the "Examples" link.

Register your O'Reilly books

Register your book at *register.oreilly.com* Why register your books? Once you've registered your O'Reilly books you can:

- Win O'Reilly books, T-shirts or discount coupons in our monthly drawing.
- Get special offers available only to registered O'Reilly customers.
- Get catalogs announcing new books (US and UK only).
- Get email notification of new editions of the O'Reilly books you own.

Join our email lists

Sign up to get topic-specific email announcements of new books and conferences, special offers, and O'Reilly Network technology newsletters at:

elists.oreilly.com

It's easy to customize your free elists subscription so you'll get exactly the O'Reilly news you want.

Get the latest news, tips, and tools

www.oreilly.com

- "Top 100 Sites on the Web"—PC Magazine
- CIO Magazine's Web Business 50 Awards

Our web site contains a library of comprehensive product information (including book excerpts and tables of contents), downloadable software, background articles, interviews with technology leaders, links to relevant sites, book cover art, and more.

Work for O'Reilly

Check out our web site for current employment opportunities:

jobs.oreilly.com

Contact us

O'Reilly Media, Inc.
1005 Gravenstein Hwy North
Sebastopol, CA 95472 USA
Tel: 707-827-7000 or 800-998-9938
　　(6am to 5pm PST)
Fax: 707-829-0104

Contact us by email

For answers to problems regarding your order or our products:
order@oreilly.com

To request a copy of our latest catalog:
catalog@oreilly.com

For book content technical questions or corrections: **booktech@oreilly.com**

For educational, library, government, and corporate sales: **corporate@oreilly.com**

To submit new book proposals to our editors and product managers:
proposals@oreilly.com

For information about our international distributors or translation queries:
international@oreilly.com

For information about academic use of O'Reilly books:
adoption@oreilly.com
or visit:
academic.oreilly.com

For a list of our distributors outside of North America check out:
international.oreilly.com/distributors.html

Order a book online

www.oreilly.com/order_new

 **O'REILLY**®